Original Reproduction

The Universal Publishing Association

P.O. Box 24027

Waco, Texas 76702

UniversalPublishing.com

ISBN: 978-1-962573-23-8

Printed in the U.S.A.

THE SHEPHERD'S ROD

By V. T. HOUTEFF

"Every scribe which is instructed unto the kingdom of heaven is like unto a man that is an householder, which bringeth forth out of his treasure things new and old." *Matt. 13:52.*

UNIVERSAL PUBLISHING ASSOCIATION

P.O. Box 24027
Waco, Texas 76702

LIST OF ILLUSTRATIONS

TOPICAL INDEX

INTRODUCTION

This book is not published to explain, or comment on truths which have been previously revealed, and accepted as such, but is to disclose realities which God has preserved through many generations, not only from becoming extinct, but also preventing their meaning from being discovered by men of wisdom. Thus, He who controls the Scriptures is able to reveal present truth to His people at a time when needed. Therefore, though such truths are originally prophetic, they become new, and stand as a direct letter from God to men at the time revealed. "Thus saith God the Lord, . . . Behold, the former things are come to pass, and new things do I declare: before they spring forth I tell you of them." (Isa. 42:5, 9.) Hence, it will prove the contents of this publication new, interesting, instructive, inspiring, and converting. The message it bears being taught by symbols and types illustrated on charts, becomes simple, and all who are searching for truth with intention to fit themselves for the heavenly garner, can easily comprehend it.

The book of "Revelation" is said to be a closed book full of symbolical mysteries, incomprehensive to human beings. This is true of **all** prophetic truths. The one who admits this fact of the book of "Revelation," automatically confesses that he does not understand the Bible; for all the books of Holy Writ meet and end in the "Revelation." Therefore, to understand **that book** is to understand the Bible. "The One who reveals the mysteries to John will give to the diligent searcher for truth a **foretaste of Heavenly things.** Those **whose hearts are open** to the reception of truth will be **enabled to understand its teachings,** and will be **granted** the blessing promised to those who 'hear the words of this prophecy, and keep those things which are written therein'."—"The Acts of the Apostles", pp. 584, 585. Thus, when the Revelation is understood, it will unlock the great Store House and bring to light all the prophetic mysteries that are stored in it.

The message in this volume was prophetically **timed** by the parable of the "Householder" who sent laborers into His "vineyard." (Matt. 20:1-16.) Proving to be the "11th hour" "call",—the last, and at the right time. The fact that this wonderful revelation of the Scriptures cannot be contradicted, proves the message correct, and its inspiration true. This prophetic call is based on the prophecies of Daniel, and its explanation made clear by the book of Revelation. Thus, it is symbolically explained. These prophetic symbols of beasts, wings, horns, heads, crowns, etc., prove to be most perfect symbols in revealing the truth represented by them and when correctly applied it is certain that their meaning cannot be misconstrued.

As the present day confusion and misunderstanding of the Scriptures among Christendom is proven by the multiplicity of sects, it is evident that the churches are in the Laodicean state: "Wretched, and miserable, and poor, and blind, and naked." And by denying the charge of this plain statement proves the words of the "True Witness" correct, **"and knowest not."** While they think they are right, the "True Witness" declares: "Thou art all wrong." What greater deception than this? (Read Rev. 3:14-18.) Since the Bible plainly says that it is the "truth" that shall make us "free", we can not too closely examine ourselves and the things we believe, for if no two of this multi-sectarian Christianity believe alike, it is evident that most, if not all, are blind. And as the Bible is correct in the words: "If the blind lead the blind, both shall fall into the ditch", then it would be useless to dispute the truth—the world is headed for the "ditch." Would not this indisputable statement arouse the professed people of God from their slumber and sleep? Past experiences prove that many will say, "It is not I." Knowing that this deception would arise in the last days, God has devised this pictorial representation of the truth, by which He is able to enlighten His church and call out His people.

While the enemy has succeeded in confusing the written Word, God lightens the earth with His glory by these symbolic revelations; and by which He discloses the entire truth and uncovers the traps of the devil! Thus through types and symbols He makes wise the simple and confounds the prudent by showing that where there is **no type** there is **no truth.**

This volume contains a complete symbolic revelation of the entire world's history, both civil and religious. The reason these wonders were portrayed by symbols is the same as that which caused Christ to teach by parables. "And the disciples came, and said unto him [Christ], Why speakest thou unto them in parables? He answered and said unto them, Because it is given unto you to know the mysteries of the kingdom of heaven, but to them it is not given." (Matt. 13:10, 11.) "But the wicked shall do wickedly: and none of the wicked shall understand; but the wise shall understand." (Dan. 12:10.) "The chief purpose of teaching by parables is that the truth may be revealed to God's children and at the same time concealed from His enemies . . . . For this same reason the prophecies that described the great antichristian powers and their work down to the end of time had to be clothed in symbolic and parabolic language to insure their preservation."—"Sabbath School Lesson Quarterly," p. 33. Second Quarter, 1932. "Christ was the foundation of the Jewish economy. The whole system of types and symbols was a compacted prophecy of the gospel, a presentation in which were bound up the promises of redemption."—"The Acts of the Apostles", p. 14.

Each of these subjects could be greatly enlarged, but had we done so, this volume would have become too voluminous, also less comprehensive. Thus we have omitted many details.

(All bold face ours.)   THE AUTHOR.

IN WHAT MANNER WERE THE SCRIPTURES GIVEN?

THE WAY GOD SPEAKS TO US

"God, who at sundry times and in divers manners spake in time past unto the fathers by the prophets, Hath in these last days spoken unto us by His **Son.**" (Heb. 1:1.) God called Abraham by His **voice.** He also conversed with him **through angels,** dreams. (Gen. 12:1; 15:12, 13;17:1-6; 18:1-22.) Jacob had the same experience. (See Gen. 28:12; 32:1, 2.) The great **I AM** spoke to His servant Moses from the burning bush. (Ex. 3:1-10.) Israel heard the voice of God from the cloud on mount Sinai. (Ex. 20:18, 19.) The ten commandments were "written with the finger of God." (Ex. 31:18.) Pharaoh king of Egypt and Nebuchadnezzar king of Babylon were given dreams, but the Spirit of God, through Joseph and Daniel revealed the secrets. (Gen. 41:28-36; Dan. 2:19.) David and Solomon wrote the Psalms and Proverbs, not by visions, dreams, or angels, but by the silent voice of the Spirit of God imprinted in the minds of His servants. God spoke to Esther and Ruth by experiences through divine providence. John received the "Revelation" by visions. God speaks to us also by types and anti-types—through the cere-monial law, by the patriarchs, and by the experiences of ancient Israel. (See Shepherd's Rod, Vol. 1, pp. 223-235.)

God used the dead and the living, the beasts of the field, the birds of the air, the fish of the sea, the land and water, sun, moon, and stars, to reveal His divine plan and to sustain His servants, etc. (See Gen. 16:7, 9; 1 Sam. 6:7-15; Num. 22:30; 1 Kings 17:4-6; Jonah 2:10; Matt. 17:27; Num. 16:32; Matt. 24:29.) God has a thousand ways whereby He can render help in a moment. Truly, what more could divine love do for fallen human beings?

How Are the Scriptures Revealed, and Properly Interpreted?

Analysis of ancient and modern history, both sacred and secular, prove that sealed, or prophetic truth has never been revealed through the educational system of the world, or by the wisdom of man, but only by the power of God. If anything is true, it is this one thing. Said Jesus: "When He, the **Spirit** of **Truth,** is **Come,** He **will** guide you into **all** truth." (John 16:13.) Christ plainly declares, that we are led into truth, not by wisdom of man but by the Spirit of God. Not into **some** truth, but in **all** truth. When God reveals truth, He is able to lead His servants in **all** truth, and does not allow such instruments to mix His truth with error. Though they may not understand all, yet the message they bear is the truth and nothing but the truth. Therefore, such truths are originally revealed by inspiration **only.** When the time divinely appointed is fulfilled, then God calls servants of His own choice, and by the Spirit of Truth reveals a portion of His Word to them. Usually in the form of a message which they must first bear to the church.

By the same power God moved upon His numerous servants, the prophets, each writing a portion of the Bible; and when compiled it made a complete book, dealing with one main subject—salvation in Christ. Though some of these writers lived hundreds of years apart, yet each portion of Scripture perfectly harmonizes,—one throwing light upon another. Thus it proves that God was the overseer of the Scriptures and skillfully led His servants in **all** truth.

Sin Against the Holy Ghost, What Is It?

As the Bible is free from error, even so its interpretation under the same Spirit of Inspiration must also be correct. Therefore, the interpretation of the Bible is true, only when it is revealed through a channel of inspiration. In no other way can God lead His people in **all** truth. Anything less than this cannot disclose Biblical truth, regardless of its simplicity. Said the Angel to Daniel: "But **I will shew thee** that which is noted in the Scripture of truth: and there is none that holdeth with me in these things, **but** Michael your prince." (Dan. 10:21.) One of the gifts for the church in the Christian dispensation, is "prophets." "And he gave some, apostles; and some prophets." (Eph. 4:11.)

Paul, again declares of the Scriptures in his time and afterwards: "Which in other ages was not made known unto the sons of men, as it is now revealed unto His holy **Apostles and Prophets by the Spirit."** (Eph. 3:5.) When the truth of the Scriptures is presented by God's servants, "the letter" can be understood by all who study it; but the same spirit is required to seal, change the heart, and direct the steps in **newness** of life. This transforming power is granted only as the receiver of the truth humbly repents from sin, renounces the world and accepts Christ. When such a message is presented, those who oppose the messenger and resist the truth, reject the Spirit, and sin against Him. The Spirit in a message is the **only** medium to awaken the conscience. When rebelled against, the sinner cuts himself off from the channel through which God communicates. "Wherefore I say unto you, **all** manner of sin and blasphemy shall be forgiven unto men: but the **Blasphemy** against the **Holy Ghost** shall not be forgiven unto men. And whosoever speaketh a word against the Son of man, it shall be forgiven him; but whosoever speaketh against the **Holy Ghost,** it shall not be forgiven him, neither in this world, neither in the world to come." (Matt. 12:31, 32.)

The antediluvian world sinned against the **Holy Ghost,** because they believed not in the message of truth sent to save them from the dreadful flood. Therefore, they perished under sin that shall never be forgiven them. The same is true when one revolts against the divine message in any generation. Men are not condemned because they have sinned, but they are condemned when they turn a deaf ear to the divine call that is to save them from their sin.

As all prophetic truths are timely revealed, it is evident that there can be nothing disclosed by the wisdom of man, no matter how simple it may be. When God reveals a portion of His holy Word through one of His chosen instruments, analysis of history prove that they are never erring as far as the message they deliver is concerned. It is also true that those who erred in their supposed message of truth, have had no truth. So the great apostle says: "But God hath revealed them unto us by His Spirit: for the Spirit searcheth all things, yea, the deep things of God. For what man knoweth the things of a man, save the spirit of man which is in him? even so the things of God knoweth **no man,** but the Spirit of God. Now we have received, not the spirit of the world, but the Spirit which is of God; that we might know the things that are freely given to us of God. Which things also we speak, not in the words which man's wisdom teacheth, but which the Holy Ghost teacheth; comparing spiritual things with spiritual. But the natural man receiveth not the things of the Spirit of God: for they are foolishness unto him: neither can he know them, because they are spiritually discerned." (1 Cor. 2:10-14.) Therefore, when a message is proclaimed, it is either all truth or there is no truth in it, save the quotations of the prophets.

"Yet the fact that God has revealed His will to men through His Word, has not rendered needless the continued presence and guiding of the HOLY SPIRIT. On the contrary, the Spirit was promised by our Saviour, to open the Word to His servants, to illuminate and apply its teachings. And since it was the Spirit of God that inspired the Bible, it is impossible that the teaching of the Spirit should ever be contrary to that of the Word."—"The Great Controversy", p. VII.

Those who are inclined to question the ability of God to lead one into all truth, are not only unconsciously denying the faithfulness of His Word, but they also minimize His power by their act, and thus have "Limited the Holy One of Israel." (Psa. 78:41.)

"The Spirit was not given—nor can it ever be bestowed—to supersede the Bible; for the Scriptures explicitly state that the Word of God is the standard by which all teaching and experience must be tested. Says the apostle John, 'Believe not every spirit, but try the spirits whether they are of God: because many false prophets are gone out into the world.' (1 John 4:1.) and Isaiah declares, 'To the law and to the testimony; if they speak not according to this word, it is because there is no light in them.' (Isa. 8:20)"—"The Great Controversy", p. VII.

"The term 'prophet' as used in the Bible . . . is employed to designate men and women engaged in a wide range of service in connection with the work of God. Some of these never uttered a prophecy as that term is generally understood . . . . Some were used only for a special occasion, others for a long series of years. Some wrote out the message God revealed to them, and others gave them orally. To some, as in the case of Daniel and others, were committed prophecies reaching into the distant future, portions of which are still unfulfilled.

"Some were God's messengers raised up in periods of great crisis, to warn the church and the world of threatened judgments, and to call men back to allegiance to God. Such were Samuel, Elijah, John the Baptist, and others. John disclaimed the prophetic title, claiming rather that he was a voice or a messenger of God, sent to prepare the way of the Lord in calling Israel to repentance. But as God's messenger he was declared by Christ to be a prophet, and 'even more than a prophet.' Luke 7:26. 'Surely the Lord will do nothing, but He revealeth His secrets unto His servants the prophets.' Amos 3:7."—"The Present Truth," Vol. 5, No. 72.

"In the highest sense the prophet was one who spoke by direct inspiration, communicating to the people the messages he had received from God. But the name was given also to those who, though not so directly inspired, were divinely called to instruct the people in the works and ways of God."—"Education," p. 46.

These heavenly messengers usually were men and women of a humble character; some could neither read nor write. Though not having the advantages that great men do, these instruments in the hand of Omnipotence, caused human knowledge and worldly greatness to sink into insignificance. Thus

God sought by these methods to reveal His transforming power in the human machine; both in intellect and in character. To rebel against God's chosen instruments is to renounce His power in preference to the human, placing the finite above the infinite, who can transmit more knowledge in a moment, than the human could in a lifetime.

Though truths are revealed through inspired channels, the instrument of iniquity has often mixed them with error. Such iniquitous workers oft times resort to the use of portions of divine revelation, unlawfully using them as an entering wedge to pass on error and thus deceive the simple. Let none flatter themselves that they can escape the clutches of the devil by the studious effort of another. Everyone must study for himself to understand his own position, and with candid mind be ready to listen to all with a teachable spirit of a child. "Verily I say unto you, Whoever shall not receive the kingdom of God as a little child, he shall not enter therein." (Mark 10:15.) Prejudice, has beguiled and ruined more souls than any trap ever devised by the great deceiver. The one who refuses to listen to reasons offered by another, is the most ignorant. Such a man is usually prejudiced because the argument presented contradicts his view of the subject, or it may be that he considers himself more intellectual or of superior social standing. Others will not hear the truth because it hurts their sinful conscience and for fear that they must part from some selfish lust. This class is under the power of the devil, and on the way to everlasting ruin —sinning against the **Holy Ghost.** Those who are sincere in their errors are the very ones who are found in the bottom of the devil's kidnaping bag. This class is the hardest to convince that they are on the way to hell.

INTRODUCING CHRIST OUR SAVIOUR

THREE DAYS AND THREE NIGHTS IN THE HEART OF THE EARTH

The question as to how long Christ remained in the tomb, and the day on which He was buried and resurrected, has been as widely discussed as any other Biblical subject. A number of theories have been advanced and doubtless much valuable time has been wasted; however, confusion upon the subject has not lessened, but rather increased.

Some one has asked, "What has that to do with our salvation?" It may not have much to do with the salvation of some, but it seems that with others it has a great deal to do. A certain sister said: "I believe all the S—— denomination teaches, but I cannot agree with the position Sister W—— holds on the subject of Christ's burial and resurrection. I know that Christ was three days and three nights in the tomb, but Sister W—— states He was buried on Friday evening and resurrected on Sunday morning. Therefore, I cannot believe in all her writings, and for this reason I have not, and will not, become a member of your church."

The misunderstanding of this question has kept this sister from connecting with the church. Now, if that particular denomination has the truth for the world at this present time, and this sister's misunderstanding has kept her from accepting it, then we must concede that this widely discussed subject has something to do with the salvation of some people, to say the least.

Said Jesus: "Ask, and it shall be given you; seek, and ye shall find; knock, and it shall be opened unto you: For everyone that asketh receiveth; and he that seeketh findeth; and to him that knocketh it shall be opened." (Matt. 7:7, 8.)

There could be nothing more pleasing to God than for one of His children to ask in faith the way of truth. If there is any power in the words of Jesus, then surely he who desires to know the truth and is willing to obey it, though it may demand that he sell all and give to the poor, renounce the world and all its inducements, it would be impossible for that soul to remain in darkness. Let the searcher after truth make just such a vow to God and thus try out His power and never failing promises through the words of His Son. But though it be possible to deceive men, we can never impose upon God, for He knows what is in the heart.

One of the chief reasons why confusion arises among Bible students is because they do not entirely depend on the Biblical expression of the words. They think themselves wiser than the prophets who were inspired with the Spirit of God, and thus wish to correct the words and meaning of the Holy Bible! Hence finite mortals have attempted to rectify and correct the Infinite One, whose wisdom, power, and vision is unsearchable! Though they know their interpretation of a text is not altogether in harmony with the whole tenor of the book and law, they see no injury, and fear not God. And when the fact is revealed they refuse to exchange error for truth because it contradicts their false theology. We invite the earnest attention of the reader upon this subject, and that he take notice of the wonderful harmony of the Scriptures and the great wisdom used in them.

The sister was asked: "Where is your evidence that Christ was three days and three nights in the tomb?" "My answer is," she said, "in Matthew 12:40, 'For as Jonas was three days and three nights in the whale's belly; so shall the Son of man be three days and three nights in the heart of the earth'." Again she was asked, "On what day do you think Christ died?" She said, "John 19:31 has the answer: 'The Jews therefore, because it was the preparation, that the bodies should not remain upon the cross on the Sabbath day, (for that Sabbath was an high day,) besought Pilate that their legs might be broken, and that they might be taken away.'" Here she explained that it could not have been the preparation for the seventh-day Sabbath, for that Sabbath was an "High" day, so it was the preparation for the passover—Wednesday. Then she began to count, "Thursday (1), Friday (2), Saturday (3); Wednesday night (1), Thursday night (2), Friday night (3). Thus there are three days and three nights."

According to this sister's reasoning she thinks her explanation is unquestionably correct. But note that Christ died at the ninth hour, just three hours before the end of the day (Matt. 27:46-50) and was buried at sunset—12 o'clock. (Luke 23:52-56.)

If He was buried on Wednesday, He would have been three full days and four full nights in the tomb, for the Bible plainly declares: "In the end of the Sabbath, as it began to dawn [daybreak] toward the first day of the week, [Sunday A.M.] came Mary Magdalene and the other Mary to see the sepulchre." (Matt. 28:1.) Again we quote from Mark 16:9, "Now when

Jesus was risen **early** the **first day** of the week, He appeared first to Mary Magdalene."

Let us examine the theory from another angle. Said Jesus: "Ye know that after two days is the feast of the passover, and the Son of man is betrayed to be crucified." (Matt. 26:2) "Then [after the two days] assembled together the chief priests . . . and consulted that they might take Jesus by subtilty, and kill him." (Verses 3, 4.) The time Christ said the words: "Ye know after two days is the feast of the passover," could not have been later than the beginning of Tuesday, if the feast of the passover was on Thursday. Then all that took place in connection with His judgment, crucifixion, death, and burial, had to be accomplished from late Tuesday morning to sunset Wednesday, which would have been impossible according to the Biblical time table as we shall endeavor to set forth.

Note the following Scriptures: "Now the first day of the feast of unleavened bread the disciples came to Jesus, saying unto him, Where wilt thou that we prepare for thee to eat the passover?" This was the preparation day for the feast of the Passover. "And He said, Go into the city to such a man, and say to him, The Master saith, My time is at hand; I will keep the **passover** at thy house **with** my disciples. And the disciples did as Jesus had appointed them; and they made ready the passover. Now when the even was come, he sat down with the twelve. And as they **did eat,** he said, Verily I say unto you, that one of you shall betray me." (Matt. 26:17-22.) The passover feast can only be observed after sunset at the beginning of the first day of unleavened bread: "In the fourteenth day of the first month **at even** is the Lord's passover." (Lev. 23:5.) This is the last day of preparation for the passover. Therefore, Jesus was not yet in the hands of the priests on the preparation for the passover feast, and much less crucified. Furthermore, Matthew is altogether clear on the subject and leaves no room for argument: "And as they **did eat,** [the passover] he said, Verily I say unto you, that one of you shall betray me." (Matt. 26:21.) How could Jesus eat the passover with the twelve had he been crucified and buried? We are ready to accept truth, but when the theory is contradicted by the Scriptures, then we must not submit to erroneous conclusions, for, he who believes a lie is an abomination unto God.

Permit us to clear the controversy by facts that can stand the test. Let the reader bear in mind that the passover is a **seven-day** affair, or what is called the "passover **week.**" We quote Lev. 23:4-8: "These are the feasts of the Lord, even holy convocations, which ye shall proclaim in their season. In the

fourteenth day of the first month at even **is** the Lord's **Passover**. And on the fifteenth day of the same month is the feast of unleavened bread unto the Lord: **Seven Days** ye must eat unleavened bread. In the first day ye shall have an holy convocation: ye shall do no servile work therein. But ye shall offer an offering made by fire unto the Lord **seven days:** in the **seventh day** is an holy convocation: ye shall do no servile work therein."

Now mark, the seventh-day Sabbath is controlled by the weekly cycle, and the passover by the monthly calendar. Therefore, in each passover week there is a seventh-day Sabbath, and it may fall on any one of the **seven** paschal days. Again, mark that the fourteenth day is called the **"Passover"** day, but the fifteenth is the **Passover "Feast."** (See Num. 28:17; Joshua 5:11.) The seventh-day Sabbath is called, "The Sabbath." The sheaf offering was the first fruits of the harvest and it was to be offered before the Lord on the morrow **after** the Sabbath; that is, on the **first day** of the week, commonly called Sunday. (See Lev. 23:11.) The sheaf offering was a type of the resurrection—the first fruits. Said the apostle: "But now is Christ risen from the dead, and become the first fruits of them that slept"—those whom He raised. (1 Cor. 15:20; also Matt. 27:52, 53.)

Thus Christ "led captivity captive" on the very day to which the type pointed.

The Passover Preparation

The passover is a feast of seven days; therefore, the preparation for the week required longer than a day. Quoting Ex. 12:3, 6, "In the tenth day of this month [the first] they shall take to them every man a lamb . . . And ye shall **keep it** up until the **fourteenth day** of the same month." The people were commanded to commence the preparation on the **tenth day** of the month. On the **fourteenth** day, before sunset, all leaven was to be put out from their houses. Then the fifteenth day drew on, being the first day of unleavened bread, and the passover **week** commenced by killing the passover lamb. "Seven days shall ye eat unleavened bread; even the first day ye shall put away leaven out of your houses." (Verse 15.) Therefore, the fourteenth day was the last day of preparation, and the fifteenth, or the first day of the feast, was a holy convocation, and they were to do no servile work therein. Matthew 26:17, has reference to the same day upon which Jesus ate the passover with the twelve. (See verses 20, 21.)

The only possible days for the passover week would be as

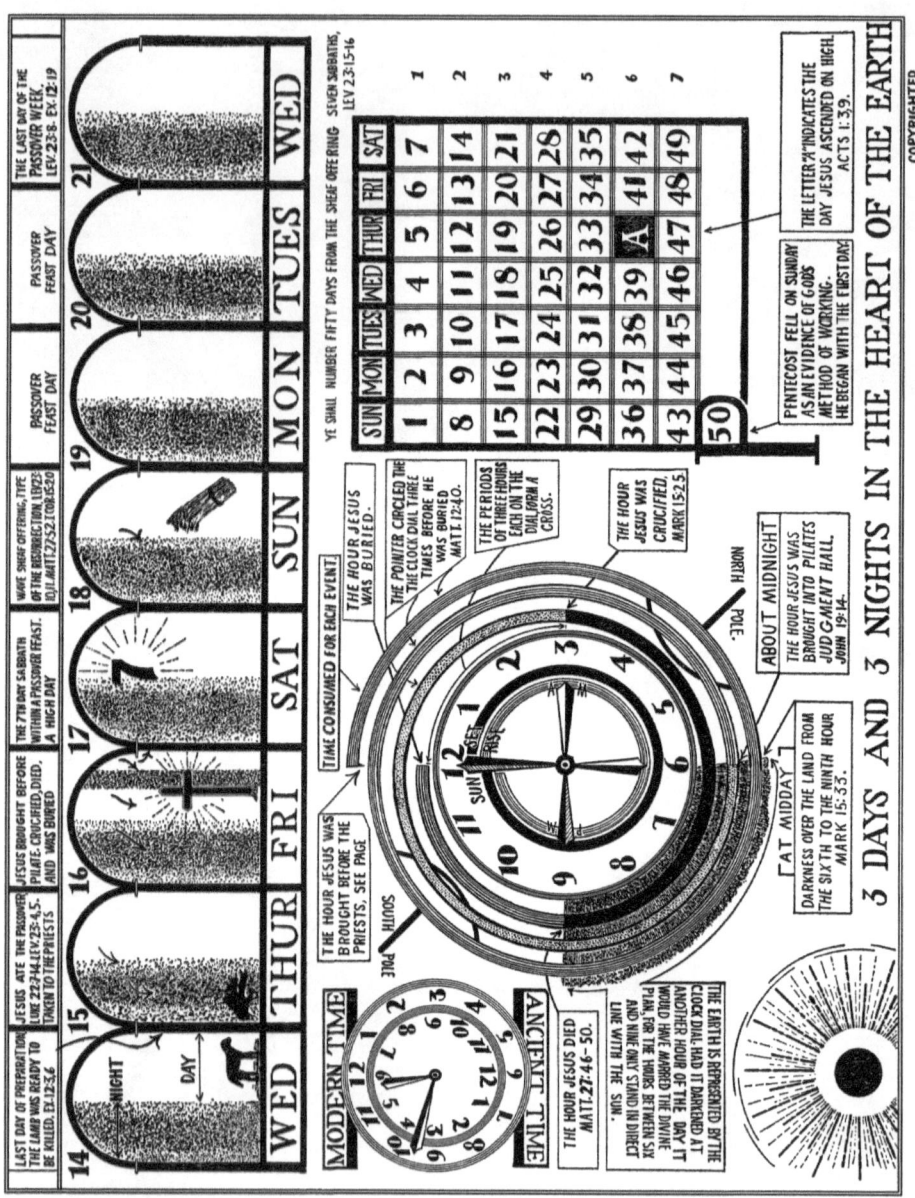

3 DAYS AND 3 NIGHTS IN THE HEART OF THE EARTH

22

follows: The fourteenth day of the first month that year was on Wednesday, and the day ended at sunset (even). The first day of the passover feast (15th day of the month) came on Thursday; the second, on Friday; the third, on Saturday (Sabbath); the fourth, on Sunday; the fifth, on Monday; the sixth, on Tuesday; the seventh and the last of the feast on Wednesday the 21st day of the month. (Follow chart on page 22).

Time Table From Passover To the Resurrection

The lamb could not be killed before the fourteenth day at even and be called **"The Passover Lamb"** according to the instruction given in the following Scriptures: "And the whole assembly of the congregation of Israel shall kill It [the lamb] in the evening." (Ex. 12:6.) Suppose everything was ready and the lamb was killed as soon as the sun went down. It would take about fifteen minutes for it to die; then the pelt must be removed. In addition to this every part of it had to be dressed, washed, and placed back in the sacrifice and the opening sewed together, for there was not any part of it to be thrown away, save the waste. Therefore, the preparation for roasting the sacrifice would require not less than an hour. Thus we read: "Eat not of it raw, nor sodden at all with water, but roast with fire; his head with legs, and with the purtenance thereof." (Verse 9.)

The ancient method of roasting required more time than our modern way. A rod was drawn through the sacrifice, then it was placed over coals of fire, and kept continually turning about by means of the rod. This method of roasting would require about four hours. To eat the passover, ordain the Lord's supper, and the ordinance of humility, then sing a hymn, would have added another hour and a half. Afterwards they went to the mount of Olives. (See Mark 14:26.) The mount is about one half mile east of the third wall of the city. Therefore, it was some distance from the place where the passover was celebrated. Thus it would have taken them close to half an hour to get there on foot; after which Jesus took the three to the garden of Gethsemane.

There could not have been less than an hour and a half spent on the mount and in the garden while Jesus prayed; after which the apostles were told to take their rest in sleep; for Jesus went out to pray three times, and on returning, twice He found them sleeping, "and He cometh unto the disciples, and findeth them asleep, and saith unto Peter, What, could ye not watch with me **One Hour?"** (Matt. 26:40.) We may suppose they spent at least an hour in sleeping, otherwise the words of the Master on His third return: "Take your rest" (Verse 45), would have been spoken in vain. After these experiences Judas arrived with the multitude and there was a little time spent in taking Jesus; and by the time they led Him to the priests it must have consumed not less than two hours. According to this computation of time, the total of hours spent from sunset Wednesday evening (beginning of the passover by killing the lamb) to the time Jesus was led to the high priest could not have taken less than twelve hours.

The analysis of the foregoing time table, proves that when Jesus was led to Caiaphas, the high priest, it was about the twelfth hour, or shortly before daylight on Thursday morning; and after His trial before the high priest, "Then led they Jesus **from** Caiaphas **unto** the hall of judgment: and it was early." (John 18:28.) "And it was the **Preparation** of the passover, and about the **sixth** hour: and he [Pilate] saith unto the Jews, Behold your King!" (John 19:14.) As John states that it was **early** when they led Him **from** Caiaphas to the hall of judgment, and as he also states that it was about the **sixth** hour (either midnight, or midday according to ancient time), then it must have been shortly after midnight (about the sixth hour) when Pilate said to the Jews, "Behold your King," for John would not call midday, **early**. Therefore, after He had been judged by the Sanhedrin they called Pilate, and then went **to** the hall of judgment. This was done on the morning of the day following, after they had taken Jesus from the garden—**early Friday** morning.

Says John, "And it was the preparation of the passover." We have previously explained that the preparation for the passover lamb was not **one** day, but rather a four day affair.

Furthermore, Matthew plainly says: "They **made** ready the **Passover.** Now when even was come, He [Christ] **sat down** with the twelve. And . . . they **did eat.**" (Matt. 26:19-21.) Therefore, the passover preparation mentioned by John, **cannot** be the preparation for the passover lamb, but rather the preparation for the passover Sabbath (the seventh-day), called the passover preparation, because it was in the passover **week,** as it occurred only once a year. So then, that Friday is called "the **preparation** of the passover." Thus, the seventh-day Sabbath in the passover week was called a **"High Day,"** because **it** was a Sabbath **within** a Sabbath—the highest day in the year.

According to time tabulation, the Jewish rulers tried Jesus from twelve o'clock Thursday morning, to about six o'clock Friday morning (ancient time). Nine hours later—at the third hour (Friday), Jesus was crucified. (See Mark 15:25.) After

He had been on the cross for three hours the sun was darkened (at **six** o'clock—noon. See Mark 15:33.) Three hours later Jesus died and the sun again gave light. (See Matt. 27:45-50.) In the three remaining hours to sunset, very hasty preparation was made and the Saviour was placed in Joseph's new tomb just before the seventh-day Sabbath drew on. We quote Luke 23:53-56: "And he took it down, and wrapped it in linen, and laid it in a sepulchre that was hewn in stone, wherein never man before was laid. And that day was the preparation, and the Sabbath drew on. And the women also, which came with Him from Galilee, followed after, and beheld the sepulchre, and how His body was laid. And they returned, and prepared spices and ointments; and rested the Sabbath day according to the commandment." Thus Jesus remained in the tomb from twelve o'clock Friday evening to about twelve o'clock Sunday morning. This is also proven by Mark 16:9, "Now when Jesus had risen **early the first day** of the week." Therefore, a total of about thirty six hours in the tomb; and a grand total of eighty-four hours from the commencement of the passover to the resurrection.

Now mark, that from the time the Jews laid hands on Christ (Thursday the 12th hour) to His resurrection (Sunday the 12th hour), there were exactly seventy-two hours or three days and three nights. Thus fulfilling the words of Jesus: "For as Jonas was three days and three nights in the whale's belly; so shall the Son of man be three days and three nights in the heart of the earth." (Matt. 12:40.) The idea that in the "heart of the earth" means in the grave, is man's supposition without Bible foundation. If the Saviour had in mind His experience in the grave, He would have said so. If His grave was in the center of the earth—about 8,000 miles beneath its surface (the heart of the earth) then one may suppose He meant the heart of the earth. Jesus used the expression to indicate that He was to be three days and three nights in the hands of sinners, and in the grave. Why are sinners called "The heart of the earth"? Because man was made of it according to Gen. 3:19, "For dust thou art, and unto dust shalt thou return."

At this point we draw the reader's attention to the **chart** on page 22. Take notice of the infinite wisdom used to devise the picture of the great sacrifice (the Cross) for human beings, which is an evidence of boundless love Divine. Note first, that the hand on the clock dial made its round three times. Mark that each event was three hours apart (3 x 9 and 6 x 12), making the cross.

Now observe that the position of the cross as it is on the dial, does not show the proper proportion. But if the reader will turn the diagram upside down as it were, which would show the way the ancient clock measured time—being regulated by sunset at twelve o'clock, then the cross appears in its perfect form; thus we have another view of divine perfection.

The line across the dial between the hours of four and five, ten and eleven—marked north and south pole, gives the exact position of the globe as it travels on its yearly orbit. Now look to the upper right at the sun as it was then in its proper relation to the earth, as it darkened from the sixth to the ninth hour and we see the sun stood in accurate position over the hours that remained in darkness! Is not this picture perfect—beyond question? If so, could an intelligent being imagine that this all happened by accident? Does not this show unmistakable evidence that God had pre-ordained it all, and that by His mighty power it has come to pass to teach His children His plan, and the salvation that is offered to them? Said Paul, "The works were finished from the foundation of the world." (Heb. 4:3.) John also declares that the lamb was slain from the foundation of the world. (See Rev. 13:8.) Sinner, "Behold the Lamb of God, which taketh away the sin of the world!"

Though the passover lamb typified the crucifixion of Christ, it was not intended that He should be offered on the very day the lamb was killed. This fact is self-evident, for the lamb was killed in the evening and Christ was crucified in the morning—three hours after sunrise,—and died three hours before the evening.

THE PROPHECY OF DANIEL AND THE REVELATION OF JOHN CONTAIN THE WORLD'S HISTORY

"Blessed is he that readeth, and they that hear the words of this prophecy, and keep those things which are written therein: for the time is at hand." (Rev. 1:3.)

"Let none think, because they cannot expound the meaning of every symbol in the Revelation, that it is useless for them to search this book in an effort to know the meaning of the truth it contains. The one who revealed these mysteries to John will give to the diligent searcher for truth a foretaste of heavenly things. Those whose hearts are open to the reception of truth will be enabled to understand its teachings, and will be granted the blessing promised to those who 'hear the words of this prophecy, and keep those things which are written therein.'"—"The Acts of the Apostles," p. 584.

"In the Revelation all the books of the Bible meet and end. Here is the complement of the book of Daniel. One is a prophecy; the other a revelation. The book that was sealed is not the Revelation, but that portion of the prophecy of Daniel relating to the last days. The angel commanded, 'But thou, O Daniel, shut up the words, and seal the book, even to the time of the end'."—Id. p. 585.

"The number seven indicates completeness. . . . while the symbols used **reveal the condition of the church** at different periods in the history of the world."—Id. p. 585.

"Finite men should beware of seeking to control their fellow men, taking the place assigned to the Holy Spirit. Let not men feel that it is their prerogative to give to the world what they suppose to be truth, and refuse that anything should be given contrary to their ideas. This is not their work. Many things will appear distinctly as truth, which will not be acceptable to those who think their own interpretation of the Scriptures always right. **Most decided changes** will have to be made in regard to **ideas which some have accepted as without a flaw.**"—"Testimonies to Ministers," p. 76.

A large portion of Christendom agree that we are living in the last days of this world's history. When Jesus was asked by his disciples for the signs of His return to earth again, and of the end of the world, one of the many signs He gave was; "When ye therefore shall see the abomination of desolation, spoken of by Daniel the prophet, stand in the holy place, (whoso readeth, let him understand:).'' (Matthew 24:15.) It is evident from the words of the Master that the book of Daniel contains information regarding the signs of the times and of the end of the world. The prophecies of Daniel were of little worth to the disciples and the early Christian church, for Daniel says the book was sealed to the time of the end. (Dan. 12:4.) And since the book is now open it is evident that we are living in the time of the end. (Rev. 22:6-10.) But the book was to be open to one class of people and shut to another, for He added, "Many shall be purified and made white, and tried; but the wicked shall do wickedly: and none of the wicked shall understand; but the wise shall understand." (Dan. 12:10.) Therefore, it is important that we should be free from all wickedness and obedient to the divine requirements, if we would understand and receive the blessings contained in the book.

The intention of this publication is not to explain the symbols which have heretofore been fully explained in various publications and proved to be correct in general outline up to the present, but our intention is to clear certain features which have been hidden by the **Spirit** of **God** for a time. The outstanding symbols which are so familiar to Bible students, will be briefly visualized, sufficient only to connect the thought with the symbols that are to be explained. We shall endeavor to prove that the symbols of the book of Daniel and Revelation contain the entire world's history, both civil and religious, from creation to redemption.

In the second chapter of Daniel, beginning with the first universal kingdom (Babylon) after the flood, we have the world's history from thence to the second coming of Christ, or to the end of the present world, represented in one great metallic image. "Thou, O king, sawest, and behold a great image. This great image, whose brightness was excellent, stood before thee; and the form thereof was terrible. This image's head was of fine gold, his breast and his arms of silver, and his thighs of brass, his legs of iron, his feet part of iron and part of clay. Thou sawest till a stone was cut out without hands, which smote the image upon his feet that were of iron and clay, and brake them to pieces. . . . And in the days of these kings shall the God of heaven set up a kingdom, which shall never be destroyed: and the kingdom shall not be left to other people, but it shall break in pieces and consume all these kingdoms, and it shall stand forever. Forasmuch as thou sawest that stone was cut out of the mountain without hands, and that it brake in pieces the iron, the brass, the clay, the silver, and the gold: the great God hath made known to the king what shall come to pass

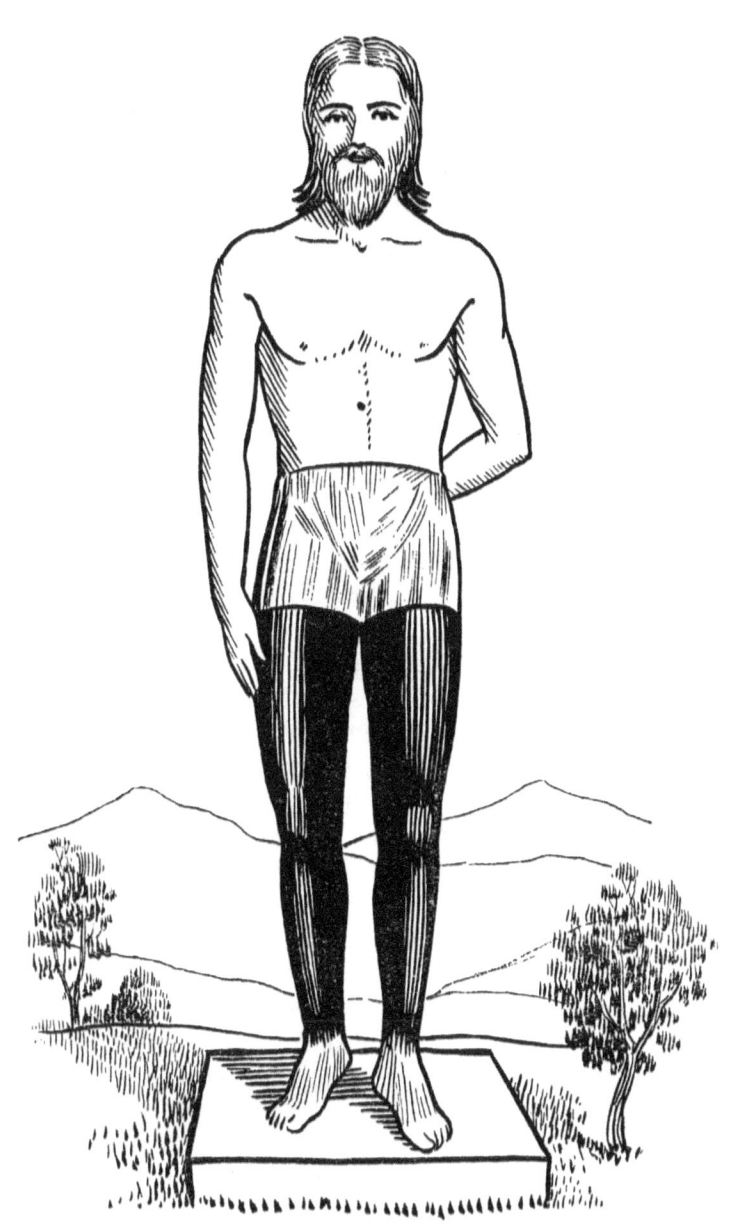

THE SYMBOL OF THE WORLD
DANIEL 2

hereafter: and the dream is certain, and the interpretation thereof sure." (Dan. 2:31-34, 44, 45.)

The gold, silver, brass, and iron have been interpreted to represent Babylon, Medo-Persia, Grecia and Rome. The mixture of iron and clay—the feet and the toes—the present kingdoms succeeding the fall of Rome. Wonderful prophecy it is, so simple and so true. But this great image only reveals the framework, as it were, of our world's history.

In the seventh chapter of Daniel we have the same chronological arrangement in symbols of various beasts. The reason for the duplication is to reveal in detail the historical events which were to transpire within the framework of the great image. "Daniel spake and said, I saw in my vision by night, and, behold, the four winds of the heaven strove upon the great sea. And four great beasts came up from the sea, diverse one from another. The first was like a lion, and it had eagle's wings: I beheld till the wings thereof were plucked, and it was lifted up from the earth, and made to stand upon the feet as a man, and a man's heart was given to it. And behold another beast, a second, like to a bear, and it raised up itself on one side, and it had three ribs in the mouth of it between the teeth of it: and they said thus unto it, Arise, devour much flesh. After this I beheld, and lo another, like a leopard, which had upon the back of it four wings of a fowl; the beast had also four heads; and dominion was given to it. After this I saw in the night visions, and beheld a fourth beast, dreadful and terrible, and strong exceedingly; and it had great iron teeth: and it devoured and break in pieces, and stamped the residue with the feet of it: and it was diverse from all the beasts that were before it; and it had ten horns. I considered the horns, and, behold, there came up among them another little horn, before whom there were three of the first horns plucked up by the roots: and, behold, in this horn were eyes like the eyes of a man, and a mouth speaking great things." (Dan. 7:2-8.)

The lion, the bear, the leopard, and the non-descript beast depict the same kingdoms as the gold, the silver, brass and iron. The unnatural and peculiar symbols connected with the beasts, namely, the wings, ribs, horns, and heads, are capable of disclosing the mysteries of historical occurrences which were to transpire within the great prophetic periods. The most wonderful thing about these prophetic symbols is that they are perfectly capable of revealing the truth, and once understood aright, they cannot be contradicted. Any interpretation of symbolical prophecies that do not perfectly fit the explanation given is never to be depended upon. The interpretation of such symbols must not

DANIEL 7:2,4.

DANIEL 7:5.

DANIEL 7:6

DANIEL 7:7.

THE WORLD'S HISTORY IN SYMBOLS OF BEASTS

31

only be in harmony with the whole tenor of God's book and law, but it must point out some important lesson for God's people; and when such an explanation, as referred to, is derived from the scriptures, then only we have the truth.

While the head of gold on the great image represented the kingdom of Babylon at the height of her glory, the lion covers a greater period according to Genesis 10:8-10: "And Cush begat Nimrod: he began to be a mighty one in the earth. He was a mighty hunter before the Lord: Wherefore it is said, Even as Nimrod the mighty hunter before the Lord. And the beginning of his kingdom was Babel, and Erech, and Accad, and Calneh, in the land of Shinar." The beginning of Nimrod's kingdom was "Babel," or as it is in the Greek, "Babylon." His dominion extended over the four cities of the plain; namely, Babylon, Erech, Accad, and Calneh. If the reader will turn to Genesis 10:1-8 and carefully count the persons born from the family of Noah after going out from the ark of the deluge to the birth of Nimrod, it will be noticed that Nimrod is the 26th person born after the flood. The location of the city was in the land of Shinar, as in Genesis 11:2: "And it came to pass, as they journeyed from the east, that they found a plain in the land of **Shinar;** and they dwelt there."

The name Babel (Babylon in Greek) originated at the time the tower of Babel was in building, after which God confounded the multitude by diversity of speech. According to Daniel, the capitol of Babylon stood on the same plain: "And the Lord gave Jehoiakim, king of Judah into his hand [The king of Babylon], . . . which he carried into the land of **Shinar."** (Dan. 1:2.) Therefore Babylon was founded immediately after the flood, perhaps somewhere between 2400 and 2300 B.C., and had reached her height as a universal empire between 400 or 500 B.C. Babylon, in her development, had consumed a period of about 1800 years or more. Certainly no one would think that Babylon made very rapid **speed** in conquering the ancient world.

Symbol of Wings and Ribs

We may now inquire the meaning of the wings on the lion and on the leopard; also the ribs in the mouth of the bear. The wings on the lion certainly cannot represent speed, as some have taught. If wings were to represent rapidity they should have been on the bear, for Cyrus and Darius conquered old Babylon over night. Furthermore, if wings represent speed on one beast, they must likewise represent the same on the other. Could they represent speed on the four-headed leopard beast? Certainly not. A careful observation of the symbols show that the leopard beast had nothing to do with Alexander's conquest of Medo-Persia. The leopard represents the kingdom after the conquest was accomplished. The four heads are the four Grecian divisions after the death of Alexander; namely, "Cassander, Lysimachus, Ptolemy, and Seleucus."

The conflict and conquest between Medo-Persia and Grecia is brought to our attention in Daniel 8:5-7: "And as I was considering, behold, an he goat came from the west on the face of the whole earth and touched not the ground: and the goat had a notable horn between his eyes. And he came to the ram which had two horns, which I had seen standing before the river, and ran into him in the fury of his power. And I saw him come close unto the ram, and he was moved with choler against him, and smote the ram, and brake his two horns: and there was no power in the ram to stand before him, but he cast him down to the ground, and stamped upon him: and there was none that could deliver the ram out of his hand."

In verses 20, 21, Daniel was told by the angel that the **he goat** "is Grecia," the **ram,** "Medo-Persia," and the **notable horn** between his eyes, is "the first king." Therefore, Alexander's swift conquest is represented by the "he goat" which touched not the ground. If wings were to represent speed they should have been on the "he goat" and not on the leopard. Since the truth of what has been said cannot be denied, and as the thought that has been entertained by some is contradictory to the symbols, we must look elsewhere for the application of the "wings." We think it is far safer and wiser, as well as more reasonable for one to admit his mistake—as we mortals are apt to make many of them—rather than to become involved in contradictory interpretations of the Word of God.

First, we must understand that Inspiration is recording by means of these symbols the entire world's history. Let us not forget that there was a world before the flood. If one of us should undertake this wonderful architectural feat to devise a blue-print, or chart, of this world's history, we certainly would take into consideration a complete account of all its parts. God being infinite in wisdom, as well as in power, would certainly not overlook or thoughtlessly neglect in His great chart of historical events to consider His world before the flood.

A record of a divine survey of this world's history from creation to redemption would be of great importance at this present time. In an age of infidelity, atheism, and hypocrisy, men who profess to be wise in secular, as well as religious matters, have lost sight of the source of true wisdom and knowledge. "Because that, when they knew God, they glorified Him not as God, neither

DANIEL 7: 2,4.

DANIEL 7: 5.

DANIEL 7:6

were thankful; but became vain in their imaginations, and their foolish heart was darkened. Professing themselves to be wise, they became fools." (Rom. 1:21, 22.) Even those who profess to be teachers of righteousness, have forfeited their faith in the Biblical reckoning of creation. God having knowledge of the present deceptive denial of His holy Word, has devised a prophetic blue-print in symbols of beasts, wings, ribs, horns, heads, crowns, etc., by which He points out in this prophetic panorama, the facts, with a force that should humiliate men and show them their utter ignorance and lack of wisdom.

According to Biblical reckoning the flood came more than 1600 years after creation. God originated the human race through Adam and Eve. Therefore, one people, one race, one language and nation from creation to the flood. The rulership given to Adam we call the first universal Adamic empire. Babylon was the second; Medo-Persia is the third; Grecia the fourth; Rome the fifth; the broken state of Rome (symbolized by the feet and toes of the great image of Daniel 2, which is the present unstable civilization) is the sixth; and from the close of the millennium after the resurrection of the wicked to their second death, is the seventh and last. Thus the Biblical number seven, as always, signifies, completeness. Therefore, seven such universal empires, revealing a complete history of the world, denote the end of sin and its dominion.

If we mortals were to devise such a chart by symbols of beasts, it is certain we would have sufficient intelligence to number every beast in his regular order. We may not suppose that God is less thoughtful in His marvelous perfection. Therefore, He has numbered every beast. We must first consider those which represented the Old Testament time, by the great metallic image; namely, the Gold—Babylon; the silver—Medo-Persia; the brass—Grecia. Gold is the chief of metals which would stand as number one; silver is second to gold, therefore number two; brass is third to gold, meaning number three. The lion, the bear, and the leopard are numbered in like manner. The lion is king or chief of beasts, therefore number one, corresponding with the gold. The bear is second to a lion, therefore number two, corresponding with silver. The leopard is third to a lion, hence number three, corresponding with the brass. These are the first set of numbers, but there is yet another set of which we must speak.

These would bring us back to our subject of what is the meaning of the wings on the lion as well as on the leopard, and the ribs in the mouth of the bear. God certainly would not have mapped out the world's history, from the flood to the end, and failed to take into account all its parts. There must be something in this chart of historical events to indicate that He had a universal empire before the flood, as previously explained. That empire being the first, naturally stands as number one; Babylon, number two; Medo-Persia, number three; and Grecia, number four. If this claim is correct, we must find this set of numbers on the lion, bear and leopard.

The wings on the lion denote empire number two. The lion by nature is first— first from the flood but (unnaturally) by two wings, second from creation. The ribs in the mouth of the bear signify empire number three. The bear by nature is second from the flood, but (unnaturally), by three ribs he is third from creation; ribs are used, for wings go in pairs. The four wings on the leopard denote that Grecia is the fourth universal empire. The leopard by nature is third from the flood, but (unnaturally), by the wings, fourth from creation. History flies, therefore wings make a perfect symbol.

"Arise, Devour Much Flesh"

"Arise, devour much flesh," said the ribs to the bear. (Dan. 7:5.)   The Medo-Persia opened the way for imperial wars, therefore: "Arise, devour much flesh."   Thus empire after empire plunged into bloody wars. The ribs in the mouth of the bear cannot mean nations, as some have taught, for nations are symbolized by horns, and not by ribs. Neither can they denote certain provinces that Medo-Persia could not have conquered, for he has them in his mouth, and it would be inconsistent to suppose that the Persians would have oppressed certain states more than others. Had that been the case, the bear would have stamped upon them as did the non-descript beast. (Verse 7.) The symbol is contrary to such suppositions, and there is neither proof nor lesson that could be derived by any such theory.

Plucked the Lion's Wings

Coming back to the lion, symbol of Babylon, Daniel says: "The first was like a lion, and had eagle's wings: I beheld till the wings thereof were plucked, and it was lifted up from the earth, and made to stand upon the feet as a man, and a man's heart was given to it." (Dan. 7:4.)   "His wings were plucked." The symbol denotes the same as the plucking of the three horns from the non-descript beast. (Verse 8.) If the plucking up of the horns denotes their kingdom was taken from them, then plucking the wings signifies that Babylon, as empire number two was to pass away, fulfilling Daniel's interpretation of the

handwriting on the wall: "This is the interpretation of the thing: **Mene;** God hath numbered thy kingdom, and finished it." (Dan. 5:26.) Therefore, Babylon fell into the hands of the Medo-Persian kings. Thus his wings "were plucked," and the Medo-Persian empire, number three, succeeded the lion, number two.

Man's Heart Given to It

After the wings of the lion were plucked, says Daniel: "He was made to stand upon his feet as a man, and a man's heart was given to it." Whatever is meant by the position of the beast and the exchange of heart, its application is after Babylon had fallen under Medo-Persian rule, for he stood as a man **after** the wings "were plucked." If we are to acquire the understanding of the symbol, we must first consider the function of the heart, for the symbol itself must be perfect, otherwise the truth cannot be determined.

The function of a heart is to preserve the life energy in the body. Let the heart stop and all is lost. This most vital organ is a governor of the body. As an empire is composed of numerous individuals, and their necessities, just so is the living body composed of a multitude of life cells, and all their essentials. As the duty of a king is to preserve the life energy in his kingdom, also punish or uproot the evil and to supervise the good, just so does the heart. By contraction and expansion it controls and imparts the flowing, living energy in the form of pure blood. The evidence gathered thus far proves that the heart is a fitting symbol of a king. But we must specify the difference between the human and the beastly heart. Daniel 4:16, speaking of the penalty that was to fall upon the king before he was driven from his throne to the field with the beasts, says: "Let his heart be changed from a man's and let a beast's heart be given unto him; and let seven times pass over him." After the king's heart was changed, he lost his reason, and by nature became equal to an ox. "The same hour was the thing fulfilled upon Nebuchadnezzar: and he was driven from men, and did eat grass as an oxen and his body was wet with the dew of heaven, till his hairs were grown like eagles' feathers, and his nails like birds' claws." (Dan. 4:33.)

The human intellect does not consist in the external image of mankind, but it rather exists in the human heart. This thought is very emphatically entertained by the scriptures: "For out of the abundance of the heart the mouth speaketh." Therefore, the symbol (man's heart) may denote intelligence. However, the symbol cannot infer human vision, but rather a proper understanding of God, for the Bible says: "The fool hath said in his heart, there is no God." (Psa. 53:1.) Obtaining a clear vision of the infinite power of the Eternal **One** is what God calls true education. The sum of the symbol is, Babylon was forced to acknowledge the existence of the Most High by removing one king (beast's heart) and setting up another (man's heart).

Having made clear what the symbol seems to indicate, we must take a brief survey of the ancient monarchy to see if this interpretation can be fully supported by the symbolical heart. As the everlasting example set forth by the flood for future generations had failed to teach the Chaldean rulers God's power and existence, the Creator of mankind in His mercy, patience and long suffering, not willing that any should perish, made a supreme effort to save that nation. "The Lord is not slack concerning His promise, as some men count slackness; but is long suffering to us-ward, not willing that any should perish, but that all should come to repentance." (2 Peter 3:9.)

When the dream of the great image was given to Nebuchadnezzar his memory of the object was blotted out, but the impression left in his mind was greatly increased. After the urgent demand from the wise men had failed to reveal the king's dream, Daniel, by divine revelation, unmasked the mysterious phenomena by interpreting the dream. This wonderful miracle should have converted the king and all the wise men of Babylon to the Hebrew worship, for by the power of Daniel's God they had escaped the death penalty; but there was no change for the better. Though the king honored God with his lips, his heart drew away from Him. The king destroyed not the idols in the land, but in his blindness proceeded to set up superior ones; for shortly after the interpretation of the dream he demanded of all his subjects the worship of the "golden image" which he had set up in the plain of Dura. (Read the third chapter of Daniel.)

The refusal of the three Hebrews to bow down to the idol, and the miracle by which they were saved from the fiery furnace, had deeply affected the minds of the rulers, but it too, failed to change the king's heart. Again he honored the God of gods with his lips but not by his deeds. The king's ungodly deeds made it necessary for a supernatural penalty. Hence a tremendous effort to bring him to a realization of his dependence upon the Creator was necessary. The dream given him (in chapter four), of the great tree—a symbol of himself—and its interpretation by Daniel, had convinced the hard-hearted monarch of its truth, and the judgment that was to fall upon him, except he repent. Daniel said: "Wherefore, O king, let my counsel be acceptable unto thee, and break off thy sins by righteousness, and thine iniquities by shewing mercy to the poor; if it be a lengthening of thy tranquility. . . . At the end of twelve months he walked in the palace of the kingdom of Babylon. . . . The same hour was the thing fulfilled upon Nebuchadnezzar; and he was driven from men, and did eat grass as oxen, and his body was wet with the dew of heaven, till his hairs were grown like eagles' feathers, and his nails like birds' claws." (Chap. 4:27, 29, 33.)

At the end of the painful experience, the king said: "Now I Nebuchadnezzar praise and extol and honour the King of heaven, all whose works are truth, and His ways judgment: and those that walk in pride He is able to abase." (Verse 37.) Though he acknowledged the power of the Eternal **One,** worshipped Him, and uttered words of praise with a most sublime expression, the king failed to surrender his heathen heart and renounce the pagan system of worship. He failed to embrace the great importance of imparting the knowledge of Jehovah to his posterity for the tranquility and endurance of his kingdom.

These wonderful experiences were for an object lesson to future kings. Shortly after the fulfillment of the dream, the kings' grandson had ascended the throne. In his heathen custom he ventured to defy the God of gods, and the King of kings, who is able to make oxen out of kings and kings out of oxen, and rulers out of slaves. "For promotion cometh neither from the east, nor from the west, nor the south. But God is the judge: He putteth down one, and setteth up another." (Psa. 75:6, 7.)

The sacred vessels had never before been defiled by any king as in Belshazzar's drunken feast. God will forbear until man steps over the boundary line. This Belshazzar did by bringing the sacred vessels before his lords, concubines, and heathen gods. At the appearance of the hand writing on the wall his guilty conscience troubled him; his loins were loosed, and his knees smote one against the other. Belshazzar, like his father, ignored Daniel and summoned the wise men of Babylon to interpret the writing; though he should have known their inability to reveal the secret. At last Daniel was called and at his appearance he said: "This is the interpretation of the thing: **Mene;** God hath numbered thy kingdom, and finished it. **Tekel;** Thou art weighed in the balances, and art found wanting. **Peres;** Thy kingdom is divided, and given to the Medes and Persians." (Dan. 5:26-28.) The priceless experiences of his father that were at his access could have been everlasting blessings, but by ignoring the power of God the king reversed the benefits from a blessing to a curse, and brought a final end to his kingdom. Every resource to make the lion (Babylon) stand up like a man under the rule of the Chaldean kings had been exhausted, and every effort failed.

Therefore, the time had come for the Lord to apply the last remedy to the lion kingdom.

Cyrus, of whom God had spoken by His prophet many years in advance, was granted to enter the capital city of the Chaldean king. (See Isa. 45:1.) Babylon as empire number two passed away, and the symbol of the "plucked" wings met its fulfillment. "In that night was Belshazzar the king of the Chaldean's slain." The lion's heart is a symbol of the heathen king—Belshazzar who was slain— and thus the beastly heart was removed. Man proposes, but oftentimes another power over which he has no control, disposes.

Daniel was made first president over the 120 princes because an "excellent spirit was found in him." Both Cyrus and Darius were converted to the worship of the true God. Therefore, the everlasting Arm which intervenes in the affairs of mankind, set up a king of His own choice.

In this manner the symbols met their fulfillment and the lion "was lifted up from the earth, and **made** to stand upon the feet as a man, and a man's heart was given to it."

The heart is a fitting emblem of a ruler of a nation. The contrast between a godly and an ungodly king is as vastly different as between the human and the beastly heart. The heart is the life-giving energy to the human body, just as a king is the head of a nation.

After freedom had been granted to the Jews, Cyrus, in his proclamation said: "Thus saith Cyrus king of Persia, The Lord God of heaven hath given me all the kingdoms of the earth; and He hath charged me to build him an house at Jerusalem, which is in Judah. Who is there among you of all His people? His God be with him, and let him go up to Jerusalem, which is in Judah, and build the house of the Lord God of Israel, (He is the God,) which is in Jerusalem." (Ezra 1:2, 3.) This godly influence of the kings of Medo-Persia did not wear out until years later. The decree made by Cyrus was written in a roll and placed at Achmetha, in the palace that is in the province of the Medes. Years later the roll being found by Darius, the edict was immediately carried out. Cyrus had decreed that all should make a free will offering, and the king himself contributed without limit. He said: "Moreover I make a decree what ye shall do to the elders of these Jews for the building of this house of God: that of the king's goods, even of the tribute beyond the river, forthwith expenses to be given to these men, that they be not hindered." (Ezra 6:8.) He further decreed that all the needs to maintain the sacrificial services "be given them day by day without fail." Then he added "That they may offer sacrifices of sweet savours unto the God of heaven, and pray for the life of the king, and of his sons." (Ezra 6:10.) Nebuchadnezzar professed conversion after his wonderful experience with the God of heaven, and declared: "And all the inhabitants of the earth are reputed as nothing: and He doeth according to His will in the army of heaven, and among the inhabitants of the earth: and none can stay His hand, or say unto Him, What doest thou? At the same time my reason returned unto me; and for the glory of my kingdom, mine honor and brightness returned unto me, and my counsellors and my lords sought unto me; and I was established in my kingdom, and excellent majesty was added unto me. Now I Nebuchadnezzar praise and extol and honour the King of heaven, all whose works are truth, and His way judgment: and those that walk in pride He is able to abase." (Dan. 4:35-37.)

Though the sublime words spoken by the Chaldean king seems to reveal a change of heart, his works showed failure in what his lips proclaimed. What a contrast between the Babylonian monarch, and the Medo-Persian kings! Nebuchadnezzar declined to set God's people free, he refused to restore the sacred vessels to the King of heaven; he made no decree for the rebuilding of the house of God; he gave no gift of any kind to the King of kings; he imparted not the knowledge of Jehovah to his people; he left his children and his household to worship the heathen gods of wood and stone; he made no effort to give God the glory, save with his lips.

Though we have these living examples before us, yet how often we admit by our lips that which is right and true, and make no move to reach for the stretched out Arm of divine love. Multitudes are aping the standard set by the ancient monarch. "This people draweth nigh unto me with their mouth, and honoureth me with their lips; but their heart is far from me." (Matt. 15:8.)

Though Nebuchadnezzar failed in these sacred things, God, in His great mercy saved the King. God bore long with the Babylonian king, but "the once proud monarch had become a humble child of God; the tyrannical, overbearing ruler, a wise and compassionate king. He who had defied and blasphemed the God of heaven, now acknowledged the power of the Most High, and earnestly sought to promote the fear of Jehovah and the happiness of his subjects. Under the rebuke of Him who is King of kings and Lord of lords, Nebuchadnezzar had learned at last the lesson which all rulers need to learn."—"Prophets and Kings," p. 521.

THE BEAR AND THE LEOPARD

The example made of the Babylonian monarchs should have an object lesson to all successive kings. The godly influence of Cyrus might also have been retained, but the kings of Medo-Persia, like the Chaldeans, were looking forward to worldly glory without fear of Him who can set up Kingdoms, and depose kings.

The priceless lesson taught by the punishment of the Chaldean kings, should have been a blessing to them, but in their vain imagination they departed from the source of true wisdom and from power that is never failing. Thus that which was intended as a blessing became a condemnation. Therefore, the kings of Medo-Persia grew worse than the kings of Grecia whose idols were their gods, and perverse appetite their only rule of life. Thus again the time had come for the **ribs** in the mouth of the bear to speak, "Arise and devour much flesh." Therefore, the arm of Omnipotence was withdrawn from the Persian king, and Alexander, with the swiftness of an eagle marched upon his prey. So, Medo-Persia opened the gateway for the bloodiest wars in our world's history. In this manner the words, "Arise, devour much flesh," met their fulfillment.

Says Daniel: "And as I was considering, behold, an he goat came from the west on the face of the whole earth, and touched not the ground: and the goat had a notable horn between his eyes. And he came to the ram that had two horns, which I had seen standing before the river, and ran into him in the fury of his power. And I saw him come close unto the ram, and he was moved with choler against him, and he smote the ram, and brake his two horns: and there was no power in the ram to stand before him, but he cast him down to the ground, and stamped upon him: and there was none that could deliver the ram out of his hand. . . . The ram which thou sawest having two horns are the kings of Media and Persia. And the rough goat is the king of Grecia; and the great horn that is between his eyes is the first king." (Dan. 8:5-7, 20, 21.) Therefore, Alexander, whose love for conquest knew no bounds, was the first to successfully lead the west against the east.

But no sooner had Alexander conquered the empire, than he engaged in a drunken debauch and passed away while yet in his youth. Thus the horn of the "he goat" was broken off from between his eyes, "And for it came up four notable ones towards

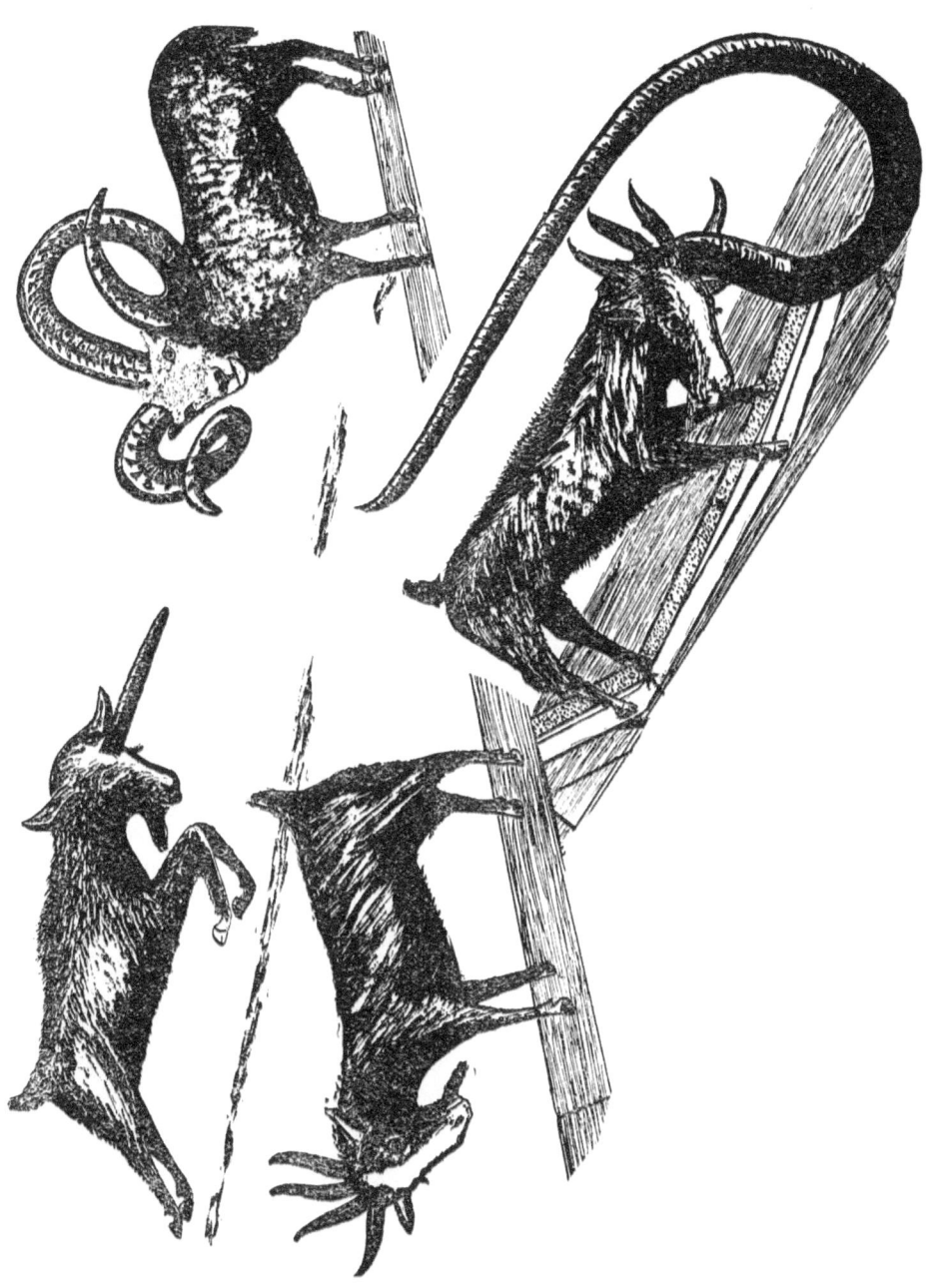

the four winds of heaven." Alexander not having a successor to inherit the throne, the kingdom was divided between his four generals; namely, Cassander, Lysimachus, Ptolemy, and Seleucus. Thus time and providence brought about the four-headed leopard beast.

The Ram and the He Goat

The **entire conflict** between the nations is symbolized by the ram and the goat, with various horns coming up and breaking off. Why a ram and a goat? Why not some other species of animals? Jesus gives the answer: "And before him shall be gathered all nations: and he shall separate them one from an-other, as a shepherd divideth his sheep from the goats: And he shall set the sheep on his right hand, but the goats on the left." (Matt. 25:32, 33.)

By these domestic beasts inspiration conveys the thought that the inhabitants of earth are but sheep and goats—true and false religion. It also signifies that wars are a strife between good and evil. But why Medo-Persia by a ram, and Grecia by a goat? Why not the reverse? The kings of the Medo-Persian empire became believers in the true God as previously explained; thus having principles contrary to those of Grecia. For that reason Medo-Persia was represented by a ram and Grecia by a goat. Wonderful it is to note how perfect and thoughtful was the great wisdom and care of the Infinite **One,** as exercised to devise these symbols. Only **omnipotence** can invent such perfect prophetic art, foretelling historical events.

Kingdom of Brass Rules the World

It has been previously explained that the lion, the bear, and the leopard beasts are divinely numbered. The leopard being the **fourth** empire from creation, and as the numbers in that fashion stop with him, naturally the question would arise: Why not continue the numerical order with the beasts that followed the leopard? There are several reasons for the change with that particular beast. As Rome was slowly rising from within the Grecian empire she finally absorbed the last Grecian division and the Ptolemy dynasty became a province of the Roman state about 27 B. C. Thus the Old Testament closed with Grecia and with Rome the New began. Therefore, between Grecia and Rome lies the dividing line. It is also noted that the beasts representing the Old Testament are hornless, but the ones in the New are with horns. All of which signifying the close of the typical and the commencement of the anti-typical period.

The numerals of the Bible are like rich veins of metal beneath the surface of the earth. Thousands walk over these unknown treasures until some unseen power brings them to the surface. We know that the Trinity is best expressed by the use of the terms, Father, Son and Holy Ghost. Likewise we express God's attributes in three terms, namely, omnipresence, omniscience, and omnipotence. This feature could be greatly enlarged upon.

If **three** is the symbol of the Triune Jehovah, **four** must designate that which proceeds from Him, as revealed in creation. The cherubims consist of four living creatures, each having the face of a lion, a calf, a man, and an eagle, respectively. There are four regions of the earth: East, North, South and West, which is expressive of the completeness of direction; likewise: winter, spring, summer and autumn covers a complete circle of the seasons. We have already observed that there were four universal empires in the history of the world from creation to the crucifixion. We may also note the fact in connection with this subject that there is a combination of the three-fold with the four-fold as clearly seen in the work of creation in which the first four days were employed in forming the sphere, and the remaining three in the creation of the living creatures and culminating in a Sabbath rest. The fourth day saw the material substance of creation finished, and on the fifth and sixth days, was the peopling of the earth. In the book of Revelation under the head of the seven seals, we observe that the first four seals were clearly separated from the last three by the symbols of four horses. Thus it appears that the four-fold measure in each case precedes the three-fold, just as in creation order: each division culminating in the seven of perfection. For this reason there are four sections in the great image of Daniel Two, four beast's in Daniel's vision, four wings and four heads on the leopard with whom the numbers in that fashion ceased. Thus it is evident that the Old Testament closed with a symbolic number— four (the leopard-beast). Showing that all the necessary provision for the salvation of the human family was completed under the dispensation of this prominent number, "four", as it terminated about the time of the crucifixion. Thus this number is used in connection with incidences to signify earthwide.

Blow ye the trumpet in Zion, and sound an alarm in my holy mountain; let all the inhabitants of the land tremble; for the day of the Lord cometh, for it is nigh at hand. (Joel 2:1.)

THE NON-DESCRIPT BEAST
DANIEL 7:7

Following the four-headed leopard comes the non-descript beast of Daniel 7:7, representing the fourth universal empire from the flood, but the fifth one from creation. Rome is represented by a more terrible symbol than the kingdoms before it. There must be a special reason why the Roman monarchy is represented by a non-descript beast. The symbol reveals that the Roman system of government was an arrangement that could not be described. The nearest approach to a correct name is the term—non-descript.

We shall now consider its government administration. The crucifixion of Christ and the martyrdom of the Christians give evidence that the Roman executive authority was vested in paganism, which was at war with Christianity. As these Christians were put to death for refusal to worship the gods of the people, it is obvious that the Jews used the civil arm of Rome to try and enforce their own religious customs; Jesus being an example, for He was crucified as a result of religious controversy. Rome in the first century persecuted the Christians, but after adopting Christianity, she ill-treated the pagans; compelling them to join the so-called Christian church. From the evidence gathered, it is plain to see that the Roman monarchy was a tool for either Pagan, Jew, or Christian; alternating in favor of one, and then of the other. Inasmuch as the character of the Imperial Roman jurisdiction could not be defined as Pagan, Jewish, or Christian, "non-descript" is the only fitting symbol. It is said of Constantine at his death that his subjects knew not what kind of burial to give him, since he was a professed Christian, but at heart a Pagan. Perhaps many nations as well as some professed Christians at this present time are non-descript like the Romans, for the apostle has described their condition thusly: "For the time will come when they will not endure sound doctrine; but after their own lusts shall they heap to themselves teachers having itching ears; and they shall turn away their ears from the truth, and shall be turned unto fables." (2 Tim. 4:3, 4.)

Attempts To Establish Ecclesiastical Governments

The question may arise: What hindered Satan from establishing an ecclesiastical monarchy before the closing period of

DANIEL 7: 7.

DANIEL 7:25

the Old Testament? The only answer that can be given, is, the Jewish nation permitted him to becloud their eyes. They were told not to make a confederacy with the world, but, unmindful of the command they made a league with the Romans, and that is what helped Satan to accomplish his scheme.

The following will show that this great enemy of mankind tried this same procedure in the days of Babylon: "Nebuchadnezzar the king made an image of gold, whose height was three-score cubits, and the breadth thereof six cubits: he set it up in the plain of Dura, in the province of Babylon. Then an herald cried aloud, To you it is commanded, O people, nations, and languages . . . ye fall down and worship the golden image that Nebuchadnezzar the king hath set up: And whoso falleth not down and worshippeth shall the same hour be cast in the midst of a burning fiery furnace. . . . The nations, and the languages, fell down and worshipped the golden image." (Dan. 3:1, 4-7.) But there were three Hebrews found who rebelled against the king's command and refused to bow down to the idol. "Shadrach, Meshach, and Abednego, answered and said to the king, O Nebuchadnezzar, we are **not** careful to answer thee in this matter. If it be so, our God whom we serve is able to deliver us from the burning fiery furnace, and He will deliver us out of thine hand, O king. But if not, be it known unto thee, O king, that we will not serve thy gods, nor worship the golden image which thou hast set up . . . And he commanded the most mighty men that were in his army to bind Shadrach, Meshach, and Abednego, and to cast them into the burning fiery furnace . . . Therefore because the king's commandment was urgent, and the furnace exceeding hot, the flame of the fire slew those men that took up Shadrach, Meshach, and Abednego. And these three men, Shadrach, Meshach, and Abednego, fell down bound into the midst of the burning fiery furnace. Then Nebuchadnezzar . . . answered and said, Lo, I see four men loose, walking in the midst of the fire, and they have no hurt; and the form of the fourth is like the Son of God. Then Nebuchadnezzar came near to the mouth of the burning fiery furnace, and spake, and said, Shadrach, Meshach, and Abednego, ye servants of the most high God, come forth, and come hither." (Verses 16-18, 20, 22-26.)

Then these men came forth unhurt. It is wonderful what God accomplished with but three slaves against a world's empire. These three men, with faith in God, broke the Satanic contrivance, abolished the establishment of an ecclesiastical government and brought the king's decree to naught.

Satan worked out a similar plot in the Medo-Persian government with plans that were carried out by intrigue, taking the king unawares. Though Daniel was cast into the lion's den, he too, came out unharmed, but his enemies perished as did those who threw the three Hebrews into the fiery furnace. Thus Satan's power was broken in both of these ancient empires. Had there been such men as these Hebrews in the days of the establishment of the Roman monarchy, or at the closing of the Old Testament history and during the commencement of the New, conditions would have been entirely different. The world is in urgent need at this time of men like the three Hebrews, who would rather yield this present life than to offend their God—men like Daniel, who looked with strong faith to the Lord and was without fault in his religious and secular duties. By such men as these the world has been blessed with everlasting benefits and rewards that no human lips can describe.

"How beautiful upon the mountains are the feet of him that bringeth good tidings, that publisheth peace; that bringeth good tidings of good, that publisheth salvation; that saith unto Zion, Thy God reigneth! Thy watchmen shall lift up the voice; with the voice together shall they sing: for they shall see eye to eye, when the Lord shall bring again Zion." (Isa. 52:7, 8.)

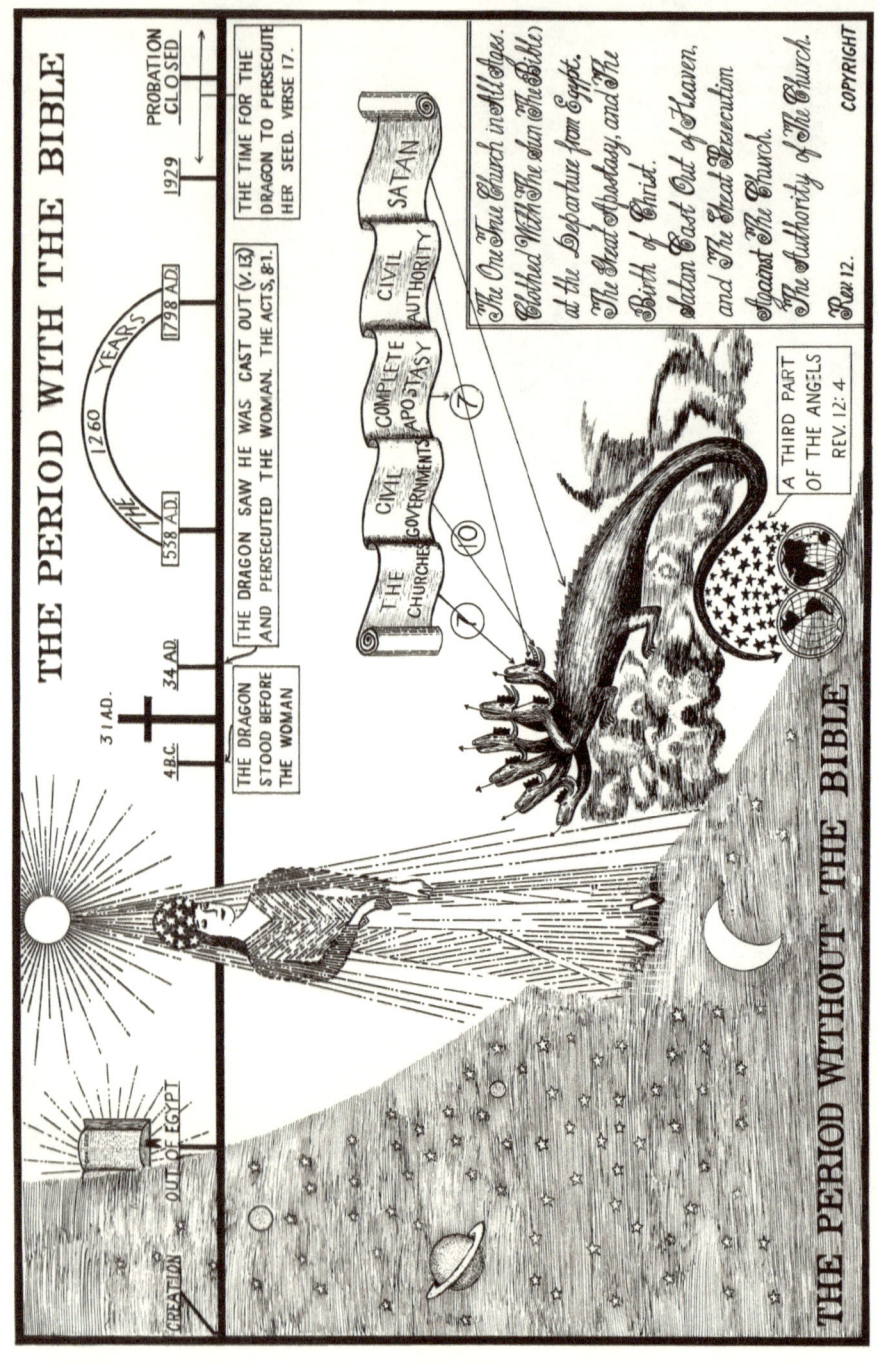

THE PERIOD WITH THE BIBLE

PROBATION CLOSED

1929

THE TIME FOR THE DRAGON TO PERSECUTE HER SEED. VERSE 17.

1798 A.D.

1260 YEARS

538 A.D.

THE DRAGON SAW HE WAS CAST OUT (V.13) AND PERSECUTED THE WOMAN. THE ACTS, 8:1.

34 A.D.

31 A.D.

4 B.C.

THE DRAGON STOOD BEFORE THE WOMAN

CREATION

OUT OF EGYPT

SATAN

CIVIL AUTHORITY

COMPLETE APOSTASY

7

CIVIL GOVERNMENTS

10

THE CHURCHES

1

The One True Church in All Ages. Clothed With The Sun The Bible, at the Departure from Egypt. The Great Apostasy, and The Birth of Christ. Satan Cast Out of Heaven, and The Great Persecution Against The Church. The Authority of The Church. Rev. 12.

A THIRD PART OF THE ANGELS REV. 12: 4

THE PERIOD WITHOUT THE BIBLE

64

THE RED DRAGON
REV. 12:3

"And there appeared a great wonder in heaven; a woman clothed with the sun, and the moon under her feet, and upon her head a crown of twelves stars: and she being with child cried, travailing in birth, and pained to be delivered. And there appeared another wonder in heaven; and behold a great red dragon, having seven heads and ten horns, and seven crowns upon his heads. And his tail drew the third part of the stars of heaven, and did cast them to the earth; and the dragon stood before the woman which was ready to be delivered, for to devour her child as soon as it was born. . . . And the great dragon was cast out that old serpent, called the Devil, and Satan, which deceiveth the whole world: he was cast out into the earth, and his angels were cast out with him." (Verses 1-4, 9.) The dragon was seen in heaven and being "cast out," it is obvious that the symbol is of heavenly origin. Of him it is said: "That old serpent, called the Devil, and Satan." Note that the dragon is a symbol of Satan, even as the Lamb having "seven horns and seven eyes" is a symbol of Christ. (Rev. 5:6.)

Since the numerous beasts form an unbreakable chain of the world empires, the dragon cannot intersect between the links as the symbol of a separate earthly system; thus he represents just what the Scripture says: "The Devil, and Satan." The figure is given to reveal Satan's scheme at a certain time in our world's history.

The "woman clothed with the sun" is understood to be God's church. The child to which she gave birth was Christ. The twelve stars that comprise the woman's crown were originally symbols of the twelve patriarchs. This will be made plain in another study. Therefore, we shall endeavor to make clear the time of the dragon and his work. It will be noticed that the dragon stood ready to devour the child (Christ) as soon as He was born. It is evident, that the old serpent armed himself with seven heads and ten horns prior to the birth of Christ.

"And his tail drew a third part of the stars of Heaven." The Scripture is self explanatory as to who the symbolical stars are, for Inspiration says: "He was cast out into the earth, and his **Angels** were **cast out with him."**

Therefore, the "third part of the stars" represent the angels who were deceived by Satan's controversy. Quoting "Testimonies for the Church," Vol. 3, p. 115: "Satan, in his rebellion, took a third part of the angels. They turned from the Father and from His Son, and united with the instigator of rebellion." The question may arise: Why draw them with his **tail** and not some other way? The symbol is perfectly capable of indicating the manner in which Satan drew them to the earth. Had it been done with his claws, it would denote that Satan defeated Michael (Christ), and by force dragged out a third of the angels. But since he drew them with his tail, the significance is that a third part of the angels joined him in rebellion against Michael. For when the dragon was cast out, naturally he was coming head first, and as he drew them with his tail, it reveals that they voluntarily followed him. Thus Christ could do nothing for them.

War In Heaven

"And there was war in heaven: Michael and His angels fought against the dragon; and the dragon fought and his angels, And prevailed not; neither was there place found any more in heaven." (Verses 7, 8.) The conflict was in heaven. The name "Michael" means **who is like God**; hence it is one of the many titles of Christ. Daniel calls Him "Michael the **Great Prince** which standeth for the children of thy people." (Dan. 12:1.) Christ has numerous titles, each bearing a definition of a certain phase, or character of His work. The angel said to Joseph, "and thou shalt call His name Jesus, for he shall save His people from their sins." He is also called "Emmanuel", meaning, "God with us." etc.

Time Cast Out

Satan could not have been cast out of heaven immediately after he sinned, or when he deceived Adam and Eve, for in Job 1:6, 7, we read: "Now there was a day when the sons of God came to present themselves before the Lord, and Satan came also among them. And the Lord said unto Satan, whence comest thou? Then Satan answered the Lord, and said, From going to and fro in the earth, and walking up and down in it." "The sons of God" are the representatives of unfallen worlds; equal to Adam before he sinned, created by the hand of God, and representatives in the same capacity as Adam could have been had he not fallen from his throne by sin. Quoting from The Spirit of Prophecy: "The commanders of the angel hosts, the sons of God the representatives of the unfallen worlds, are assembled. The heavenly council before which Lucifer had accused **God** and **His Son,** the **representatives of those sinless realms** over which

Satan had thought to establish his dominion."—"The Desire of Ages", p. 833.

Satan still had access to heaven in Job's time. Therefore, he must have been cast out at a later date. Says John: "And when the dragon saw that he was cast unto the earth, he persecuted the woman which brought forth the man child." (Rev. 12:13.) The next necessary step is to find when the dragon first persecuted the "woman" (Christian Church); we shall then have the truth of the time Satan was cast out. That time of persecution is recorded in The Acts 8:1, "And Saul was consenting unto his [Stephen's] death. And at that time there was a great persecution against the church which was at Jerusalem; and they were all scattered abroad throughout the regions of Judea and Samaria, except the apostles." Thus the great persecution against the church was about 34 A.D. It is true that Satan persecuted Christ before that time, but Christ is not the "woman." He is the "Child" whom Satan wished to "devour." Therefore, Satan was cast out immediately after Christ ascended on High. The Spirit of Prophecy speaking of the occasion says:

"All are there to welcome the Redeemer. They are eager to celebrate His triumph and to glorify their King. . . . He presents to God the wave-sheaf, those raised with Him as representatives of that great multitude who shall come forth from the grave at His second coming. . . . The voice of God is heard proclaiming that justice is satisfied. Satan is **vanquished**. Christ's toiling, struggling ones on earth are 'accepted in the Beloved.' Before the heavenly angels and the representatives of unfallen worlds, they are declared justified.

"Satan saw that his disguise was torn away. His administration was laid open before the unfallen angels and before the heavenly universe. He had revealed himself as a murderer. By shedding the blood of the Son of God, he had uprooted himself from the sympathies of the heavenly beings. Henceforth his work was restricted. Whatever attitude he might assume, he could no longer await the angels as they came from the heavenly courts, and before them accuse Christ's brethren of being clothed with the garments of blackness and the defilement of sin. The **last link** of sympathy between Satan and the heavenly world was broken."—"The Desire of Ages," pp. 833, 834, 761.

The time he drew a third part of the stars (angels) from heaven, and the time of the war in heaven, were two distinct occasions. He drew the angels when they followed him from heaven to earth and sought to devour Christ. "And when the dragon **saw** that he was cast out into the earth"; that is, after Christ was crucified, Satan at his return to heaven was forbidden an entrance. Thus he **"saw"**—understood that he was cast out. **Then** he persecuted the church.

The Dragon's Horns and Heads

The only possible time for the application of the symbolical horns, heads, and crowns would be with the closing of the **old** dispensation, and at the commencement of the New. For, the dragon appeared in that form when Christ was to be born. The horns represent the same as they do on any symbolical beast. Being **ten** in number the symbol denotes that the effect of his scheme was universally felt. It also signifies that Satan had obtained full control of the nations which were symbolized by the **ten** horns of the non-descript beast of Daniel 7; and thus he moved upon Herod to kill the children at the birth of Christ with the hope of destroying the Saviour—devouring the "Child."

Let us not overlook the fact that all the horns, heads, and crowns, were present when he stood ready "to devour her Child." Consequently, whatever the meaning by these symbols, all must be in existence at the same time. Had this not been so, the symbols of heads and horns would have so indicated by coming up one after another like the beasts, and also like the horns of the ram and of the goat of Daniel 8. The same is true with the non-descript beast of Daniel 7:7, from which **three** of the **ten** horns were "plucked up by the roots." Where systems and governments do not all exist at the same time, the symbols appear one after another in their correct order. Thus we see that Inspiration is perfect in every respect, and faultless in revealing the truth intended. Therefore, it would be inconsistent for one to conclude that the "horns" as well as the "heads" could represent a consecutive order of systems as long as they all appear in a group, and in oneness with the beast that carries them.

It is also impossible that both horns and heads could represent civil governments, or kings. If the horns stand for political systems, then the heads cannot. If the wounded head on the leopard-like beast of Revelation 13:1-3 represents a religious organization, then all the heads must stand for religious systems. However, there is an exception with the four-headed leopard of Daniel 7:6, for he is without horns and his heads are proven to be civil by the four horns of the goat. It is an unmistakable fact that the symbols are intended to reveal the civil and religious phases during the period represented by the non-descript beast in both his stages—imperial and papal Rome.

As crowns denote civil authority and as they appear on the heads instead of on the horns, it is evident that the church in that period was using civil dictatorial power to propagate her dogmas. Thus the lessons embodied in these symbols are far greater than we can comprehend in a moment. As the facts brought forth regarding the nature of the symbols cannot be questioned, we have a positive foundation for their application.

The dragon with his seven heads and ten horns, with the crowns on the heads, appeared at the birth of Christ as previously explained, and occupies the period parallel with the nondescript beast. The heads are represented by the Biblical number "seven," meaning "completeness," and embrace every religious system in the days of Christ. As the dragon represents the devil who controls the heads, the symbol unmistakably denotes a complete apostasy. It is not intended to reveal that the pagan system of worship was headed by the devil, for it has never been otherwise. It was the Jewish church that had apostatized, and that is what made the Biblical number "seven heads." Just such an apostasy had gripped the world in the days of Noah; and its wickedness made the continuation of the world impossible. Therefore, necessity, for the good of mankind, brought about the flood. The terrible apostasy of the Jews made unavoidable another disaster similar to the dreadful deluge. As God could not overthrow the world by water the second time, and yet keep His never failing promise to his faithful servant Noah, He sent His Son to die in the world's stead. Therefore, the world perished not, because of the supreme sacrifice of the Son of God; and the world exists today because Christ arose from the dead.

The Dragon's Crowns

Next we note the crowns and their significance. It has been explained that the crowns denote civil authority. The heads being crowned, it reveals that the churches of that time employed the civil arm of the state. Had this not been true, the Jews could not have crucified the Lord of glory; neither could they have stoned Stephen, or beheaded and killed the others. It was the civil arm of Rome, headed by the dragon, through which the Jews committed these terrible crimes; resulting in their own destruction.

The Accuser of the Brethren

After the dragon was cast down from heaven according to the Vision, says John: "And I heard a loud voice saying in heaven, Now is come salvation, and strength, and the kingdom of our God, and the power of His Christ: for the accuser of our brethren is cast down, which accused them before our God day and night." (Rev. 12:10.) "Satan's accusations against those who seek the Lord are not prompted by displeasure at their sin. He exults in their defective characters: for he knows that only through their transgression of God's law can he obtain power over them."—Prophets and Kings, pp. 585, 586. When the Spirit of God prompts to reprove, He will reveal sin and rebuke the sinner. But Satan, encourages the sinner to unconsciously commit himself in transgression, then he accuses him before the great Judge **in Heaven,** as "being clothed with the garments of blackness and the defilement of sin," to **secure** his condemnation. God's people must learn to detect the voice of the Spirit of Christ, as well as the spirit of Satan. When the two clash, the One will strive for obedience to God's Word, but the other will excuse the sin and sympathize with the sinner. In this way Satan gains ground, for the sinner loves his sin.

THE CHURCH OF GOD IN SYMBOL OF A WOMAN
REVELATION 12

"And there appeared a great wonder in heaven; a woman clothed with the sun, and the moon under her feet, and upon her head a crown of twelve stars: And she being with child cried, travailing in birth, and pained to be delivered. And there appeared another wonder in heaven; and behold a great red dragon, having seven heads and ten horns, and seven crowns upon his heads. And his tail drew a third part of the stars of heaven, and did cast them to the earth: and the dragon stood before the woman which was ready to be delivered, for to devour her child as soon as it was born. And she brought forth a man child, who was to rule all nations with a rod of iron: and her child was caught up unto God, and to His throne. And the woman fled into the wilderness, where she had a place prepared of God, that they should feed her there a thousand two hundred and three score days." (Verses 1-6.)

Note that the objects shown in the vision were in heaven, not on earth. Therefore, what ever these symbols may imply, they must be of a heavenly origin. Again note that her only clothing is the sun, and that her crown is composed solely of **"twelve stars."** Observe that she is **not standing** on the **"moon,"** for the Revelator says, She had "the moon **under** her feet." We must carefully study the character of these symbols, for thus only can we learn their significance. Also mark that she **was** to be delivered of a man child, and that the same **was** "caught up to God and to His throne."

It is an admitted fact that the child was Christ, Who ascended on High after His resurrection. (Mark 16:19.) The symbol being of heavenly origin, the "woman" cannot represent Mary, the mother of Christ, but she denotes the church ("woman") that was to bring forth, or into which Christ was to be born. Thus John in vision was looking back beyond the birth of Christ.

It has been taught by some that the "woman" is a symbol of the Christian church, and that the moon under her feet is to denote the Mosaic dispensation or sacrificial ceremonial system that had passed away, and being clothed with the sun, to mean the glory of the gospel in the new dispensation. According to the following, these claims prove incorrect.

If the "woman" represents the Christian church, how could the same church (woman) travail in birth with Christ, by whom the church was founded thirty years later? If we say she represents the Jewish church, how could she fly into the wilderness and remain there from 538 to 1798, in the Christian dispensation? If the "moon" under her feet indicates the end of the Mosaic sacrificial system, why did it not end before the birth of Christ, since the moon stood under her feet before He was born. If it had ended at that time, could it have been a symbol of the death of Christ? If her garment of sunlight is a symbol of the gospel in the Christian dispensation, how could the church (woman) be clothed with it years before the gospel dispensation began, having been clothed with it before the child was born? Which one of the two churches, Jewish or Christian, gave birth to Christ? If it were the Jewish church, then how could the light with which she was clothed be applied to the Christian church? If these questions cannot be answered, then we are obliged to go deeper into the subject.

The idea advanced that the "woman" is a symbol of the Christian church only, and the "moon" of the Jewish ceremonial system, proves incorrect. The Christian church was founded about 31 A. D., or not earlier than 27, at which time Christ began to preach; being about thirty years of age. Therefore the symbol points back at least thirty-one years before the beginning of the Christian church, for the "woman" (church) "was travailing in birth, and pained to be delivered."

Thus it was the Jewish church that "brought forth" the Son of God and not the Christian. Therefore, "she [the Jewish church] being with child, cried, travailing in birth, and pained to be delivered"; that is, the promise was made to Israel that the Messiah was to be born through that nation by that particular church ("woman"). The old dragon, knowing the channel through which the "child" was to come, closely watched with the intention of destroying the promised **One** as soon as **He** was born. It was then, that the dragon by the hand of Herod, "slew all the children that were in Bethlehem and in all the coasts thereof," hoping to do away with the coming King. (See Matt. 2:16.)

The evidence proves that the symbol of the "woman" takes in both periods, B.C. and A.D. Therefore, as the moon was under her feet **before** the birth of Christ, it must be a symbol of a period of time which had preceded the Jewish church. As the "woman" was "clothed with the sun" before she brought forth the "Child," it is evident that the symbol, "**clothed** with the sun," was fulfilled before the birth of Christ. If the moon is

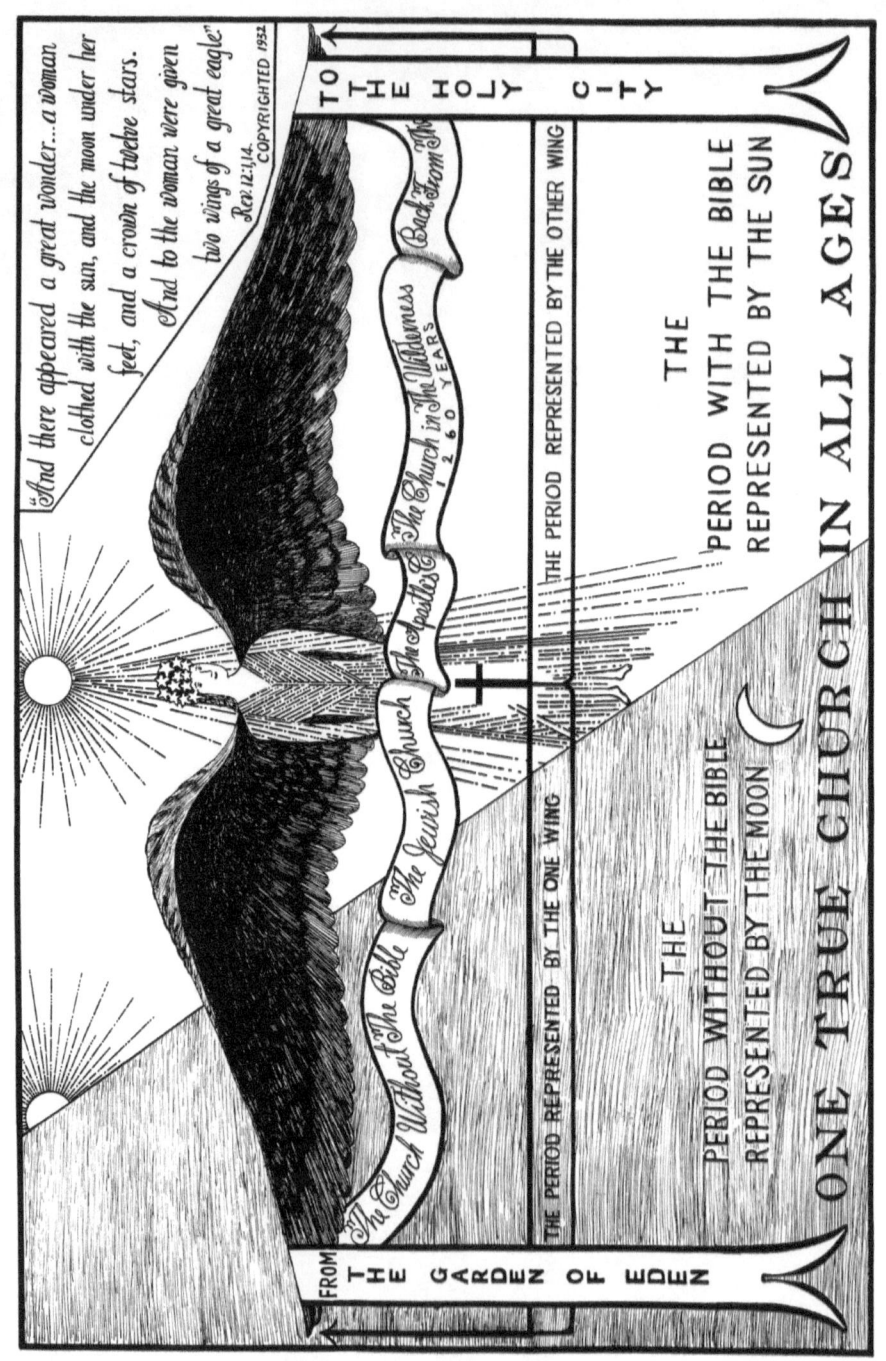

"And there appeared a great wonder...a woman clothed with the sun, and the moon under her feet, and a crown of twelve stars. And to the woman were given two wings of a great eagle"

Rev. 12:1,14.

COPYRIGHTED 1952.

TO THE HOLY CITY

Back From The Wilderness

The Church in The Wilderness 1260 YEARS

The Apostles

The Jewish Church

The Church Without The Bible

THE PERIOD REPRESENTED BY THE OTHER WING

THE PERIOD WITH THE BIBLE REPRESENTED BY THE SUN

THE PERIOD REPRESENTED BY THE ONE WING

THE PERIOD WITHOUT THE BIBLE REPRESENTED BY THE MOON

FROM THE GARDEN OF EDEN

ONE TRUE CHURCH IN ALL AGES

74

symbolical, then, the symbol of the "sun" must be the main object, for, the "moon" depends on the sun for light, and the "woman" **was** clothed with it. Thus, "sun" and "moon," must be taken into consideration. In Genesis 1:16, we are told that the sun and the moon are to rule the day and the night. The "sun" therefore must denote a period into which God's church had been given great light, and the "moon" must be a symbol of the preceding period. The great light cannot be the gospel of Christ in the New Testament. Neither can the "moon" represent the ceremonial system under the Jewish economy, for the "woman" was clothed with the "sun," and the "moon was **under** her feet" while the ceremonial system was yet in existence, for the **child** was born after the "woman" had been clothed with the "sun." Christ Himself, by **eating** the **Passover** just before His crucifixion, established the fact that the ceremonial law was still in existence 34 years after His birth. (See Matt. 26:18-21.)

If the above statement is correct, then we must find two such periods that would perfectly fit the symbols. The first is the one before the Bible came into existence, and the second is the one with the Bible—"clothed with Light"—the written Word of God. Thus symbolically, the first period may be called, night, ruled by the "moon," and the second, day, ruled by the "sun." Therefore, the "woman clothed with the sun," and "travailing with child," is the period after Israel went out of Egypt, and at that time the period without the Bible, "moon," was passing away.

We shall bring forth another proof from a different angle, making doubly sure of the idea that the "woman" represents both periods—before and after Christ. Revelation 12:14 states: "And to the woman were given two wings of a great eagle, that she might fly into the wilderness, into her place, where she is nourished for a time, and times, and half a time, from the face of the serpent." Note that she was given **two** wings of a **great** eagle. If the wings were not symbolical, what their object? As the wings of the lion and the four-headed leopard of Daniel 7 represented periods, as previously explained on pages 33-34, then the two **great** wings must denote two great periods of church history. The eagle being king of birds, and as it is emphasized that they were of a **"great eagle,"** it is evident that the symbol must apprehend each period from its beginning. Thus one of the wings takes in the entire church history from the fall of Adam to the crucifixion of Christ, and the other from His crucifixion to the end of this present world (His second coming). Thus it proves that there is only **one** true church in all ages.

Her crown of **twelve stars** originally represented the twelve

patriarchs and later the twelve tribes after they went out of Egypt, at which time the wonderful light shining from the written Word of God (the Bible), clothed the church (woman) while she was travailing with the **"child"** (the promise of the Messiah). But the crown of **twelve** stars in the New Testament period stand for the twelve apostles. Number twelve is a symbol of government. Jesus said to them: "Ye also shall sit upon twelve thrones, judging the twelve tribes of Israel." (Matt. 19:28.) This fact is proven by the type (the twelve tribes). It will be noticed that in the reckoning of the tribes of Spiritual Israel (the 144,000) by the type (Israel after the flesh) as in Revelation 7:5-8, the tribe of Dan is missing, and instead the tribe of Manasseh, the first born son of Joseph is numbered. The type corresponds perfectly with the anti-type, for Judas Iscariot being one of the "twelve apostles," was cast aside, of whom Dan is a figure. And in his stead Paul of Tarsus was added, of whom Manasses is a figure. Therefore, we see perfect harmony in type and anti-type. The lesson in this instance by these unmistakable symbols, teaches that God has had only one church, one truth, and one way of salvation for all generations. The same is also expressed in the words of Paul: "There is one body, and one Spirit, even as ye are called in one hope of your calling; **one** Lord, **one** faith, **one** baptism, **one** God and Father of all." (Eph. 4:4-6.)

God's church has been symbolized also by earthly objects; we speak of the symbols by women; namely, Hagar, and Sarah. The former is a symbol of the Jewish, and the latter of the Christian Church. (See "The Shepherd's Rod," Vol. 1, p. 136.) These earthly symbols point out God's church in different sections and conditions. But the "woman clothed with the sun" and her "eagle's wings" being of heavenly origin, denote God's true church (truth) in one continuous line, and her Child, our only Saviour and Redeemer in both periods—before and after Christ.

The Crown of Twelve Stars in the New Testament Period

John's vision in the twelfth chapter of Revelation, deals with two main subjects; namely, the "woman clothed with the sun," and the "red dragon." The latter has been explained. (See pages 65-69.) The symbol of the "woman" in the New Testament time covers three divisions: 1st, the apostolic period; 2nd, her absence from civilization (in the wilderness) for 1260 days (years of papal persecution, verses 6, 14); 3rd, the last period of the church while in conflict with the dragon. (Verses 15-17.) The first and second period shall be explained in connection with another study. An explanation of the third period is found in "The Shepherd's Rod," Vol. 1, pp. 151, 152.

Therefore, our intention in is this chapter is to briefly visualize the lesson taught by her "crown of twelve stars." We ask the question: Who appointed these present day self-styled apostolic authorities? It is said that after the apostles passed away, another set of the same number have a right to be apostles. Suppose the claim is true; there are hundreds of churches, and if each one of them had twelve apostles, there would be a multiplicity of thousands of them at one time, and if that act had been repeated in every age, there would be an innumerable multitude of apostles at the appearance of Christ. If there have been thousands of apostles, it is evident by the following Scripture that they shall never enter into the city of God as apostles, for Inspiration says: "And the wall of the city had **twelve** foundations, and in them the name of the **twelve** apostles of the Lamb." (Rev. 21:14.)

What is the difference between an apostle and a minister of the gospel? If there is no difference then there should have been more than twelve apostles in the early church, for there were more than twelve engaged in the ministry. Christ had appointed twelve, but Judas was counted out, leaving only eleven. After Christ ascended on high, the eleven agreed to appoint another in Judas' place: "And the lot fell upon Matthias; and he was numbered with the eleven apostles." (The Acts 1:26.) Therefore, they made up the number. Now if Matthias took Judas' place, then there must be thirteen such men according to Romans 1:1, "Paul, a servant of Jesus Christ, **called** to be an **Apostle**, separated unto the gospel of God."

Mark carefully that the "woman's" crown has only "twelve stars," and in the foundation of the city there are **only** the names of the **twelve** apostles. Which one of the two, Matthias or Paul, is not recognized by Him, who laid the precious foundation of the Holy City? If we say Paul, we make him a liar. If we say Matthias, then his ordination by the eleven had no effect in appointing an apostle. What then? In The Acts 1:26, is the first and last we hear of Matthias, but not so of Paul. If Matthias is the apostle, then he surely is not as worthy as Paul. Which one of the ordinations would be most honorable? Is it Paul's by Christ Himself as He met him on the way to Damascus, or Matthias', by the hands of the apostles?

The question is clear. No man's hands are qualified to ordain an apostle, regardless of his high standing in connection with the gospel. The holy hands of Christ and His personal presence only can appoint one for such an office. This is unimpeachable evidence, for the "woman" has a crown of only **"twelve stars."** Therefore, who has the power to ordain another and thus multiply the "stars"?

What is an apostle? Answer.—One that is "separated unto the gospel of God." But if this is the only meaning of the title, then all who are engaged in the proclamation of the gospel, being separated, must be apostles. Therefore, the word, "apostle," must have a special significance and a deeper meaning than simply separated unto the gospel of God. The apostle Paul was called to be an apostle for the Gentiles. Thus he, with the eleven became the earthly founders of the church of the Gentiles, and Christ the divine head. Speaking of the gifts in the church, apostles are the first, for without a founder there would be no organization, thus the rest of the gifts follow. (See 1 Cor. 12:28.)

The crown is her glory, and the stars (twelve apostles) are her only earthly authority. Here is a striking evidence that the present day apostles are falsely so-called. A prophet may claim authority as a prophet but never as an apostle. However, there is a difference between the prophets of the Old Testament and the ones of the New; the latter being under the authority of the former; in other words, he may be an interpreter or revealer of the Bible: "For all the prophets and the law [ceremonial—in type] prophesied until John." (Matt. 11:13.) Interpretation is correct only when inspired by the same Spirit, thus timely utterances are revealed. Not only do the annals of history prove this, but the Bible is very emphatic on the subject, for it plainly says that we are, "Built upon the foundation of the apostles and prophets, Jesus Christ himself being the chief corner stone." (Eph. 2:20.) Again we read: "Howbeit **when** He the Spirit of **truth**, is **come**, He will guide you into **all truth:** for He **shall not** speak of **himself;** but whatsoever He shall **hear, that shall** He speak; and He will **shew** you things to come." (John 16:13.) Where is the need for such apostles? Are not the words of the apostles in the Bible? If we should appoint a set of such men, would we not set aside the "woman" and her "twelve star crown"? If we set aside the "crown" by voluntary election of apostles, what will we do with the gospel committed to the church by Christ's ordained apostles? Hear the authority by the crown of stars: "But though we, or an angel from heaven, preach any **other** gospel unto you than that which **we** have preached unto you, let him be accursed. As we said before, so say I now again. If any man preach any other gospel unto you than that ye have received let him be accursed." (Gal. 1:8, 9.) "For such are false apostles, deceitful workers, transforming themselves into apostles of Christ." (2 Cor. 11:13.) The world is filled with so-called apostles and sects of every kind, is it not? It is time for God's people to fall on their knees before their Creator, and study the Scriptures for themselves, that they may know what is truth. Why should one accept the decision of another? By so doing we are robbed of an experience of our own. If so, may we not ask the question, What is the future outlook of the world? No one is saved because he may admit the evidence of the truth, or because he may belong to the right church, or creed. It is only by an experience of his own, based upon evidences of truth, received into the heart, that can renew the mind, and regenerate the soul, so that he can walk in newness of life. It is utterly impossible to enter into the kingdom of Christ without a personal touch of divine glory. Jesus said: "Verily, verily, I say unto thee, Except a man be born again, he **cannot** see the kingdom of God." (John 3:3.) The following Scriptures bear the same evidence. "For he is not a Jew which is one outwardly; neither is that circumcision, which is outward in the flesh: But he is a Jew, which is one inwardly; and circumcision is that of the heart, in the spirit, and not in the letter; whose praise is not of men, but of God." (Rom. 2:28, 29.)

"Circumcision is nothing, and uncircumcision is nothing, but the **keeping** of the **Commandments** of God." (1 Cor. 7:19.) "And rend your **heart** and **not** your garments, and turn unto the Lord your God: for He is gracious and merciful, slow to anger, and of great kindness, and repenteth him of evil." (Joel 2:13.) "For they that are such serve not our Lord Jesus Christ, but their own belly; and by **good words** and **fair speeches** deceive the hearts of the **simple**." (Romans 16:18.)

Returning to our original thought: The eleven were allowed to perform the ordination of Matthias for a lesson to this present day with its new-modeled religion, showing that God has committed to no man apostolic authority—save to the **twelve**. The commission to the ministry is: "Go ye therefore, and teach all nations, baptizing them in the name of the Father, and of the Son, and of the Holy Ghost: Teaching them to observe **all** things whatsoever I have commanded you: and, lo, I am with you alway, even unto the end of the world." (Matt. 28:19, 20.) "So thou, O son of man, I have set thee a watchman unto the house of Israel; therefore thou shalt hear the word at **my** mouth, and warn them for **Me**. When I say unto the wicked, O wicked man, thou shalt surely die; if **thou** dost not speak to warn the wicked from his way, that wicked man shall **die** in his iniquity; but **his** blood will I require at **thine** hand." (Ezek. 33:7, 8.)

In reality the twelve "stars" on the "woman's crown" originally represented the twelve patriarchs; later the twelve tribes of fleshly Israel; after that the twelve apostles; and last the twelve tribes of Spiritual Israel (the 144,000). Thus again it proves number "four" to be an important number, and that by the "woman" these four periods are represented.

God who foresaw the selfishness of men, commanded the prophet to write the following: "Ye eat the fat, and Ye clothe you with wool, Ye kill them that are fed: but Ye **feed not** the flock. The diseased have ye **not** strengthened, **neither** have ye healed that which was sick, **neither** have ye bound up that which was broken, **neither** have ye brought again that which was driven away, **neither** have ye sought that which was lost; but **with** force and with cruelty have **ye ruled** them. And they **were** scattered, because there was **no** shepherd; and they became meat to all the beasts of the field, when they were scattered. My sheep wandered through **all** the mountains, and upon **every** high hill: yea, **My** flock was scattered upon **all** the face of the earth, and **none** did search or seek after them. Therefore, **ye shepherds,** hear the word of the Lord; As I live, saith the Lord God, surely because **My** flock became a prey, and **My** flock became meat to every beast of the field because there was **no** shepherd, **neither** did **My** shepherds search for my flock, but the shepherds **fed themselves**, and **fed not My** flock; Therefore, O ye shepherds, hear the word of the Lord; Thus saith the Lord God: Behold, **I am** against the **shepherds:** and **I will** require **My flock** at **their** hand, and cause them to **cease** from **feeding** the **flock; neither** shall the **Shepherds** feed **themselves any more;** for I will **deliver** my flock from **their mouth, that** they may **not** be meat for **them.** For thus saith the **Lord God;** Behold, I even I, will both **search** my sheep, and **seek** them out." (Ezek. 34:3-11.)

As a comparison the Spirit of God drew a literal picture from the flock of sheep and shepherds; God's people as the flock; and the ministry as the shepherds. God's true people will imitate the sheep, and His watchmen **will** imitate the good shepherd who cares for his sheep. Anything less than this is an abomination in God's sight. If we are to learn the lesson intended we must first acquire a clear understanding of the type (shepherds and flocks), for, the anti-type (ministers and church members) are asked to copy after the pattern.

The picture is drawn from the ancient method of herding the flock. The open pasture of the mountains and hills required the shepherd's continual care over the sheep. The vast territory drew the sheep and shepherds a considerable distance from home, and the continual moving over the landscape made it impossible to obtain a permanent shelter of any kind for the sheep, or shepherds. Consequently, other help was needed. Each shepherd had a certain num-ber of dogs, depending on the size of the flock, for the safety of the sheep from man and beast. As one thing called for another, an ass was used to carry the necessary supplies for the sheep, dogs and shepherds. These consisted of cloth-ing, night coverings, food for the shepherds as well as for the dogs, medicines, bandages, etc. The faithful animal carried the load on his back throughout each day of the year. At the end of the day the shepherd counted his sheep. If one was missing, he went to search for it at once, as it was not safe for one to wander apart from the flock.

The excellent condition of the sheep was the evidence of the Shepherd's fidelity and worthiness of his hire. He not only had to seek good pasture, but act as veterinarian as well. Often a sheep would break its leg and it was the shepherd's duty to skillfully set, splinter and bandage the wound. In traveling over the rough surface of the land, where there were rocks and brush, accidents were frequent. Sometimes a thorn would prick the flesh, or other minor injury occur, that probably caused no pain, and would not be noticed by the shepherd, yet a fly might have deposited her eggs in the open sore, and larva would soon develop and work their way under the skin and to the bone; this was a common occurrence. At such a time the shepherd's attention is turned to the ailment of the sheep and he must then give it special care and bandage the wound.

When a lamb, or even a sheep was sick and too weak to follow the flock it was the shepherd's duty to care for and carry them. If he should have a lamb in his arms, the mother sheep is constantly by his side gazing at, and speaking to it. These noble creatures care, feed, and keep their lambs spotlessly clean. Are you mothers doing as much for your children? Are you shepherds (ministers) of the flock of God doing all the ancient shepherd did for his sheep? Or do you feed and care for yourselves more than you do for the flock of God? Are you worthy of your hire?

The ancient shepherd had to give a complete account of the flock, even to the smallest details. Do you think God will require less of you? Are not His sheep of much greater value? David risked his life for a lamb, but God delivered him from the lion and the bear. David, for God's honor, and for the safety of His people, endangered his own life, faced the Giant Goliath, but God delivered the Philistine into David's hands, and made David king over His nation. Do you think He will do less for you, if you, too, imitate the Good Shepherd?

Said Jesus: "I am the good shepherd: the good shepherd

giveth **his life for the sheep.** But he that is an hireling, and not the shepherd, whose own the sheep are not, seeth the wolf coming, and leaveth the sheep, and fleeth; and the wolf catcheth them, and scattereth the sheep. The **hireling fleeth,** because he is an hireling, and careth not for the sheep. I am the good shepherd, and **know** my sheep and am **known** of **mine**. As the Father knoweth me, even so know I the Father: and I lay down my life **for** the **sheep."** (John 10:11-15.)

The prophet Isaiah looking forward to the present day conditions says: "Yea, they are greedy dogs which **can never have enough,** and they are shepherds that **cannot understand:** they all look to their own way, **every** one for **his gain,** from **his** quarter." (Isa. 56:11.)

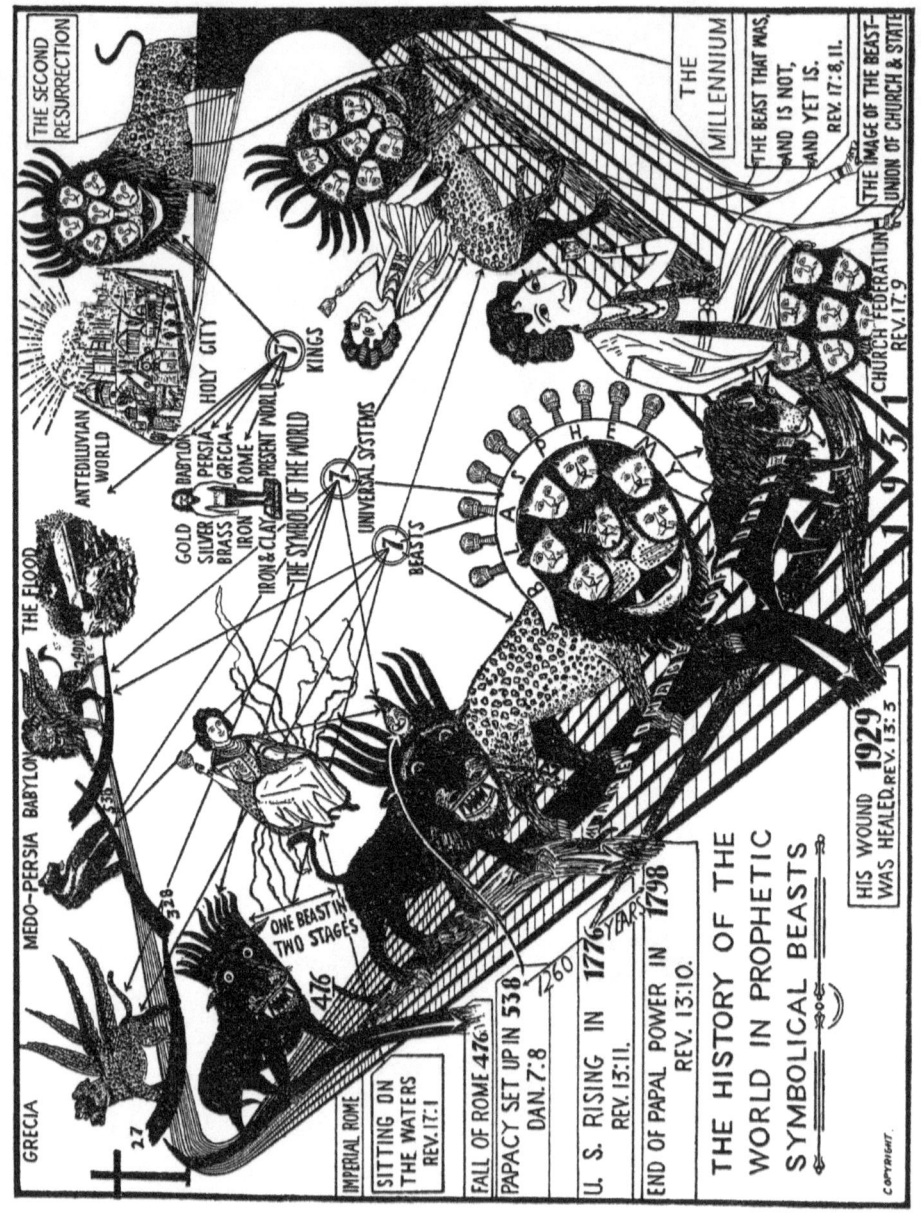

THE HISTORY OF THE WORLD IN PROPHETIC SYMBOLICAL BEASTS

84

THE LEOPARD-LIKE BEAST
REV. 13:1-10

The non-descript beast of Daniel 7, representing Rome in his first stage, shows prophetically by his ten horns that there were ten kings to arise out of Rome. In his second stage it is shown that the papacy was to arise, subdue three kings, and wear out the saints of the most High for the space of 1260 years. But it tells not of the **fall** of the Roman monarchy or the papacy. It is silent concerning the **reformation** that came before or after 1798 A.D. Therefore, the lack of information by the symbols of this beast, must be found somewhere else in the prophetic Word of God. This must be sought in the book of Revelation, for **it** is the complement to Daniel's prophecies.

The leopard-like beast of Revelation 13:1-10 is the only symbolical prophecy that tells of the fall of the Roman monarchy, the crowning of the ten kings, the wound of the papacy, the reformation and rise of Protestantism, and the captivity of the pope.

"And I stood upon the sand of the sea, and saw a beast rise up out of the sea, having seven heads and ten horns, and upon his horns ten crowns, and upon his heads the name of blasphemy." (Rev. 13:1.) Note this beast has the same number of horns as the "non-descript" in his first stage (imperial Rome). Daniel says, the ten horns on the beast representing Rome are "ten kings that shall arise." (Dan. 7:24.) The horns symbolizing the Roman world in its imperial state, also pointed forward to the time when the empire would be divided into ten parts, or kingdoms. In other words, while the horns primarily represented the Roman world in its imperial form, they secondarily denote the present world in its divided state since the fall of Rome—corresponding with the ten toes on the great image of Daniel 2.

The non-descript beast in his first stage has ten horns. As in his second stage the little horn came up, and three of the ten were plucked up by the roots, it denotes that they can never be reinstated as kings. The horns being reduced to the Biblical number **seven**, signified that the papacy was to have complete sway over the entire world as far as the Christian church is concerned. Therefore, the ten horns on the leopard-like beast of Revelation 13:1, cannot signify that the three uprooted ones have assumed their authority the second time.

As the same number of horns appear on each succeeding beast; namely, the non-descript (Dan. 7:7); the leopard-like

(Rev. 13:1); and the scarlet colored (Rev. 17:3); representing the entire New Testament era, it is evident by the facts gathered that the number of horns are intended to denote universal. As they are absent from the beast of Revelation 13:11-18, it verifies the fact that the two-horned beast denotes a local system. Therefore, it is unquestionably clear that the fixed number of horns (ten) are designed to universally symbolize the peoples and governments. (Follow the chart on page 84.)

Inasmuch as the lion, the bear, the four-headed leopard, and the non-descript beast (the symbols of Babylon, Medo-Persia, Grecia and Rome) are linked to each other, the unbreakable chain of beasts make it impossible for another universal beast (system) to intersect their consecutive order. Consequently, the leopard-like beast of Revelation 13:1-9, must follow the non-descript beast (Rome).

Verses 2, 3: "And the beast which I saw was like unto a leopard, and his feet were as the feet of a bear, and his mouth as the mouth of a lion; and the dragon gave him his power, and his seat, and great authority. And I saw one of his heads as it were wounded to death; and his deadly wound was healed: and all the world wondered after the beast." The composition of the beast reveals the fact that he is a descendant from the four beasts before him. The mouth of a lion, the feet of a bear, the body of a leopard, and the number of horns, all point back to his hereditary characteristics as descending from Babylon, Medo-Persia, Grecia, and Rome. This indisputable fact proves that he is the fifth universal beast.

The leopard-like beast arises out of the sea in the same manner as the four beasts before it. (Daniel 7:3.) Therefore, the beast of Revelation 13:1-9 is created from the result of war and commotion among the nations, in the same manner as Babylon, Medo-Persia, Grecia, and Rome. Since the evidence revealed by the symbol cannot be questioned, the leopard-like beast assumes the period after the fall of imperial Rome, corresponding to the feet and toes—iron and clay of the great image in Daniel 2. In other words, the leopard-like beast arrives with the closing period represented by the first stage of the non-descript beast, while the second stage of the latter (papal Rome) continues up to 1798. Consequently, the unfolding process of the one, overlaps the downward course of the other. To John the leopard-like beast was shown not in its unfolding process, but rather in its closing act for he says, "And his deadly wound **was** healed." He saw in vision the beast after the deadly wound had been healed, for he uses the past tense, "was." But in Daniel's vision the work of the non-descript beast was all in the future. Said the Prophet: "And he **shall** speak great words against the **most high,** and **shall** wear out the saints of the most **high,** and **think** to change times and laws: and they **shall** be given into his hand until a time and times and the dividing of time." (Dan. 7:25.) Daniel in vision viewed the history represented by the beasts, forward; while John looked backward; or in other words, Daniel saw what the beast **was to do,** while John was shown what the beast **had** done.

The Crowns and the Horns

Of the beast "having seven heads and ten horns, and **upon his horns ten crowns"** John says, "And I saw one of his heads as it were wounded to death." The wounded head represents the papacy, wounded by Martin Luther which was originally symbolized by the horn-head of the non-descript beast showing **only** the papal power and the authority. But the "leopard-like" shows the papacy in her wounded state, and the imprisonment of the pope. Thus, the two beasts (the non-descript and the leopard-like) overlap each other, from the fall of imperial Rome to 1798. Therefore, while the non-descript beast in its second stage represents the papacy, she is secondarily described by the "leopard-like." The one reveals the tyrannical authority, and the other describes her downfall. For the little horn was to have power and wear out the saints of the most High for 1260 years (Dan. 7:25.) But the leopard-like also "opened his mouth in Blasphemy", and power was given unto him to "continue forty and two months." (Rev. 13:6, 5.) The number of months is equivalent to "time and times and the dividing of time"—1260 days (years), figuring 30 days to the month.

With the imprisonment of Pope Pius VI, and his death on Aug. 19, 1799, a certain transaction occurred between the non-descript and the leopard-like beasts. The head and horns were removed from one to the other, so to speak. In making the change the little horn "having the eyes of a man and a mouth speaking great things," was transposed from horn-head to a common wounded head, showing the papacy had lost her ecclesiastical authority, and was no longer represented by a **horn-head** (combination of church and state).

As that event terminated the prophetic period of the 1260 years of Daniel 7:25 and Revelation 13:5, it completely crowned the horns of the leopard-like beast, signifying that the state is now independent of the church. The crowns on his horns denote the fall of the Roman monarchy, showing that the ten kings which were symbolized by the ten horns of the non-descript beast, have received their kingdom.

Horns and Heads All Present

"I John saw the beast having seven heads and ten horns, and upon his horns ten crowns." Let us not overlook the fact that **all** horns, crowns, and heads are present on the beast. Therefore, whatever meaning is derived by the symbol, all must be in existence at the time his deadly wound was healed. Had it not been so, the symbols of heads and horns would have come one after another as it was with the little horn and the other three that were "plucked up" from the non-descript beast of Daniel 7:7. A similar method is observed with the "he goat." **After the notable horn (Alexander)** was broken off, four came up to take its place (the four divisions of Grecia), and after these came up the exceeding great horn which primarily represented Rome. (Dan. 8:8, 9.)

Where systems and governments do not all exist at the same time, the symbols show their consecutive order. Another factor to be noted that every symbol of the entire procession of the beasts point out facts that were to transpire within the period represented by each beast, and not one of them refers to anything in the past, save the hereditary ancestrial characteristics.

Therefore, heads or horns have no reference to anything before or after the period represented by the beast. It is also unnatural for heads (members of the beast) to exist before or after the beast himself. Therefore, it would be inconsistent to conclude that the horns as well as the heads could denote a consecutive order of systems so long as they all appear at the time of the closing act of the beast. The leopard-like beast in his wounded state must be intended to prophetically point out the existing condition with the present civilization.

The Symbol of the Heads

It is impossible that both horns and heads could stand for civil governments or kings. If the horns represent the political side, then the heads cannot. John says of the leopard-like beast, "I saw one of his heads as it were wounded to death." As the "head" that was "wounded" represents a religious system, then all seven must represent religious organizations, for all heads are alike, save the wound. Thus it is an unmistakable fact that the symbols are intended to reveal both the civil and religious side of the present world.

The crowns represent civil authority as previously explained. Had they been on the heads like on the dragon of Revelation 12:3, it would denote that the churches are using the civil arm of the state to propagate their dogma as in the days of imperial and papal Rome, represented by the dragon. But since the crowns are on the horns, and the state is independent from the church, it proves the symbol by the crowns to be correct. As the facts brought forth regarding the nature of the symbols cannot be questioned, it is evident that we have a positive foundation for their application.

The leopard-like beast is a descendant of the four ancient empires. Therefore, he represents the world, but more particularly the entire western civilization, with their civil and religious systems. Consequently the heads represent Christendom only. John says: "The beast having seven heads and ten horns and upon his horns ten crowns, **and upon his heads the name of blasphemy.**" The fact that there is the name of blasphemy on the heads is an additional proof that they can only represent religious organizations, for blasphemy is equivalent to hypocrisy, and hypocrisy means an attempt to mix the sacred with the common. But the Lord says: "I know the **blasphemy** of them which say they are Jews [Christians], and are **not,** but are the synagogue of Satan." (Rev. 2:9.) "Of whom is Hymenaeus and Alexander; whom I have delivered unto Satan, that they may learn not to blaspheme." (1 Tim. 1:20.) "Therefore, son of man, speak unto the house of Israel, and say unto them, Thus saith the Lord God; Yet in this your fathers have **blasphemed** me, in that they have **committed a trespass against me.**" (Ezek. 20:27.) "Your iniquities, and the iniquities of your fathers together, saith the Lord, which have **burned incense** upon the mountains, **and blasphemed me** upon the hills: therefore will I measure their former work into their bosom." (Isa. 65:7.) Disobedience to the Word of God is blasphemy.

Naturally the question arises, who could these blasphemous denominations be? They can certainly be many; consider the multiplicity of sects. The prophetic word of God, speaking of this present time says: "Knowing this first, that there shall come **in the last days** scoffers, walking after their own lusts." (2 Pet. 3:3.) "For the time will come when they will **not endure sound doctrine;** but after their own lusts they shall **heap to themselves teachers, having itching ears;** And they shall **turn away** their ears **from the truth,** and shall be turned unto fables." (2 Tim. 4:3, 4.)

What has brought the present day confusion? Because they have departed from sound Bible truth is the only answer that can be given. Is it possible that all can be right when no two believe alike, with but one Bible, one gospel, one Lord, one hell to shun and one heaven to gain? Jesus said: "And other sheep

I have, which are not of this fold: them also I must bring, and they shall hear my voice; and there shall be **one fold,** and **one shepherd.**" (John 10:16.)

Such Satanic confusion as the one at the present time was about to arise in the days of Paul. As the Spirit of God moved upon him, he uttered the words with a sharp rebuke: "Now I beseech you, brethren, by the name of Our Lord Jesus Christ, that **ye all speak the same thing,** and that there be **no divisions** among you; but that ye be **perfectly joined** together in the same mind and in the same judgment. For it hath been declared unto me of you, my brethren, by them which are of the house of Chloe, that there are contentions among you. Now this I say, that every one of you saith, I am of Paul; and I of Apollos; and I of Cephas; and I of Christ. Is Christ divided? was Paul crucified for you? or were ye baptized in the name of Paul?" (I Cor. 1:10-13.) How great the contrast between the position taken by the Spirit-filled servant of God, and the present day self-styled apostles.

Jesus said, "And these things will they do unto you, because they have **not known the Father, nor me.**" (John 16:3.) Had all these so-called Christian leaders been led by the Spirit of God, they would imitate the example set forth by the prophets and the apostles; then there could have been no division in Biblical truth. The Present-day condition is indeed a blasphemy and fulfills the words of the Master: "For there shall arise false Christs, and false prophets, and shall shew great signs and wonders; insomuch that, if it were possible, they shall deceive the very elect." (Matt. 24:24.)

In view of this great confusion there is apparent difficulty to immediately determine who is right and who is wrong. Jesus said: "Again I say unto you, That if two of you shall agree on earth as touching anything that they shall ask, it shall be done for them of my Father which is in heaven." (Matt. 18:19.) There could be nothing more pleasing to God than for one of His children to ask in sincerity the way of truth; therefore, such a one **shall not** be left in darkness: "Ask, and it shall be given you; seek and ye shall find; knock, and it shall be opened unto you." (Matt. 7:7.) If people care to find the truth, it can easily be done. But the fact of the matter is that they do not care. People would rather be deceived than to ask God to show them His truth. Yes, they pray, but their prayers are not heard, for: "He that turneth away his ear **from hearing the law,** even **his prayer shall be abomination**." (Prov. 28:9.) The so-called Christians of this day, say, "That Scripture is in the Old Testament and for the

Jews only." We turn to the New Testament for light upon the subject: "Whosoever therefore shall **break** one of these **least** commandments, and shall **teach** men so, he shall be called the **least** in the kingdom of heaven: but whosoever **shall do and teach** them, the same shall be called **great** in the kingdom of heaven." (Matt. 5:19.) The honest in heart, with surprise, hear the word from the impious scoffer of the day: "That does not mean the law of God; it is the commandment of Jesus: 'Thou shalt love thy neighbor as thyself'." True, but which one of the ten commandments can you break and yet fulfill the commandments of Jesus? And if you love your neighbor, will you dishonor your God? Are not the first four kept to show honor to God; and the last six to test our love to men?

Said Jesus: "On these two commandments hang all the law and the prophets." (Matt. 22:40.) Is the begotten Son of God working in opposition to His Father? "The Revelation of Jesus Christ, **which God gave unto Him,** to shew unto his servants things which must shortly come to pass, and he sent and signified it by his angel unto his servant John." (Rev. 1:1.) "Here is the patience of the **Saints:** here are they that **keep** the **commandments of God,** and the **faith of Jesus."** (Rev. 14:12.) Has not Jesus said that His saints keep the commandments of God? Again the carnal mind raises an objection, "They keep the commandments of God, and not the law." But the Spirit declares: "If ye have respect of persons, ye commit sin, and are convinced of the **law** as transgressors. For whosoever shall keep the whole **law,** and yet **offend in one point,** he is **guilty of all.** For he that said, Do not commit adultery, said also, Do not kill. Now if thou commit no adultery, yet if thou kill, thou art become a transgressor of the **law.** So speak ye, and so do, as they that shall be judged by the **law** of liberty." (Jas. 2:9-12.) "Blessed are they that do his commandments, that they may have right to the tree of life, and may enter in through the gates into the city." (Rev. 22:14.)

The keeping of His commandments is the ticket to heaven. "To the law and to the testimony: if they speak not according to this word, it is because there is no light in them." (Isa. 8:20.) "Because the **carnal mind** is enmity against God: for **it is not subject to the law of God,** neither indeed can be." (Rom. 8:7.) "He that saith, I know Him, and keepeth not His commandments, is a liar, and the truth is not in him." (1 John 2:4.) After loosing one devilish loophole, the carnal mind takes hold of another; determined to serve the devil and deceive himself, and with his nose in the air he utters the words, "We are not to keep the law according to the letter but according to the Spirit,

'For the letter killeth but the Spirit giveth life.'" His misconception of what truth is, leads him to believe that to keep the Law according to the Spirit he must disregard the written Word of God, and keep the **Divine Law** according to his own ways, and in harmony with his carnal mind; making void Jehovah's own inscription (see Ex. 31:18), thus exalting the finite above the Infinite! What greater blasphemy can one commit? We give here a brief explanation of the subject.

To keep the law according to the letter is to build a wall around it as the proud Pharisees did. We quote 1 John 3:15, "Whosoever hateth his brother is a murderer." Therefore, though we kill not, and yet hate our brother we have kept the law blameless according to the **letter,** but **not** according to the Spirit. The keeping of the law according to the Spirit has a broader significance than the carnal mind can conceive. If I must keep the whole law, I must keep the **whole** Word of God in every respect, otherwise, I would dishonor Him, and would become a transgressor of the law as a disobedient son dishonors his earthly father, and becomes guilty of the fifth commandment in the law.

"**Are** we saved by the law?" No, indeed! We are judged by the law. So, if we willfully disobey the Word of God, we fall under the condemnation of the law. "For if we sin willfully after that we have received the knowledge of the truth, there remaineth no more sacrifice for sins." (Heb. 10:26.) But if we love the righteousness of God as expressed in His law, and determine to obey His **Holy Word** where ever found (Bible or Spirit of Prophecy) according to the revelation by His Spirit, then we receive the power which enables us to fulfill the divine purpose, and thereby our sins are blotted out by the blood of Christ, and thus we are made free from the law and its condemnation—placed under divine grace.

It is true that people like to be deceived, flattering themselves that they are on the way to heaven, while Satan winks at their ignorance. The Word of God says: "And many shall follow their pernicious ways; by reason of whom the way of truth shall be evil spoken of . . . . But these, as natural brute beasts, made to be taken and destroyed, speak evil of the things that they **understand not;** and shall utterly perish in their own corruption." (2 Peter 2:2, 12.) This proves how sectarianism sprung up.

As it has been proven, and generally accepted that the "seven Churches" of Revelation, chapters two and three, represented the history of the church in the Christian era, it is evident that the church was split in seven sections. The Laodicean being the last, she is also in danger of falling according to the testimony of the true Witness: "So then because thou art lukewarm, and neither cold nor hot, **I will spue thee** out of my mouth." (Rev. 3:16.) God has sent message after message to give light upon His written Word. They were intended to correct error, rebuke sin, and reprove the sinner; but the leaders of each section threw out the messages, and the few who were willing to sacrifice all for the truth were forced to part from the churches and march on with the light. Were the leaders willing to correct their errors and purify the church, there would have been but one section. **By** the denial of the truth each section cut itself off from the mighty arm of God. Thus, not one of these churches have had additional light on the Scriptures other than that which was imparted to them by the founders of each movement. This fact proves the prophetic Word of God correct, and the older the section the greater the condemnation. Therefore, these churches are represented by the "heads"; the "blasphemy" over them, denotes their fall. Should they refuse this **last** call also, then the revelation of these facts would be against them, and will bring their final ruin.

The message regarding the 144,000, and a call for reformation presented to the Seventh-day Adventist church in 1930 was in like manner rejected. Therefore, as the leadership of the churches have never accepted a message at any time, they are certainly fulfilling the following prophecy: **"The wise men** are ashamed, they are **dismayed and taken:** lo, they **have rejected the word of the Lord;** and **what wisdom** is in them? . . . . For the **pastors** are become brutish, and have not sought the Lord: therefore they shall not prosper, and all their flocks shall be scattered." (Jer. 8:9; 10:21.)

The "seven heads" of the "leopard-like beast" represent this mystery of ungodliness and hypocrisy, showing how each one fell into the trap as they came to it. Therefore, since Luther's time and on, God permitted that His people should be cast out by Satan's flood (the unconverted.) Thus, He has been calling His church from one movement to another.

Therefore, they who lower the standard, and refuse to reform at the sounding of the trumpet, are the very ones who cause division in the church of God! "Now I beseech you brethren, mark them which cause divisions and offenses contrary to the doctrine which ye have learned; and avoid them. For they that are such serve not our Lord Jesus Christ, but **their own belly;** and by **good** words and **fair** speeches deceive the hearts of the simple." (Rom. 16:17, 18.)

Since the history of the church is such, and the last section

(Laodiceans) is in a worse condition, and under greater condemnation than any previous one, and as there is no time left for calling out a new movement, then a message of amazing light and stern rebuke through the Word of God, with manifestations of divine judgments, is the only remedy that can bring true conversion and reformation. Thus preparing a church to stand "without spot, wrinkle or any such thing," of which only can be said: "And the dragon was wroth with the **woman** [the church as a body] and went to make war with the remnant of her seed, **which keep the commandments of God,** and **have the testimony of Jesus Christ."** (Rev. 12:17.) It is the purity of the church that incurs the wrath of the dragon.

These "seven churches" were also symbolized by "seven candlesticks", and the leadership of the same churches, by "seven angels." So we read: "The mystery of the seven stars which thou sawest in my right hand, and the seven golden candlesticks. The **seven stars are the angels of the seven churches: and the seven candlesticks** which thou sawest **are the seven churches."** (Rev. 1:20.) "And **unto the Angel** of the church of the Laodiceans **write."** (Rev. 3:14.) Note the message is addressed to the **Angel** (leadership), and not to the candlestick (the church as a body.) Therefore, the condemnation is not to the candlestick, but to the angel. "Because **thou** sayest, I am rich, and increased with goods, and have need of nothing; and knowest not that thou art wretched, and miserable, and poor, and blind, and naked." (Rev. 3:17.) My brethren, this is not against you, for it is Christ speaking who died for you, but it will be, if you change not your course of action.

If Christ by assembling these seven churches in a group of seven candlesticks and giving the blackest record to the last one, is not calling the Laodiceans Babylon, then neither is the interpretation of the "heads" doing so. It is not because the Laodiceans are better that they are not called Babylon, for their record is worse, but it is to show that on account of their increased light, He is to deal differently with them. It is to prove that if the "angel" (leadership) of the church of the Laodiceans should reject the message of the "True Witness," He cannot call the 144,000 out from the midst of them into another movement by the call of Revelation 18: "Come out of her my people, that ye be not partakers of her sins, and that ye receive not of her plagues," (verse 4), but rather by the message of Revelation 7 and Ezekiel 9. Thus speedily releasing His people, and quickly "finish the work, and cut it short in righteousness: because a short work will the Lord make upon the earth." (Rom. 9:28.)

Disobedience to the Word of God is blasphemy, and blasphemy is hypocrisy; that is to say, they are not what they profess to be. Hypocrisy hides the crying sins under the appearance of virtue. This sin of hypocrisy is difficult to cure in that it is not easily discovered by men. We cannot understand the hearts of others nor discern between the cloak of hypocrisy and the life of holiness. A spiritual deception has its beginning from a being other than human. Therefore, the scheme is so cunning that it cannot be discerned by finite observation. This kind of deception can only be recognized under the close scrutiny of the holy Word of God and by the aid of His Spirit.

"The effectual means to cure such a well devised plan of deception is a steadfast belief in that there is an all-seeing eye of God; who sees sin wherever it is, and will bring it into judgment. A hypocrite may hide his sin from the eyes of others and sometimes from his own conscience, but can never impose upon God." Paul, looking forward to such a time as this, says: "For the time will come when they will not endure sound doctrine; but after their own lusts shall they heap to themselves teachers, having itching ears; And they shall **turn away their ears from the truth,** and shall be turned unto fables." (2 Tim. 4:3, 4.) "Thou therefore which teachest another, teachest thou not thyself? Thou that preachest a man should not steal, dost thou steal? Thou that sayest a man should not commit adultery, dost thou commit adultery? Thou that abhorrest idols, dost thou commit sacrilege? Thou that makest thy boast of the law, through breaking the law dishonourest thou God?" (Rom. 2:21-23.) To the careless and indifferent, Job comments as follows: "It shall devour the strength of his skin: even the first born of death shall devour his strength." (Job 18:13.)

The seven heads are to symbolically point out these "high places" ruled by unsanctified leaders who have attempted to mix the sacred with the common, and refuse to hear the Word of the Lord. The Biblical number "seven," denoting completeness, naturally would comprise all Christendom at the time the prophetic truth is made known. Such apostasy is not a strange thing in the history of God's people, for time and again the church has fallen under a satanic flood. In Luther's day conditions were as bad as when the church crucified Christ. If this generation is more wicked than any before it, what would immunize the church from just such an apostasy? It is accepted by most Bible students that prophecies of this nature are understood only when the prophetic object in view is fully developed. Therefore, this is the time of which the symbols speak. However, there is another angle to this, by which we shall prove that the facts presented are true.

One Head Wounded Unto Death

John says: "I saw one of his heads as it were wounded to death." As the wounded head has reference to the stroke delivered to the papacy by Luther, the exile of the pope in 1798 was a sign of the completeness of the wound and that the prophetic period had ended. Thus fulfilling the words: "He that leadeth into captivity shall go into captivity." (Rev. 13:10.) Had not the papacy received the deadly wound by Luther, the pope could not have been put into prison by the French general, for before the pontifical authority received Luther's sword, the pope reigned supreme. But the blow weakened his power, and the result was that Protestantism came upon the stage of action. The continual infliction began to irritate the "head," until finally the pope landed behind the prison bars. The annoyance continued until 1870, when ultimately the temporal power of the pope was taken away. That being the last vexation of the "head," it showed that it was left to heal its "deadly wound."

Quoting the words of Luther explaining how the papacy was wounded: "I put forward God's word; I preached and wrote—this was all I did. And yet while I was asleep, . . . the word that I had preached overthrew popery, so that neither **prince nor emperor** has done it **so much harm.** And yet I did nothing; the Word alone did it all."—"The Great Controversy," page 190. "I began this work in God's name," said Luther, "it will be ended **without me, and by His might.**"—Id. p. 142. Let none misunderstand the following statement for the same author has recorded them both. Therefore it would be unjust to miscon-strue the one statement, for by so doing we would throw out of harmony the other. Speaking of the 1260 years we read: "This period, as stated in preceding chapters, began with the supremacy of the papacy, A.D. 538, and terminated in 1798. At that time, the pope was made captive by the French army, and the Papal power received its deadly wound, and **the prediction was fulfilled, 'He that leadeth into captivity shall go into captivity!'"**—Id., p. 439. Note that the aim of the author in this statement is not to tell how the wound was received, but to show that the prophetic period ended with the imprisonment of the pope, which fulfilled not the words, "And I saw one of his heads as it were wounded unto death" (verse 3); but rather the Scripture quoted, **"He that leadeth into captivity shall go into captivity."** (Verse 10.) Shall we ignore God and His Spirit, and give to Berthier the credit, thus justifying stupidity?

His Deadly Wound Was Healed

"And I saw one of his heads as it were wounded to death; **and his deadly wound was healed:** and all the world wondered after the beast." (Rev. 13:3.) William Miller proclaimed the prophetic peri-od of the 2300 days prior to 1844. That wonderful prophecy was delivered to Christendom with great power by the Spirit of God. Though the leaders of the nominal churches could not contradict the truth presented by Miller, they turned a deaf ear to the doctrine taught by him.

But as the disappointment came in 1844 through the misunderstanding of what was to transpire at the end of the prophetic period, the movement created by Miller came to its end. The second angel's Message of Revelation 14:8, had announced that Babylon (the churches prior to 1844) had fallen. That is to say that God would let no light shine upon His word through these fallen churches. Had God not called forth another Protestant movement the deadly wound would have been healed at that time.

By the divinely called movement, and aided by the writings of the "Spirit of Prophecy," God's intention was to keep the "deadly wound" on the "head." But the prophetic Word of God says: "His deadly wound was **healed**." Since God's Holy Word declares that the wound was healed, and as the prophecy cannot be broken, it is positive that the wound is "healed."

But if Protestantism, by obedience to God's Word, is what inflicted the wound, then **true Protestantism only** can keep the painful sore on the head. If the wound is healed, then it is evident that they to whom God had committed the message for a perishing world have been defeated in the same manner as ev-ery movement since the world began. It is a most wonderful thing to note how the old enemy has succeeded in defiling the church in every age through its leadership. The highest human intellect has been continually led into error and thus have served Satan to their own downfall. Will God's people never profit by these historical and biblical facts? Are not these things written for our ad-monition upon whom the ends of the world are come? God, by His Holy Word, commands: "Cease ye from man, whose breath is in his nostrils: for wherein is he to be accounted of?" (Isa. 2:22.)

As it has been accepted that the exile of the pope in 1798 was a signal that the infliction had been accomplished, so then as he has gained back his temporal power it further proves that the deadly wound **is healed.** These facts cannot be denied, for it is admitted that the incident of 1798 is true; therefore the one in 1929 cannot be refuted. That being so, this is the time to which the prophetic symbol speaks, "his deadly wound was healed." Read "The Shepherd's Rod," Vol. 1, for the entire volume deals with that subject.

All the World Wondered After the Beast

"His deadly wound was healed," John says, **"And all the world wondered after the beast."** Note that the world wondered after the beast and not after the head. Therefore, it cannot mean that the world would necessarily have to enroll in the membership of the system represented by the head. The significance is that **all** the world has partaken of the spirit of the beast—worldliness. The world in general has never been otherwise. It could not be said that "**all** the world wondered after the beast" if the people whom God has entrusted with the gospel are free from the spirit of the beast. But it must be that they have betrayed their trust, and partaken of its spirit. Where is the distinction between the church and the world!

The Name of Blasphemy

"And upon his heads the name of blasphemy." That is, resistance of known truth, expression of defiant impiety and irreverence towards God, or things held sacred—mocking God's personality and authority. The prophet Isaiah, looking forward to this time of wholesale deception, headed by so-called spiritual guides, says: "And **in that day seven women shall take hold of one man,** saying, We will eat our own bread, and wear our own apparel: only let us be called by thy name, to take away our reproach." (Isa. 4:1.)

It is an admitted fact among Bible students that churches are symbolized by "women." Pure woman—pure church, as in Jeremiah 6:2, Revelation 12:1; vile woman—corrupt church, as in Revelation 17:4, 5. Isaiah says, there are "seven" women. The number comprises these same churches. They say, "We will eat our own bread." That is, they want to have their own way; they care not for God's way (Word). "We will wear our own apparel"; that is, they want their own plans in preference to God's plans or His righteousness. Thereby, they clothed them selves with self-righteousness. Their aim is to be called by the **one man's name**; that is, by the name of Christ (Christians) to take away their reproach. People have come to suppose they can do most anything under the guise of Christianity and get away with it. God will let them continue their course until they, like Belshazzar, have passed the boundary line of divine grace, and then He will call them to account.

"And they worshipped the dragon which gave power unto the beast: and they worshipped the beast, saying, Who is like unto the beast? who is able to make war with him?" (Rev. 13:4.) The question may be asked, How can professed Christians worship the dragon? The answer is easy, and the worship of the dragon can be clearly seen. The present system of worship by so-called Christian institutions is unquestionably pagan. Sunday, Christmas, and Easter keeping, etc., originated in ancient Babylon, from the old pagan religion in honor of the sun god. Christians, in modern times, assume to honor the most High God with pagan customs calling them "Christian Doctrines." Protestantism has taken a grip on these pagan festivals as a leech on a human body. As the sluggard sucks the blood unaware that his satisfaction brings him to destruction, just so with protestants and their pagan commemoratives; even daring to call them by the name of Christ. Blasphemy indeed! Every student of ancient history knows this to be true; likewise every Bible student knows these so-called Christian festivals are unbiblical as well as unchristian. If these institutions were Christian, or Biblical, they would certainly have been spoken of in the Bible. But since they are not found in the Word of God, Christians had better leave them alone lest they be found worshiping the dragon.

Jeremiah, looking forward to this time of apostasy, says: "Thus saith the Lord, Learn not the way of the heathen, and be not dismayed at the signs of heaven; for the heathen are dismayed at them. For the customs of the people are vain: for one **cutteth a tree** out of the forest, the work of the hands of the workman, with the axe. They **deck it with silver and with gold;** they fasten it with nails and with hammers, that it move not." (Jer. 10:2-4.) Though the Word declares, "Learn not the ways of the heathen," professed ministers of the gospel will cut a tree from the forest and deck it with silver and gold, then dare call it by the name of Christ—Christmas tree. What greater blasphemy can one do? Are ministers and religious teachers ignorant of these things? Jesus said, "God is a Spirit: and they that worship him must worship him **in spirit and in truth.**"

John heard the men defying God, saying, "Who is like unto the beast? Who is able to make war with him?" That is, who can abolish this pagan system of worship; is there one? They challenge God's authority. It may not be said by words, but it is most decidedly expressed by action. Men's discernment is blunted by sin, and when an attempt is made to associate the sacred with the common or pagan, they see no evil. Though the Word of God declares: "But in all things approving ourselves as the ministers of God, in much patience, in afflictions, in necessities, in distresses, In stripes, in imprisonments, in tumults, in labours, in watchings, in fastings; By pureness, by knowledge, by longsuffering, by kindness, by the Holy Ghost, by love unfeigned, By the word of truth, by the power of God, by the armour of righteousness on the right hand and on the left, By honor and dishonor, by evil report and good report: as deceivers, and yet as true; As unknown, and yet well known; as dying, and, behold we live; as chastened, and yet not killed; As sorrowful, yet always rejoicing; as poor, yet making many rich: as having nothing, and yet possessing all things. O ye Corinthians, our mouth is open unto you, our heart is enlarged. . . . Be ye not unequally yoked together with unbelievers: for what fellowship hath righteousness with unrighteousness? and what communion hath light with darkness? And what concord hath Christ with Belial? or what part hath he that believeth with an infidel? And what agreement hath the temple of God with idols? For ye are the temple of the living God; as God hath said, I will dwell in them and walk in them; and I will be their God, and they shall be my people. Wherefore come out from among them, and be ye separate, saith the Lord, and touch not the unclean thing; and I will receive you, And will be a Father unto you, and ye shall be my sons and daughters, saith the Lord Almighty." (2 Cor. 6:4-11, 14-18.)

It is open disobedience to the plain "thus saith the Lord" that has brought about confusion and disgrace in the Christian world at the present time. True the reformers saw not all these errors, and were not responsible, for they had no light upon them. As God has given light upon His Word, by degrees, making it possible to grasp the truth, He expects us to receive it, and thus lead us to the victory.

But one may say, if God could save others with less light, why should He give us more light? Of the many reasons we shall comment on only two. By increased light on the Word, God is able to save a multitude instead of a few. The second reason is, as the last part of the church will be translated instead of resurrected, we need sufficient light to prepare us to meet God and immortal beings.

Just such ignorance of God's Word in the days of Noah brought the world to its destruction by water. A similar wicked condition reduced to ashes the cities of Sodom and Gomorrah. If in the days of Christ, just such hypocrisy, under the appearance of virtue, required the life of the Son of God to preserve the world from destruction, what would the outcome be at this present time? God cannot destroy the world, for He has a multitude to save. He has no other Son for a gift to the church, for Christ is the "**only** begotten" Son of God. If God's ideal is to bless the world through the medium of His church on earth, and they to whom the gospel for the world is committed have left the sheep and are serving the devil, in the person of themselves, where is the hope of the world? The only answer that can be given is, **woe to the sinners in Zion.** God will gather His sheep. He will have a church; but what will be the reward of those who were instructed to feed the lambs and are feeding themselves? Christ, who sees the end from the beginning, and with his all-seeing eye focused on present day conditions, has said: "Who then is a faithful and wise servant, whom his lord hath made ruler over his household, to give them meat in due season? Blessed is that servant, whom his lord when he cometh shall find so doing. Verily I say unto you, that he shall make him ruler over all his goods. But and if that evil servant shall say in his heart, My lord delayeth his coming; And shall begin to smite his fellow servants, and to eat and drink with the drunken; The lord of that servant shall come in a day when he looketh not for him, and in an hour that he is not aware of, and shall cut him asunder, and appoint him his portion with the hypocrites [with the heads of the beasts]; there shall be weeping and gnashing of teeth." (Matt. 24:45-51.)

Separating the Tares from the Wheat

Peter saw a time when God will judge the church: "For the time is come that judgment must begin at the house of God; and if it first begin at us, what shall the end be of them that obey not the Gospel of God?" (1 Pet. 4:17.) What would be the end of him who enters not the ark of safety, but dares bar the way of others? As the prophet saw the day of vengeance upon the sinner in Zion, and the Lord returning from the slaughter, he asked: "Who is this that cometh from Edom, with dyed garments from Bozrah? this that is glorious in his apparel, traveling in the greatness of his strength? I that speak in righteousness, mighty to save. . . . For the day of vengeance is in mine heart, and the year of my redeemed is come. And I looked, and there was none to help; and I wondered that there was none to uphold: therefore mine own arm brought salvation unto me; and my fury, it upheld me. And I will tread down the people in mine anger, and make them drunk in my fury, and I will bring down their strength to the earth." (Isa. 63:1, 4-6.)

Fearful is the day that is soon to fall upon the watchman on the walls of Zion, for the righteous only shall be preserved. "Those who would rather die than perform a wrong act are the only ones who will be found faithful."—"Testimonies for the Church," Vol 5, p. 53. The separation of the pure from the impure is well described by Ezekiel. Those who are worthy to escape the ruin will be marked by the man with the writer's inkhorn, after which the five men with the slaughter weapons shall smite the class who are left without the mark. Said the Lord: "Slay utterly old and young, both maids, and little children, and women: but come not near any man upon whom is the mark; and begin at my sanctuary. Then they began at the ancient men which were before the house. And he said unto them, Defile the house, and fill the courts with the slain: go ye forth. And they went forth, and slew in the city." (Ezek. 9:6, 7.) At this time the tares are separated from the wheat according to the words of Christ: "Let both grow together until the harvest: and in the time of harvest I will say to the reapers, Gather ye together first the tares, and bind them into bundles to burn them: but gather the wheat into my barn." (Matt. 13:30.)

The purification of God's church marks the harvest or the "Loud cry" of the Third Angel's Message, for the Lord of the harvest declares, "Let both grow together **until** the harvest." The wheat gathered at the commencement of the harvest and at the separation from the tares in the church, is called the first-fruits of the harvest. As John looked upon the company he heard a melody of joy, inexpressible by human lips: "And they sung as it were a new song before the throne, and before the four beasts, and the elders: an no man could learn that song but the hundred and forty and four thousand, which were redeemed from the earth. These are they which were not defiled with women; for they are virgins. These are they which follow the lamb whithersoever he goeth. These were redeemed from among men, being the **first fruits** unto God and to the Lamb." (Rev. 14:3, 4.) "And no man could learn that song." Experience only can tell the joy in one's heart at a time when rescued from everlasting ruin, and granted everlasting life without tasting death—merged into eternity's ceaseless ages!—a life that measures with the life of God.

Confidence in Men is Satan's Sure Trap

We may search as far back as we desire and it is certain that we shall discover to our surprise and sorrow, that the church leadership has been so greatly deceived that in each period they failed to recognize the unrolling of the scroll; and as the blinded multitude took the side of the corrupted leaders against the revealed truth, they split God's church in numerous sections. Thus by defeating the foremost, Satan has been able to engage them to labor for him, and thereby to overthrow the church as a body. To ascertain the accuracy of the foregoing statement it would not be necessary to comment on facts beyond the first advent of Christ. Therefore, a brief survey of the Christian era shall be considered here.

Satan had drawn the "dirt brush" over the eyes of the highest human intellect at the close of the Old Testament dispensation. Their spiritual eyes were so skillfully plastered that they could not see a bolt of lightning as bright as the sun, in the darkest night. The fulfillment of prophecy, the miracles surrounding the birth of Christ, His spotless character, His unselfish labor and wonders in every step, touch, look and act, filled the very atmosphere with divine love. Men who were destitute of the sense of sight from their birth, felt the healing power of the Infinite One. The blind saw the Lord of glory and praised God, but the religious teachers of Israel were not affected by the power that moved even inanimate objects. The earth quaked; and the sun veiled its face; the rocks were rent and the graves were opened; the dead arose and beheld the Son of God. But the proud Pharisees, priests, and rabbis, esteemed as never erring, could neither feel, see, nor hear. There is no wonder greater than the one written by the actions of the blind leaders of that age. John, speaking of the experience, says: "In Him was life and the life was the light of men. And the light shineth in darkness: and the darkness comprehended it not." (John 1:4, 5.)

Every possible ray of light pointing to the coming of the "Lamb of God" had been given to the once-chosen people; but it profited them not. Said Jesus: "If therefore the light that is in thee be darkness, how great is that darkness!" Would that these experiences could arouse the leaders and the people at this present time from self confidence and counterfeit security to an earnest search of positive Bible truth.

The early Christian church in like manner was dragged into the dark ages. As soon as the Apostles passed away Satan marshaled his agents, men of renown, into the church. The already-blinded leaders laid their hands on men, not from the viewpoint of consecration, but from distinction, and thus made them shepherds of the flock. In the darkest hour of the Christian church, God, by the hand of Luther, called the attention of the multitude to the terrible deception, but few were ready to listen to the humble monk. One would imagine that the most intellectual would have been the first to see the light in the plain "thus saith the Lord." Luther, with a great struggle, and at the risk of his life, founded the Lutheran denomination. But as he passed away, that movement in like manner was corrupted and hardened against new light on the Word of God.

As John Knox came with additional truth, the leaders of the church refused to be interested, thus necessity gave birth to the Presbyterian denomination. These experiences have been repeated with Wesley, Campbell, Miller, and White. (See "The Shepherd's Rod," Vol. 1, pp. 32-114.) "We have far more to fear from within than from without. The hindrances to strength and success are far greater from the church itself than from the world."—Review and Herald, March 22, 1887. If the danger against the church has been from within, through confidence in self-deceived leadership in every age, what would change things at the present time?

These facts concerning Satan's sure traps, echo and re-echo with the loudest wail to arouse the sleeper at this particular time. Hear the trumpet's sound: "hake thyself from the dust; arise, and sit down, O Jerusalem: loose thyself from the bands of thy neck, **O captive** daughter of Zion!" (Isa. 52:2.) Prejudice, with dependence upon men, in confidence of having all the truth and that there is need of none, has devoured more souls than any trap ever devised by the enemy of mankind. The class who accept the decisions of others without investigating for themselves, and refuse to be interested in hearing and reasoning the Scriptures, have been deceived concerning present truth in every age. "For the wisdom of this world is foolishness with God. For it is written, He taketh the wise in their own craftiness. And again, The Lord knoweth the thoughts of the wise, that they are vain." (I Cor. 3:19, 20.)

Men who are esteemed great by the world, God can seldom use. In general, the great educators of the age are carnal minded, therefore the product from the schools of men is enmity against God. "Because the carnal mind is enmity against God: for it is not subject to the law of God, neither indeed can be." (Rom. 8:7.) If God would use them they must first, with the great apostle, deny themselves. Said Paul: "To preach the gospel: not with wisdom of words, lest the cross of Christ should be made of none effect. For it is written, I will destroy the wisdom of the wise, and will bring to **nothing** the understanding of the **prudent.**" (1 Cor. 1:17, 19.) "And, I brethren, when I came to you, came **not with excellency of speech** or of **wisdom**, declaring unto you the testimony of God. For I determined not to know anything among you, save Jesus Christ, and Him crucified. And I was with you in weakness, and fear, and in much trembling. And my speech and my preaching **was not with enticing words of man's wisdom,** but in demonstration of the Spirit and of power." (1 Cor. 2:1-4.)

God took Moses to the desert and there under His supervision He trained him for forty years—when Moses unlearned all he had learned in the schools of Egypt, then only was God able to use him for an instrument of His mighty arm. When Moses felt capable to deliver Israel from Egyptian bondage he failed; but when he saw himself helpless, then he was strong. If God should give great light to a man who is high in his own esteem, and held likewise by the world, man would glorify himself and rob God of the glory. "At this time Jesus answered and said, I thank Thee, O Father, Lord of heaven and earth, because Thou hast **hid** these things from the **wise** and **prudent**, and hast **revealed** them to **babes."** (Matt. 11:25.) God reveals Himself through instruments and ways least suspected by men. Thus He performs a miracle by making impossibilities possible, revealing His power and arousing the sleeper with **light** and **voice divine.** Men of distinction have seldom accepted any light upon the Word of God simply on the value of its truth; this class generally accepts Biblical truth after it becomes popular and when preached by men esteemed higher than themselves.

Said the prophet, "Cease ye from man, whose breath is in his nostrils: for wherein is he to be accounted of ?" (Isa. 2:22.) "It is better to trust in the Lord than to put confidence in man." (Psa. 118:8.) The prophet Micah, looking forward to this time of carnal security, says, "Trust ye not in a friend put ye not confidence in a guide." (Micah 7:5.) God's people must learn to look to Him only, depending upon the plain "thus saith the Lord." He may use the human instrument to communicate light, but it will shine on the never-erring Word of God. Such light will dispel sin and rebuke the sinner, exalt Christ, glorify God, and debase men. "The lofty looks of man shall be humbled, and the haughtiness of men shall be bowed down, and the Lord alone shall be exalted in that day. For the day of the Lord of Hosts shall be upon every one that is **proud** and **lofty,** and upon every one that is **lifted up; and** he shall be **brought low."** (Isa. 2:11, 12.)

Satan knows how to deceive so that it can not be easily detected. He studies the inclination of the people, and the thing which appeals most he sets as a trap. Because the generation is trusting in human intellect and are willing that others should think for them, the **devil** will present to this class the most dazzling personality the world has ever looked upon. Said the apostle: "And no marvel; for Satan himself is transformed into an angel of light." (2 Cor. 11:14.)

God's instruments for communicating light upon His Word will be the opposite to those of Satan's. "I thank Thee, O Father, Lord of heaven and earth," said Jesus, "because Thou hast hid these things from the wise and prudent, and hast revealed them unto babes." (Matt. 11:25.) To the prophet Isaiah, it was revealed that God will use humble men to debase the proud: "For behold, the Lord the Lord of hosts, doth take away from Jerusalem and from Judah the stay and the staff, the whole stay of bread, and the whole stay of water. The mighty man, and the man of war, the judge, and the prophet, and the prudent, and the ancient, the captain of fifty, and the honorable man, and the counselor, and the cunning artificer, and the eloquent orator. And I will give **children to be their princes,** and **babes shall rule over them.** And the people shall be oppressed, every one by another, and every one by his neighbor: **The child** shall behave himself proudly **against the ancient,** and the **base against the honorable."** (Isa. 3:1-5.) Said Jesus, "Whosoever therefore shall **humble** himself **as this little child,** the same is **greatest in the kingdom of heaven.** And whoso shall receive one such little child in my name receiveth me." (Matt. 18:4, 5.)

A Brief Summary of the Leopard-like Beast

It has been previously proven that the leopard-like beast by his seven heads, and ten horns is a representation of a universal system. The four beasts of Daniel 7; namely, the lion, bear, leopard, and the non-descript were shown in the vision as four universal empires coming up one after another. Thus, prophecy as well as history proves that Babylon, Medo-Persia, Grecia and Rome succeeded each other. This unbreakable chain of four links makes it impossible to intersect any one of the four beasts with a universal system. Therefore, the leopard-like must come in line after the fourth beast. As the "ten horns" of the nondescript beast represented "ten kings" that were to arise from the Roman monarchy, the "crowns on the horns" prove that the leopard-like beast represents the period after the fall of the Roman monarchy, at which time the "ten kings" received their kingdom. As he also "came out from the **Sea,"** it is evident that he too was to be created from the result of wars. Thus the fall of the Roman monarchy gave birth to a fifth beast. His mouth of a lion, feet of a bear, body of a leopard, and ten horns, show that he is a descendant of Babylon, Medo-Persia, Grecia, and Rome.

As he opened his mouth in blasphemy for forty-two months, or 1260 years, it is undeniable that he represents the papal period from 538 A. D. to 1798 A. D.—the time in which the papal head received its deadly wound. But as his wound was to heal some time after 1798, it is evident that he also represents this world's history after the imprisonment of Pope Pius VI up to the time his "deadly wound was healed"; these periods gave birth to Catholicism and Protestantism.

It would have been unwise, and useless to devise this prophetic beast if the symbols would fail to reveal Protestantism as they do Catholicism. Before the 1260 years ended in 1798, the four Protestant denominations were already in existence; namely, Lutheran, Presbyterian, Methodist, and Christian. But after 1798 came the First-day Adventists; and the Seventh-day Adventists from 1844 to 1929 completed his seven heads. As Protestantism fell by the declaration of the Second Angel's Message after 1844, and as the symbol of Revelation 13 in 1930 revealed that the Seventh-day Adventists "wondered after the beast" (world), these two incidents healed the wound, and drew the blasphemy over all seven heads. Thus, the complete fulfillment of the symbolical prophecy revealed the truth of the beast. As all other sects are but off-shoots from these seven bodies, the heads included all Christendom up to 1930. As the prophetic word of God says, "All the world wondered after the **beast**" (worldliness), and not after the head (papacy), it denotes that they have wondered after the world and not after Catholicism. Out of this great apostasy the message of Revelation 7:1-8, will seal and save 144,000 saints, from the S.D.A. church who shall never taste death. But the message represented by the angel of Revelation 18, with whose glory the earth is to be lightened, will call out from the world the "great multitude" of Revelation 7:9.

God, who is so particular for the good of His church in revealing His truth to His people, has presented to us wonderful pictures of historical events; which is the evidence of love everlasting for Israel His chosen—the first-fruits of His harvest. Thus "the God of Jacob," thousands of years in advance, had laid His plans to present to His people a work of prophetic art with divine touch.

THE TWO-HORNED BEAST
REV. 13:11-18

As John beheld the vision with intense interest, his attention was directed to another striking object: "And I beheld another beast coming up out of the earth; and he had two horns like a lamb, and he spake as a dragon." (Verse 11.) Just about the time the second and last stage of the non-descript beast was to terminate, another earthly power was to come upon the stage of action, according to the vision. It is wonderful to note how accurate the symbols are, even to their proper time and order. The beast having lamb-like horns (promise of growth) is an unmistakable symbol of a nation "slowly arising as from a small plan to a mighty empire." "Lamb-like," is descriptive of the government arising in 1776 A. D. (See "The Great Controversy," pp. 439-441.)

This beast has been accepted as a symbol of the United States. Therefore, our intention is not to bring forth facts pertaining to its application. Our aim is, as previously stated, to briefly connect one beast with another by throwing light upon symbols which have not been understood.

It will be noticed that every beast representing the New Testament time has ten horns except this one. We repeat that the ten horns stand as a symbol of universal systems. This fact proves that the **two-horned** beast represents a local government. As civil powers or governments are symbolized by horns, this particular beast having **two,** it is evident that the nation represented by this symbol, shall have a double form of government. As John says, "The beast spake as a **dragon,**" it clearly reveals that it is to repudiate its constitution, and the God-given liberty of its subjects will be taken away. According to verse12, this power is to imitate the beast "before him" (the papal rule): "And he exerciseth all the power of the first beast before him, and causeth the earth and them which dwell therein to worship the first beast, whose deadly wound was healed." If this great nation should presume upon the conscience of its sub-jects by legislation, as to how they may, or may not worship, it would be contrary to the provisions in its constitution—speaking as a dragon. Quoting the United States constitution, the first amendment concerning religious matters, states: "Congress shall make no law respecting an establishment of religion, or prohibiting the free exercise thereof." If this country should repudiate this amendment, it will completely meet the symbolical specification.

The following verse discloses the fact that the old dragon shall exercise his power to deceive as many as possible: "And he doeth great wonders, so that he maketh fire come down from heaven on the earth in the sight of men, And deceiveth them that dwell on the earth by the means of those miracles which he had power to do in the sight of the beast; saying to them that dwell on the earth, that they should make an image to the beast, which had the wound by a sword, and did live." (Rev. 13:13, 14.) Thus he is to exercise persecutive powers as well as the working of miracles.

As the Word exposes this great deception, one would think that the world would open its eyes and refuse to be charmed by such Satanic wonders. But Satan knows that the people are unmindful of the Word of God, and that their emotions are easily moved by supernatural marvels and the eloquence of men. Therefore, he will perfect the contrivance and many will fall into it regardless of warnings. The human mind cannot comprehend that mysterious and irresistible power that is soon to spread its dreadful shadow over the inhabitants of the earth. No mortal being can stand against that supernatural, civil and religious system. Those who are students of the Word, trusting in God without reservation, and thus filled with the Holy Spirit, will escape that dreadful trap.

"Those who would rather die than perform a wrong act are the only ones who will be found faithful."—"Testimonies for the Church," Vol. 5, p. 53. Their only safety will be, "Thus saith the Lord." They must look to God as their only deliverer, as did the three Hebrews in ancient Babylon, and as Daniel in the lion's den. Let the consequence be what it may, God's people can find shelter only in taking the position of Shadrach, Meshach, and Abednego, as when they answered the king: "O, Nebuchadnezzar, we are not careful to answer thee in this matter. If it be so, our God whom we serve is able to deliver us from the burning fiery furnace, and He will deliver us out of thine hand, O king. But if not, be it known unto thee, O king, that we will not serve thy gods, nor worship the golden image which thou hast set up." (Dan. 3:16-18.)

God's people, with Daniel, will be able to say at the time of their deliverance: "My God hath sent His angel, and hath shut the lions' mouths, that they have not hurt me: forasmuch as before Him innocency was found in me; and also before thee, O king, have I done no hurt." (Dan. 6:22.) In such time of trial it shall be clearly seen who will serve God and who will not. That time of trouble shall divide the earth's inhabitants in two separate and distinct classes, as sheep and goats.

"And he had power to give life unto the image of the beast, that the image of the beast should both speak, and cause that as many as would not worship the image of the beast should be killed. And he causeth all, both small and great, rich and poor, free and bond, to receive a mark in their right hand, or in their foreheads: And that no man might buy or sell, save he that had the mark, or the name of the beast, or the number of his name." (Rev. 13:15-17.)

This drastic decree of the two-horned beast shall be adopted by the nations of the world, and the image of the beast, which will demand obedience to an ecclesiastical form of worship, will be internationally set up. The mark of the beast is Sunday observance. Under one pretext or another, the careless and in-different will worship the image of the beast, and receive the mark. Only those who have fortified themselves with faith in God, knowledge of His Word, and obedience to divine precepts through sanctification of the heart by the power of the Holy Spirit, will be able to escape the clutches of the devil. When God's people are restrained from buying and selling, their only source of sustenance will be through divine providence. One way or another, for that short time, God will provide and care for His people. But it may be in a similar circumstance as in the wilderness journey.

"The time is not far distant, when, like the early disciples, we shall be forced to seek a refuge in desolate and solitary places. As the siege of Jerusalem by the Roman armies was the signal for flight to the Judean Christians, so the as-sumption of power on the part of our nation, in the decree enforcing the papal Sabbath, will be a warning to us. It will then be time to leave the large cities, preparatory to leaving the smaller ones for retired homes in secluded places among the mountains."—"Testimonies to the Church," Vol. 5, pp. 464, 465. The 18th verse of Revelation 13, will be explained in another study.

THE SCARLET COLORED BEAST
REV. 17

"So he carried me away in the spirit into the wilderness: and I saw a woman sit upon a scarlet coloured beast, full of names of blasphemy, having seven heads and ten horns." (Verse 3.) This particular beast cannot be a symbol of Rome as some have thought. The first reason is, that the **non-descript beast** of Daniel 7, as previously explained, is a symbol of Rome, and was seen coming up from the sea; but the **scarlet colored beast**, John says, was in the **desert**. Therefore, the forces that brought the **scarlet colored** beast on the stage of action is the opposite of that which produced the **non-descript.**

The second reason is, as the angel was about to show the vision to John, he said to him, "Come hither; I will show thee the judgment of the great whore that sitteth upon many waters." (Verse 1.) Then John was carried into the wilderness and there he saw the woman riding on the beast. The reason the vision is given is to show him the judgment of the woman. But she was not judged in the days of Rome; her judgment is yet in the future, and will be executed under the "Loud Cry" angel of Revelation 18. (See verses 8, 10.) The riding on the beast is her last act; therefore, the beast must represent the period in which she is judged. There is a third reason why the beast cannot be a symbol of Rome. The book of Daniel, and the book of Revelation were written especially for the generation living at the time of the end, and not so much for the Roman world. (See Dan. 12:4.) They had no understanding of the writings that pertained to the last days, and thus could not have profited by them. Therefore, it would have been improper and unwise on the part of God to apply all the beasts to Rome, and leave the period to which the books apply without symbolical representation.

We believe that there must be more complete symbolical information for this present generation than for any previous one. Thus, it is very inconsistent and unreasonable of those who have applied the "leopard-like beast" of Revelation 13, and the "scarlet colored" of Revelation 17, in addition to the "non-descript beast" of Daniel 7, as symbols of Rome. Why so many symbols of Rome and none of the period for which the books were written? Furthermore, there are no facts to support such claims. The greatest rebuke to such assertions in that they derive the same lesson from one beast as they do from the other. If there is no special lesson in each of them, why are they given? Applying the heads, as they do the horns, to symbols of governments, shows that they had no light from the great and all-wise God. If each term means government, why did Inspiration use both horns and heads?

Note how unreasonable it is to apply the woman riding on the beast, or sitting on the heads to Catholicism in the New Testament time, and the heads to seven consecutive forms of governments in the Old Testament period. Said the angel: "The seven heads are seven mountains, on which the woman sitteth." (Verse 9.) If the papal church came into existence in 508 A. D., how could she "sit" on any government centuries before? Again, if the heads succeeded each other, where is the proof ? Are they not all present on the beast and the woman sitting on them? As the scarlet coloured beast by his ten horns and seven heads proves to be universal, the successive chain of beasts (the lion, bear, four-headed leopard, non-descript, and leopard-like) make it impossible for another universal beast to intersect their unbreakable chain of five links. Such an act would be an attempt to overthrow prophecy, and history. Therefore, the only period he can possibly represent would be the one after the "deadly wound" of the leopard-like is healed—becoming a sixth universal beast.

Since the "scarlet colored" is the last in the symbolical procession of beasts, he must possess all the characteristics of his ancestors. The ten horns of the non-descript beast, the seven heads of the leopard-like, and his own unharmed heads, show that he comes on the stage of action after the deadly wound was healed. His **scarlet** color denotes curse, as it does on the dragon (devil), in Revelation 12:3, and the words, "go into perdition," (Rev. 17:11), reveal that he is to bring this world to an end by a curse that will result in "entire ruin; utter destruction; future misery or eternal death."—"Standard Dictionary."

Therefore, if this beast represents our world at the present time, would it not be unwise on the part of God, if He should have neglected to foresee the present day multiplicity of sects, and the great confusion among Christendom, if the symbols by this beast fail to reveal the true condition of the churches? As the non-descript beast tells the fall of the church in the period he represents, so must the scarlet colored. In fact, this is the principal reason why these prophetic beasts are presented.

The scarlet colored beast is the last symbolical beast in the continuous chain of historical events. This beast does not arise from the sea like the beasts before it, but was seen in the wilderness. Therefore, the scarlet colored beast is created by an historical incident unlike the beasts before it. The symbol denotes that it is not strife and wars between the nations that brings this beast upon the stage of action, but rather a principle that is the opposite of the symbol—troubled sea.

He has ten horns and seven heads, the same as the leopard-like beast of Revelation 13:1-3. The only difference between the heads of the two beasts is the deadly wound on the leopard-like. As his "wound was healed," it is evident that the "scarlet colored" is a continuation of the "leopard-like." Says John, "And his deadly wound was healed."

Thus the scarlet colored beast has seven unharmed heads. The seven heads represent Christendom as they do on the leopard-like beast, but it is in the symbol of the scarlet colored, that they are called Babylon. As he is full of names and blasphemy, it verifies the fact that he represents an exceeding sinful period. **"Full of names,"** implies a period of great multiplicity of so-called Christian sects; "and blasphemy," because of rejecting present truth, (refusing to be corrected) and yet dare to call themselves by the name of Christ (Christians).

The "ten" horns denote the same as on the beasts before it, meaning a universal system. If the heads of the leopard-like beast represent religious organizations, then the scarlet colored embraces the entire present civilization, both civil and religious (horns and heads). Note that the dragon of Revelation 12:3, has the crowns on his heads, not on his horns. It has been previously explained that when the crowns appear on the heads, it denotes a religio-political system. But if they appear on the horns it reveals that the state is independent of the church.

It will be noticed that the scarlet-colored beast is **crownless, as the non-descript** of Daniel 7:7, 8. The ten horns in the first stage of the non-descript beast, representing imperial Rome, had no crowns because they had received no kingdom as yet. But in his second stage (after the fall of imperial Rome) in reality they should have been crowned; the "little horn" having the "eyes of a man and a mouth speaking great things" (a combination of a horn-head—union of church and state—the papacy) being supreme, the horns could have no crowns, showing the papacy was to rule over kings. The scarlet colored beast is also controlled by the woman riding on his back (church and state). Thus it denotes that she is the authority, or the crown, for she rules the beast. This is one of the reasons why the crowns are absent on this beast. The last is an image of the first verifying the fact that the scarlet colored beast represents the "image of the beast" period, fulfilling Revelation 13:12, 15: "And he exerciseth all the power of the first beast before him, and causeth the earth and them which dwell therein to worship the first beast, whose deadly wound was healed. And he had power to **give life unto the image of the beast,** that the image of the beast should both speak, and cause that as many as would not worship the image of the beast should be killed." The difference between the two drastic systems is revealed by the two symbols (horn-head on the one, and the woman riding on the other).

The non-descript beast has only one "horn-head"—a symbol of a mono-sectarian system by alliance of civil power with religious creed. But the scarlet colored beast has seven heads, which denote a multi-sectarian combination under a supreme religio-political jurisdiction (the woman). He represents our world at its end, with its sovereign authority and theoretical theology under the dominion of the "woman."

The period represented by the scarlet colored beast commenced in 1929, at which time the deadly wound was healed. But his career is not fully developed until the "woman" shall sit upon his back.

The commencement of that act will be marked when the following prediction is fully realized: "When Protestantism shall stretch forth her hand across the gulf to grasp the hand of Roman power, when she shall reach over the abyss to clasp hands with Spiritualism, when under the influence of this three-fold union, our country shall repudiate every principle of its constitution as a Protestant and Republican government, and shall make provision for the propagation of papal falsehoods and delusions, then we may know that the time has come for the marvelous working of Satan, and that the end is near."—"Testimonies for the Church," Vol. 5, p. 451.

Revelation 17:8, "The beast that thou sawest was, and is not; and they that dwell on the earth shall wonder, whose names were not written in the book of life from the foundation of the world, when they behold **the beast that was, and is not,** and yet is." "The beast that thou sawest" (the scarlet colored), said the angel, **"was and is not."** As previously explained, the beast first began to appear on the stage of history in 1929. Therefore, the word, **"was,"** represents the period from the above stated date up to the time when he will be, **"not."**

The period represented by the word **"not,"** is the thousand years of Satan's captivity—millennium: "And he laid hold on the dragon, that old serpent, which is the Devil, and Satan, and bound him a thousand years, And cast him into the bottomless pit, and shut him up, and set a seal upon him, that he should deceive the nations no more, till the thousand years should be fulfilled: and after that he must be loosed a little season." (Rev. 20:2, 3.)

This period commences with the second coming of Christ and the end of this present world. At that time the Scripture of Revelation 20:6, will be fulfilled: "Blessed and holy is he that hath part in the first resurrection: on such the second death hath no power, but they shall be priests of God and of Christ, and shall reign with him a thousand years." As the righteous dead are raised and united with the living, then the prophecy of Jeremiah shall be fully realized: "I beheld, and, lo, the fruitful place was as a wilderness, and all the cities thereof were broken down at the presence of the Lord, and by His fierce anger. For thus hath the Lord said, The whole land shall be desolate; yet will I not make a full end." (Jer. 4:26, 27.)

When the cities are broken down and the land laid waste, then the hope of the redeemed shall be accomplished: "For the Lord himself shall descend from heaven with a shout, with the voice of the archangel, and with the trump of God: and the dead in Christ shall rise first: Then we which are alive and remain shall be caught up together with them in the clouds, to meet the Lord in the air: and so shall we ever be with the Lord." (1 Thess. 4:16, 17.) At that glorious time when the saints depart, the earth will be left in darkness as described by Jeremiah: "For this shall the earth mourn, and the heavens above be black: because I have spoken it, I have purposed it, and will not repent, neither will I turn back from it. The whole city shall flee for the noise of the horsemen and bowmen; they shall go into thickets, and climb up upon the rocks: **every city shall be forsaken, and not a man dwell therein.**" (Jer. 4:28, 29.)

Then, as the saints enter in through the pearly gates John's vision will meet its fulfillment: "And I saw thrones, and they sat upon them, and judgment was given unto them: and I saw the souls of them that were beheaded for the witness of Jesus, and for the Word of God, and which had not worshipped the beast, neither his image, neither had received his mark upon their foreheads, or in their hands; and they lived and reigned with Christ a thousand years." (Rev. 20:4.) The righteous shall spend a thousand years judging the wicked dead. For further study of the millennium see "Patriarchs and Prophets," p. 103; "The Great Controversy," pp. 321, 662.

"But the rest of the dead **lived not again** until the thousand years were finished. This is the first resurrection. . . . And I saw the dead, small and great, stand before God; and the books were opened: and another book was opened, which is the book of life: and the **dead** were **judged** out of those things which were written in the books, according to their works," (Rev. 20:5, 12.) The books contain the records of the wicked; the book of life is opened and examined by the saints, and in it they behold only the names of the righteous. The names of some who once appeared in it were blotted out, while the names of others were never entered between its pages.

Coming back to our subject: "The beast that thou sawest was, and is not; and **shall ascend out of the bottomless pit."** Thus far, we have explained the first part of the Scripture quoted (**was** and is **not**). Now we note the words, "And shall ascend out of the bottomless pit." In the millennial period the wicked shall be judged; and at its close, Christ and the saints shall return to earth. John bears witness of this: "And I John saw the holy city, new Jerusalem, coming down from God out of heaven, prepared as a bride adorned for her husband." (Rev. 21:2.) As Christ with the saints and the city descend, then, the following Scripture will be fulfilled: "And the sea gave up the dead which were in it, and death and hell delivered up the dead which were in them: and they **were** judged every man according to their works." (Rev. 20:13.) Note the verb, "were", being in past tense, shows that they were judged previous to their resurrection. By the resurrection of the wicked, Satan will be loosed from his captivity for a "little season." (See Rev. 20:3.) In this manner shall the beast (world) "ascend out of the bottomless pit."

But the angel also said, the beast "goeth into perdition"; that is, after he ascended. Satan is loosed for only a short season. He and the wicked shall live for one hundred years after the resurrection. ("The Shepherd's Rod, Vol. 1, pages 164, 165.) The Bible says that at the end of the hundred years "Death and hell were cast into the lake of fire. This is the second death. And whosoever was not found written in the book of life was cast into the lake of fire." (Rev. 20:14, 15.) The second death of the wicked is an everlasting death, "and they shall be as though they had not been." (Obadiah 16.) Speaking of Satan's destruction, says the prophet: "All they that know thee among the people shall be astonished at thee: thou shalt be a terror, and never shalt thou be any more." (Ezek. 28:19.)

"For, behold, the day cometh, that shall burn as an oven; and all the proud, yea, and all that do wickedly, shall be stubble: and the day that cometh shall burn them up, saith the Lord of hosts, that it shall leave them neither root nor branch." (Mal. 4:1.) In this manner the beast shall go into perdition. (Webster's definition of the word **perdition** is: "total destruction; utter loss of the **soul** or of happiness in a future state.")

It is summarized as follows: The beast that **"was"** is the period prior to the millennium; and, **"is not"**, is during the time of the millennium; and "shall ascend out of the bottomless pit," is the period after the millennium, at which time all the wicked will be resurrected and go into perdition; that is, at the end of the **one hundred** years, the wicked, **Satan** and his angels shall be consumed by fire.

"And they that dwell on the earth shall wonder, whose names were not found written in the book of life from the foundation of the world, when they behold the beast that was, and is not, and yet is." (Rev. 17:8.) What a surprise it will be to the wicked when they witness the great multitude, as the sands of the sea for number, suddenly come to life. It will be something which has never entered their mind. Note the phrase, "From the **foundation** of the **world.**" This term includes all the wicked since the world began and proves positively that this interpretation is correct.

Verse 9, "And here is the mind which hath wisdom. The seven heads are seven mountains, on which the woman sitteth." All the heads being present on the beast, and the woman sitting on them, proves that all seven "mountains" must be in existence at the same time. They cannot be consecutive for the woman sits on them all, which denotes one great union of the heads by the medium of the woman. They are called "mountains," as God's denomination is called "mountain," in Isaiah 2:2, and Micah 4:1. The "mountain" (singular) is God's denomination, but the "mountains" (plural by both Isaiah and Micah) have reference to the same denominations represented by the heads on the beast. **Thus "the seven heads are seven mountains."**

Verse 10, "And there are seven kings: five are fallen, and one is, and the other is not yet come; and when he cometh, he must continue a short space." Note that it does not say "**they** are," but "**there** are." Therefore the "heads" cannot be symbols of the kings. The kings reign in successive order, for, **five** are **fallen,** and one **is,** and the other is **not yet come.** Note the Biblical number "seven," meaning completeness. As the beast also represents the wicked who shall arise from the dead on the other side of the millennium, and if all who lived from Cain to the end of this present generation are to be raised, then the seven kings in connection with the beast must apply to the entire world's history from creation to the end. "Who hath wrought and done it, **calling the generations from the beginning? I** the Lord, **the first,** and **with the last**; I am He." (Isa. 41:4.)

As the explanation of the symbolical prophecy is first understood at this present time, and as such prophecies are only timely revealed, and the lesson derived concerns this present generation, then the prediction is present truth. Therefore, we must consider the use of the Biblical past and present tense. This grammatical rule is followed in the Scriptures, and it is one way to recognize present truth. Let not the enemy trip you on this point by vain philosophy or theology. The Scriptures are perfect in themselves. The King James version is as dependable as any "good" translation. Take heed of explanations by translations which you yourself do not understand. Trust no man.

"And there are seven kings: five are fallen, and one is, and the other is not yet come; and when he cometh, he must continue a short space." (Rev. 17:10.) The "king," that **"is,"** must be the one in existence at this present time, and the one that is **"not yet come,"** must be in the future. Consequently, the five that are **"fallen,"** must be in the past. This would be the only fair position for one to take without doing injury to the holy Word of God. As it has reference to the entire world's history under sin, we must consider the number of universal empires, or periods, since the world began. There is one before the flood, as previously explained; the second is Babylon; the third, Medo-Persia; fourth, Grecia; and the fifth is the Roman monarchy. These **five are fallen.** The one that **"is"**, is the present civilization since the fall of Rome under the symbol of the "leopard-like" and the "scarlet colored" beasts, to the commencement of the millennium, which period is termed Rome in her broken state, represented by the feet and toes of the great image of Daniel 2. These are the six kings. "Five are fallen" and the one **"is."** The other that is **"not yet come,"** must be the period after the millennium, corresponding with the beast that is to ascend from the bottomless pit.

It is wonderful to note how God has portrayed our world's history with such perfect symbols, using numbers of completeness in each instance. Thus His divine plan, rule, and guide for His people, is revealed from generation to generation. Speaking of the seventh king, the one after the millennium, the text says, "When he cometh, he must continue a short space," corresponding with that of Revelation 20:3, "And after that he [Satan] must be loosed a little season."

Revelation 17:11, "And the beast that **was,** and **is not,** even he is the **eighth,** and is of the seven, and goeth into perdition." To unmask the apparent mystery, all that is necessary, is to count the prophetic **beasts** representing periods and nations. Beginning with the first beast and as we close with the last, he must be "the eighth" and "yet of the seven." The **lion** (Babylon) is the first; the **bear** (Medo-Persia) is the second; the four-headed **leopard** (Grecia) is the third; the **non-descript** (Rome) is the fourth; the **leopard-like** (from the fall of Rome to 1929) is the fifth; the one with the **lamb-like** horns (United States) is the sixth; the **scarlet colored** (from 1929 to the end of this present world) is the seventh; the same "scarlet colored" that shall ascend from the bottomless pit and go into perdition (from the resurrection of the wicked to their second death), is the eighth: "And the beast that was, and is not, even he is the eighth, and is of the seven, and goeth into perdition." He is the "eighth," but is "of the seven," because "He **was** and is **not,** and **yet is."** That is, the scarlet colored beast appears on the stage of action the second time (first, prior to the millennium and second, after the millennium, by the second resurrection). Therefore, he is the eighth, but is of the seven: "And goeth into perdition" (the second death of the wicked). Simple as it is, yet most perfect, it tells the truth and corrects error. Here we see another set of numbers including the entire chain of beasts. The red dragon in Revelation 12:3, cannot be numbered with the numerous beasts for he is not a symbol of a particular nation or government. He represents Satan and his schemes at certain times, for he is "called the **Devil, and Satan."** (Rev. 12:9.)

Verse 12, "And the ten horns which thou sawest are ten kings, which have received no kingdom as yet; but receive power as kings one hour with the beast." The ten horns denote exactly the same as on the non-descript beast. As the present civilization was embodied in that beast (Roman monarchy) and symbolized by the horns, just so the wicked multitude on the other side of the millennium is embodied in the scarlet beast and symbolized by the horns. Therefore, they "have received no kingdom as yet." "But received power as kings one hour with the beast." This last phrase (one hour with the beast) will be fully explained in connection with another study.

Verse 13, "These have one mind, and shall give their power and strength unto the beast." The kings that descended from the Roman monarchy have been in continual strife and will be to the end. Said the prophet: "And whereas thou sawest iron mixed with miry clay, they shall mingle themselves with the seed of men: but they **shall not cleave** one to another, even as iron is not mixed with clay." (Dan. 2:43.) "But with the innumerable company on the other side of the millennium it will not be so: "These have one mind, and shall give their power and strength unto the beast." (Rev. 17:13.)

Verse 14: "These shall make war with the Lamb, and the Lamb shall overcome them: for he is Lord of lords, and King of kings: and they that are with him are called, and chosen, and faithful." Satan shall gather the great multitude and deceive them once more. He will marshall the armies of the nations at the close of the one hundred years against the holy city—New Jerusalem, thus making war with the Lamb: "And when the thousand years are expired, Satan shall be loosed out of his prison, And shall go out to deceive the nations which are in the four quarters of the earth, Gog and Magog, to gather them together to battle: the number of whom is as the sand of the sea. And they went up on the breadth of the earth, and compassed the camp of the saints about, and the beloved city: and fire came down from God out of heaven, and devoured them. And the devil that deceived them was cast into the lake of fire and brimstone, where the beast and the false prophet are, and shall be tormented day and night forever and ever." (Rev. 20:7-10.)

"Tormented day and night forever and ever." Note that it says not tormenting, but "tormented"; that is, they are punished once for ever. "Day and night," means that they shall be punished and destroyed in the same manner as the antediluvians—by raining, "day and night,"—water in the former, and by fire in the latter.

The color of the beast (scarlet) reveals that God's people will have been called out by the message of the **"loud cry,"** and thus be separate and distinct from the world. Thus, leaving the beast "scarlet" (skimmed-separated), a sign of being under condemnation, left without excuse—ready to perish. "Full of names and blasphemy", denotes multiplicity of sects and hypocrisy. The balance of the chapter will be explained in another study.

THE WOMAN RIDING ON THE "BEAST", "HEADS" AND "WATERS"
REVELATION 17

"And there came one of the seven angels which had the seven vials, and talked with me, saying unto me, Come hither; I will shew unto thee the judgment of the great whore that sitteth upon many waters." (Verse 1.) The angel that was talking to John is one of the seven which had the seven vials of the seven last plagues. (See Rev. 15:7; 16:1.) It will be noticed that he had the vial of the plague ready, but it had not been poured out at the time he said to John, "Come hither; I will shew unto thee the **judgment** of the great whore." By the information given, it is certain that the event predicted by the symbol, the woman **sitting** on the beast, is shortly before the plagues are poured out and in the time when the "woman" is to be **judged.**

Who Is the Woman Riding On the Beast?

The reason John was shown the vision, is made clear by the words of the angel: "Come hither; I will shew unto thee the **judgment** of the great whore that sitteth upon many waters." The angel's interpretation of the **"waters"** is given in verse 15: "Peoples, and multitudes, and nations, and tongues." The woman **sitting** on **them** denotes that the inhabitants (waters) had fallen into her trap of deception (sitting on them).

"And the woman was arrayed in purple and scarlet colour, and decked with gold and precious stones and pearls, having a golden cup in her hand full of abominations and filthiness of her fornication." (Verse 4.) The woman is a symbol of a counterfeit religious system. From her cup she hands out false doctrines. Being **golden,** it has an appearance of splendor—inviting. Her costly garments of loud colors and precious ornaments vividly portray the magnificence of this most vile woman and her kingly pomp, and vain glory. By the power of her attraction, so irresistible to the human eye, she has conquered men of the strongest intellect—"With whom the kings of the earth have committed fornication." Millions with strong mental faculties, men who appear as giants among the inhabitants of the earth, have fallen helpless victims in her trap. The kings of the earth are guilty of spiritual adultery with the **"woman"** (drunk with **false doctrines**), thereby becoming entangled in her seductive snares.

Any **so called** Christian organization handing out false doctrines under an appearance of virtue, evidently is governed by the power of the **"woman."** The origin of all such fallacious teachings can be traced back into the **golden** cup. Said the angel: "The seven **heads** are seven **mountains,** on which the woman **sitteth."** It has been previously explained that the **heads** are symbols of so-called Christian denominations, and as she **sits** on them **all,** it denotes a union of churches under one head—"the woman." The Biblical number **"seven"** apprehends **all** such organizations.

If all the churches at this present time were led by the Holy Spirit, there would be no confusion among the so-called Christian sects. As it would be impossible for all to be right while no two believe alike, it is warrantable to say that those who are drinking the wine from the "cup of her fornication," are not few, for Inspiration says: "And the **inhabitants** of the earth have been made drunk with the wine of her fornication." (Verse 2, last part.)

Note that the "woman" **sits** on the "waters," also on the "heads," and on the "beast." (See Rev. 17:1, 3, 9.) As it would be impossible for one person to sit on **all** three objects at one time, the prophetic symbols reveal a spiritual fraud in three different periods. Thus John declares: "I saw a woman sit upon a scarlet colored beast." Not upon the "waters", nor upon the "heads." Before he saw her, the angel said, The woman "sitteth upon many waters." It was the angel also who added, "The seven heads are seven mountains, on which the woman **sitteth."** (See verses 1, 9.) Thus, John saw her last exploit only (sit upon the beast). Consequently, the symbol, sitting on the **"waters"** is her first act, according to the vision.

Therefore, her first achievement ("sitting on the waters"), must have been in the past from the time the prophetic symbol is revealed. Hence, the sitting on the **heads** becomes her second accomplishment, and the sitting on the **Beast** is the last; at which time she is judged.

As the Protestant churches are represented by the heads, she could not have sat on them before the reformation, for they were not as yet in existence. As the heads upon which the "woman sits" are unharmed, it is evident that the prophetic symbol is to meet its fulfillment some time after the deadly wound of the leopard-like beast of Revelation 13:3, is healed. The symbol, sitting on the heads, denotes union of churches, for she **sits** on them.

Therefore, when Catholicism, Protestantism, and Spiritualism clasp each other's hand by the medium of a league, then it could be said, "the woman sitteth on the **heads."**

The symbol of the "woman sitting on the **beast,"** will meet its fulfillment when that religious federation shall make an alliance with the powers of the world. Such an act would give the woman full control of the entire beast, horns and heads —the world. At that time the following Scripture will meet its perfect fulfillment: "And he causeth all, both small and great, rich and poor, free and bond, to receive a mark in their right hand, or in their foreheads: And that no man might buy or sell, save he that had the mark, or the name of the beast." (Rev. 13:16, 17.)

Thus the symbol of the "woman" sitting on the "waters," represents the period before the reformation. This was true during the period of papal supremacy, for at that time the papacy ruled the Roman world—"peoples, and multitudes, and nations, and tongues." Thus the "woman" sat on the "waters" during the 1260 prophetic years of Daniel 7:25, but she is yet to sit on the "heads," and on the "beast." Had she sat on the non-descript beast instead of on the "waters," it would have been wrongly symbolized, for, the "woman," by the tool of Catholicism, did not reign over **all** the world (beast), but over many "peoples, and multitudes, and nations, and tongues" (many waters). Therefore, the symbol, "sitting upon the scarlet colored beast," denotes an international religio-political system.

How Long Has the Woman Been In Existence?

This question may be answered by the following Scriptures: "And I saw the woman drunk with the blood of saints, and with the blood of the martyrs of **Jesus:** and when I saw her, I wondered with great admiration." (Verse 6.) This could truly be said of the Roman church, for, she persecuted the Christians and martyred them. Therefore, she is "drunk" with their blood. True, the Roman church has had unlawful connection with the "woman"; **was,** and **is** drunk with the wine of her fornication.

The "woman" did not originate with the Roman church, but rather **she produced** that church. Therefore, we must trace her existence beyond the beginning of the papacy. Revelation 18:24, throws light upon the subject: "And **in** her was found the blood of the **prophets,** and of the **saints,** and of **all** that were slain upon the earth." The holy Word of God declares that the **"woman"** is guilty of the blood of the martyrs in **all** ages. Therefore, the "woman" is drunk with the blood of Abel, and thus the blood of "all" the martyrs is found in her; proving that Cain was her first client by presenting a counterfeit sacrifice (false doctrine), and by slaying his brother.

There are many so-called Christians, who, like Cain, say, "It makes no difference; one thing is as good as another." But God accepts no substitute and no man's religion. That which human wisdom has devised, is man's righteousness, and not the righteousness of Christ. Therefore, it is an abomination in God's sight. The human fiber of obedience to divine requirements being weakened, and the sinful inclinations strengthened from generation to generation, the nature of man cannot be better at this present time than when the disciples asked Jesus: "Knowest thou that the Pharisees were offended, after they heard this saying?" So-called Christians, like the Pharisees, become offended when told of their errors, and rebuked for their sins. "But He answered and said, Every plant, which my heavenly Father hath not planted, shall be rooted up. Let them alone: they be blind leaders of the blind. And if the blind lead the blind, both shall fall into the ditch." (Matt. 15:12-14.)

"And upon her forehead was a name written, **Mystery, Babylon the Great, the Mother of Harlots and Abominations of the Earth.**" (Rev. 17:5.) The woman riding on the beast is the **mother.** The seven heads on the beast are the symbols of her daughters (harlots). Catholicism is her first daughter in this symbol, and as Protestantism sprang from Catholicism, then, apostate Protestantism in the multiplicity of sects, are her daughters also. Or it may be said, the woman" is the mother of Catholicism, and Catholicism is the mother of Protestantism. Says the Revelator: "I saw a woman sit upon a scarlet coloured beast, **full** of **names** of blasphemy." (Verse 3.) Thus the number of **"heads,"** and **full of names,"** include all the offshoots from Protestantism and Catholicism. Had there been no mention made of being **"full of names,"** more than seven, and **"scarlet,"** which denotes that God's people have been called out of it, therefore, **"scarlet"—skimmed**—under curse ready to perish, the Biblical number "seven heads," would have included those who are carrying God's message as in the period of the leopard-like beast of Revelation 13:1, at the time his deadly wound was **healed.** Therefore, it would have made no allowance for the church which **"keep** the **commandments** of **God,** and the **Faith of Jesus,"** and thus it would have contradicted the following Scripture: "And the dragon was wroth with the woman [God's church], and went to make war with the remnant of her seed [Israel the true—the 144,000], which keep the commandments of God, and have the testimony of Jesus Christ." (Rev. 12:17.)

God has never had more than one movement in existence at a time and it could not be otherwise now, for Christ cannot be divided. (See 1 Cor. 1:13.) God's church is well marked in every generation by obedience to present truth. The fact itself proves the claim true as there is **only** one church in the period of the beast which has the "Spirit of Prophecy" and **all** of the commandments as written by the finger of God. Said Jesus: "Whosoever therefore shall break one of these least commandments and shall teach men so, he shall be called the least in the kingdom of heaven: but whosoever shall do and teach them, the same shall be called great in the kingdom of heaven." (Matt. 5:19.) It is this divine principle that shall divide the world into two classes—the commandments of God and the traditions of men. "And before him shall be gathered all nations: and he shall separate them one from another, as a shepherd divideth his sheep from the goats: And he shall set the sheep on his right hand, but the goats on the left." (Matt. 25:32, 33.)

THE EXCEEDING GREAT HORN OF DANIEL 8:9

"Then I lifted up mine eyes, and saw, and behold, there stood before the river a ram which had two horns: and the two horns were high; but one was higher than the other, and the higher came up last. I saw the ram pushing westward, and northward, and southward; so that no beasts might stand before him, neither was there any that could deliver out of his hand; but he did according to his will, and became great. And as I was considering, behold, an he goat came from the west on the face of the whole earth, and touched not the ground: and the goat had a notable horn between his eyes. And he came to the ram that had two horns, which I had seen standing before the river, and ran unto him in the fury of his power. And I saw him come close unto the ram, and he was moved with choler against him, and smote the ram, and brake his two horns: and there was no power in the ram to stand before him, but he cast him down to the ground, and stamped upon him: and there was none that could deliver the ram out of his hand. Therefore the he goat waxed very great: and when he was strong, the great horn was broken; and for it came up four notable ones toward the four winds of heaven. And out of one of them came forth a little horn, which waxed exceeding great, toward the south, and toward the east, and toward the pleasant land." (Daniel 8:3-9.)

The angel giving the interpretation to Daniel says: "The ram which thou sawest having two horns are the kings of Media and Persia. And the rough goat is the king of Grecia: and the great horn that is between his eyes is the first king. Now that being broken, whereas four stood up for it, four kingdoms shall stand up out of the nation, but not in his power. And in the latter time of their kingdom, when the transgressors are come to the full, a king of fierce countenance, and understanding dark sentences, shall stand up." (Daniel 8:20-23.)

"And in the latter time of their kingdom [the four Grecian divisions], a king of fierce countenance . . . shall stand up." This Scripture is applicable to the Roman monarchy, for this king must stand at the end of the reign of the kings of Grecia. The Ptolemy's was the last of the four Grecian divisions to fall under the ascendancy of Rome. With the defeat of Anthony, and the death of Cleopatra about 27 B. C., the noted dynasty of the Ptolemy's came to its end, and Egypt became a province of the

Roman state. He was to stand up "when the transgressors are come to the full." The Grecians have never been anything but transgressors; therefore, the reference can be applied only to the Jewish nation, at which time the once-favored people of God would have exceeded any previous record of both moral and Spiritual corruption. The Jewish nation reached that condition at the time of the ascendency of Rome, and the first advent of Christ. Therefore, this king of "fierce countenance" is the Roman monarchy, after the "transgressors" (Jews) had come to their "full."

Rome's Power Not Her Own; Understanding Dark Sentences

"And his power shall be mighty, but not by his own power: and he shall destroy wonderfully, and shall prosper, and practice, and shall destroy the mighty and holy people. And through his policy also he shall cause craft to prosper in his hand; and he shall magnify himself in his heart, and by peace shall destroy many: he shall also stand up against the Prince of princes; but he shall be broken without hand." (Daniel 8:24, 25.)

"He shall understand dark sentences," and "his power shall be mighty, but not by his own power." His prosperity is accomplished by peace; then, if by peace, the Scripture can have no reference to ambitious conquests of territory. His power was to be directed against the holy people (the Christians). "He shall also stand against the Prince of princes" (Christ).

In order that a human being may understand dark sentences, he must use supernatural power, and that power cannot be his own. The question arises as to where he was to obtain his mighty power. If his attack is to be against Christ and His people, it would not be hard to recognize the kind of power that he would use. However, John gives us the source of this mysterious strength.

"And there appeared a great wonder in heaven; a woman clothed with the sun, and the moon under her feet, and upon her head a crown of twelve stars: and she being with child cried, travailing in birth, and pained to be delivered. And there appeared another wonder in heaven; and behold a great red dragon, having seven heads and ten horns, and seven crowns upon his heads. And his tail drew the third part of the stars of heaven, and did cast them to the earth: and the dragon stood before the woman which was ready to be delivered, for to devour her child as soon as it was born. And she brought forth a man child, who was to rule all nations with a rod of iron: and her child was caught up unto God, and to His throne." (Rev. 12:1-5.)

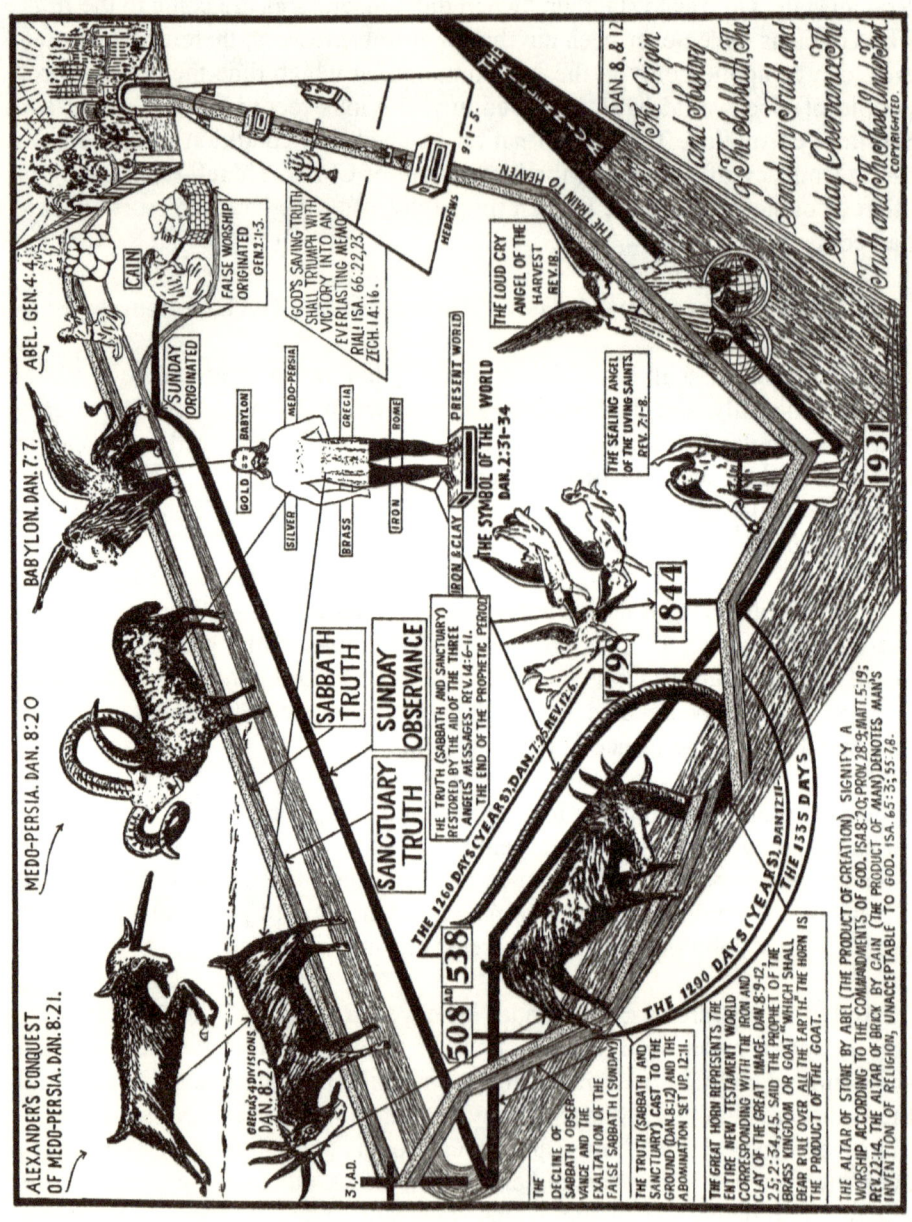

The Origin and History of The Sabbath, the Sanctuary Truth, and Sunday Observance—The Truth and Method Illustrated.

DAN. 8. & 12

128

The woman is a symbol of God's church; the crown of twelve stars is her authority or government (the twelve apostles), and the child is Christ. In the ninth verse we are told that the dragon is "the Devil, and Satan." It was under the figure of Herod that the dragon stood before the woman, ready to devour her child as soon as it was born.

"And when they were departed, behold, the angel of the Lord appeared to Joseph in a dream, saying, Arise, and take the young child and His mother, and flee into Egypt, and be thou there until I bring thee word: for Herod will seek the young child to destroy him." (Matt. 2:13.)

Therefore, the power that Rome used in her cruelty against the "holy people and the Prince of princes" was the old dragon power, and thereby the Roman emperors "understand dark sentences" through which he, the devil, was determined to destroy Christ and his followers. (Follow the chart on page 128).

The Horn Reveals That Which the Beast Fails to Do

As Medo-Persia and Grecia are each represented by the two symbols—Medo-Persia first by the ram, and second by the bear; and Grecia first by the goat and second by the four-headed leopard beast, so Rome was represented first by the exceeding great horn on the goat, and second by the non-descript beast. The first stage of the fourth beast represents imperial Rome, but the second stage, after his three horns had been plucked, describes papal Rome. (See pages 56-59.) The beast representing imperial Rome does not give much information regarding the Roman form of government, but that which is not revealed by the beast is made known by the goat's great horn. Therefore, we must consider the great horn's power and conduct.

Cast Down the Host and the Stars

Says Daniel: "Therefore, the he goat waxed very great: and when he was strong, the great horn was broken; and for it came up four notable ones towards the four winds of heaven. And it waxed great, even to the host of heaven; and it cast down some of the host and of the stars to the ground, and stamped upon them." (Dan. 8:8, 10.)

"The host of heaven" cannot refer to the Jewish nation at that time for the Jews had killed the prophets, and had rejected every message God had sent by His humble servants, until there was no remedy. Thus they had been without a prophet since the time of Malachi. Had they obeyed God's voice through His messengers, He would not have left them to fall under the Roman yoke.

The Jews reasoned as most Christians do at the present time. They took the position that they were wise and well favored of God, even though they had rejected every ray of light, and completely despised the entreaties and mercies of Jehovah. Their misconception of God's truth, and prejudice against light upon the word of God, robbed them of wisdom and knowledge of the Most High, until they were finally led into terrible sin and condemnation. When they rejected the message borne to them by the apostles with the power of the Holy Spirit, they sinned against the Holy Ghost, and thereby closed the only channel through which God could communicate with them.

Therefore, the Jews, under such condemnation, could not be termed the "host of heaven," and much less "stars." "Yea he magnified himself even to the Prince of the host." (Verse 11.) "The Prince" is Christ, and "the host" are the Christians. This is the only proper application that can be made of the expression.

"The stars" are none other than the apostles, as they were symbolized by the woman's crown of Revelation 12:1. Therefore, the "stars" that were cast down refer to the apostles, and "the host," to the Christians after the crucifixion of Christ, when Rome, together with the Jews, persecuted and martyred ("cast to the ground"). "Yea he magnified himself even to the Prince of the host; that is, the Roman power magnified itself against Christ—Prince of the Christians.

The Daily and the Sanctuary Cast Down

"And by him the daily sacrifice was taken away, and the place of his sanctuary was cast down. And an host was given him against the daily sacrifice by reason of transgression, and it cast down the truth to the ground; and it practiced and prospered." (Dan. 8:11, 12.)

The Spirit of Prophecy, commenting on the text, says: "Then I saw in relation to the 'daily', Daniel 8:12, that the word 'sacrifice' was supplied by man's wisdom, and does not belong to the text."—"Early Writings," p. 74. This being true, we must disregard the word "sacrifice," but hold to the "daily," although the word "sacrifice" is italicized, showing that it was supplied, a vision was given regarding the text, making it evident that a vital truth is involved in the words "daily," and "sanctuary." Whatever the "daily" may be, it was taken away by the "Great Horn."

In Daniel 11:31, reference is made to the same incident:

"And arms shall stand on his part, and they shall pollute the sanctuary of strength, and shall take away the daily, . . . and they shall place the abomination that maketh desolate."

The verse just quoted makes clear the idea that both the "daily" and the "sanctuary" must be a part of God's truth. This thought cannot be misconstrued without doing injury to the Scripture. Note the language used: "And they shall **pollute** the sanctuary of **strength** and shall **take away** the **"daily."** After **polluting** the "sanctuary" and **taking away** the "daily," then it says: "They shall **place** the abomination that maketh desolate." That is to say: The "sanctuary" and the "daily" were replaced by the abomination. The abomination must be some Pagan religious institution, and that Pagan doctrine ("abomination") was to make desolate. That is to say, it laid **waste** the "sanctuary," the "daily," and the **"truth";** or as it is expressed in Daniel 8:13, "Trodden under foot." "And it cast down the **truth** to the ground; and it practiced, and prospered." (Verse 12.)

Jesus, speaking of the same incident, says: "When ye therefore shall see the abomination of **desolation,** spoken of by Daniel the prophet, **stand in the holy place,** (whoso readeth, let him understand.") (Matt. 24:15.)

Jesus calls the "daily" and the "sanctuary," **"holy place."** No Pagan sanctuary would the Master call "holy place"; neither can it be polluted, for it has always been unclean. No Pagan daily can be holy. Therefore, the "daily" and the "sanctuary" must hold truth vital to the Christian church, and the prophet declared that it was to be "trodden under foot." The word "sacrifice" in relation to the "daily" was shown to be supplied by man's wisdom, as previously stated. It was also pointed out that the word "daily" is correct. Therefore, it cannot be supplemented by another word; it must remain as it is.

As Daniel was carefully watching the scene in the vision, he says: "Then I heard one saint speaking, and another saint said unto that certain saint which spake, How long shall be the vision concerning the **daily,** and the transgression of desolation, to give both the **sanctuary** and the **host** to be **trodden** under foot? And he said unto me, Unto two thousand and three hundred days; **then** shall the **sanctuary** be **cleansed."** (Dan. 8:13, 14.)

The prophetic period of the 2300 days (years), a well-known Bible truth, was first taught by William Miller prior to 1844. Therefore, we shall not give its explanation here. It is sufficient to say that the long prophetic period ended in 1844. The question was asked by one saint, How long shall be the vision concerning the **daily,** the **sanctuary,** and the **host?** Then it is answered by another saint, "Unto two thousand three hundred days." It is only necessary to ascertain what two vital truths were brought to light in 1844, and we shall have the truth of what is meant by the **"daily"** and the **"sanctuary."** They are self-explanatory in both word and time—the Sabbath and the Sanctuary truths, as they were jointly taught in 1844 A. D.

The Sabbath doctrine is the only Bible truth in the Christian dispensation that has to do with a definite day; hence, it is called **"daily."** The word "daily," in the Hebrew by Isaac Leeser is rendered "continual." Thus it clearly bears the evidence that the Sabbath (**daily** doctrine) is a continual and everlasting truth.

As the Sabbath (**daily**) was taken away, and the "abomination set up," then that which took the place of the Holy Sabbath, and the Sanctuary truth, is called "the abomination." Consequently, Sunday observance and a counterfeit priesthood are the only things to which the term "abomination" can be applied, for the seventh-day was supplanted by the first day of the week, Sunday—"the abomination that maketh desolate." That is, the Sabbath was lost sight of, or "cast to the ground," until 1844, together with the sanctuary truth. As the truth concerning the sanctuary service was "cast to the ground," (the truth of the priesthood of Christ in the heavenly sanctuary), the Pagan priesthood, or the Papal, as it is called now, was set up, thus taking away from the church the true mediatorial work of Christ. The truth of the sanctuary, jointly with the Sabbath, was brought to light in 1844, at which time the judgment (blotting out sin) began in the heavenly sanctuary, fulfilling the following prophecy:

"I beheld till thrones were cast down, and the Ancient of days did sit, whose garment was white as snow, and the hair of His head like the pure wool: His throne was like the fiery flame, and His wheels as burning fire. A fiery stream issued and came forth from before Him: thousand thousands ministered unto Him, and ten thousand times ten thousand stood before Him; the judgment was set, and the books were opened." (Daniel 7:9, 10.)

At the fulfillment of this prophecy, the first angel's message was proclaimed: "And I saw another angel fly in the midst of heaven, having the everlasting gospel to preach unto them that dwell on the earth, and to every nation, and kindred, and tongue, and people, saying with a loud voice, Fear God and give glory to Him; for the hour of His **judgment** is come." (Rev. 14:6, 7.) This is another well know Bible truth. (Read "The Great Controversy," pp. 352-356.)

The sanctuary and Sabbath truths were restored to their proper place in 1844. But the question as to the time when these two holy doctrines were "cast to the ground," or "trodden under foot," remains to be answered. The angel, speaking to Daniel relative to the time, said: "And **from** the time that the **daily** shall be **taken away,** and the abomination that maketh desolate **set up,** there **shall be a thousand two hundred and ninety days.** Blessed is he that waiteth, and cometh to the **thousand three hundred and five and thirty days."** (Dan. 12:11, 12.)

It will be noticed that there is no blessing pronounced at the termination of the 1290 prophetic days (years), but there is a special blessing promised to those who wait till the 1335 days (years) are fulfilled. Therefore, at the end of the 1335 years the **"daily"** (Sabbath) was to be restored, and the blessing is to those who shall live from that time on, if they understand and receive its truth.

To ascertain the prophetic time when the Seventh-day Sabbath ("daily"), and the "truth" ("sanctuary") were trodden underfoot, and Sunday observance with its Pagan priesthood set up in their stead, it would be necessary to subtract 1335 years from 1844, which would point back to 508 A.D., (dealing with the Hebrew calendar). In that year the "Daily" (Sabbath) and the "Sanctuary" truths were "cast to the ground," and the "Abomination" (Sunday) "set up."

In order to understand the truth of the 1290 years ("days"), add this figure to 508, which points forward to 1798 A.D. at which time the 1260 prophetic days of Daniel 7:25 terminated with the imprisonment of Pope Pius VI. Thus the prophetic treading of the **"host"** ended in 1798, but the **"sanctuary"** and the **"daily"** truths were not restored and placed in the church until after the fulfillment of the 1335 days (years) in 1844. This unquestionable evidence proves that the movement that arose in 1844 is God's true church, and divinely predicted. Hence it clears up the widespread confusion in Christendom, as to which denomination has the truth for the present time; it also weeds out all the rest as false, for it is the only movement that has the truth of the sanctuary.

As the truth of the two inseparable doctrines were thrown down in 508 A.D., preliminary to the setting up of the papacy, just so the imprisonment of the pope in 1798 was preparatory to the restoration of the jointly taught Bible truths, the Sabbath and the Sanctuary. The accountability that rests on the papacy is not the observance of the day, but rather, the desire to change the law of God, as shown in Daniel 7:25: "Think to change times and laws." The papacy thought to erase the Seventh-day Sabbath from the **eternal** law, and to inscribe the first day of the week in its place.

How Was the Church Paganized?

It was the Roman emperors who paganized the church, and as the pagans always observed Sunday, the Sabbath was set aside as far as the church authorities, the priests and the emperors, were concerned. The pagans cared nothing for the Sabbath. They were not taught its sacredness, and the few Christians who tried to keep the holy day were lost in the multitude. Soon the Sabbath services were a thing of the past. This was accomplished by 508 A. D. This satanic act paved the way, and the papacy was set up in 538. The pope was made the absolute ruler, king of kings, and a corrector of heretics by his so-called divine authority. The scheme was for the perpetuity of the false doctrines, and to keep the truth underfoot forever. It is a most mysterious thing, the way the old enemy of mankind has succeeded in deceiving the strongest intellects. He enthralls them to their own destruction. Thus it has been in every age.

As previously explained, Rome at first persecuted the Christians. But when the old dragon saw that persecution could not overthrow their faith, he reversed his plan, and devised a more subtle satanic scheme to destroy the church. He worked, as always, through the natural heart, using the human tool to carry out a deception unseen by mortal eye.

"Gibbon's Rome," Vol. 2, pp. 273, 274, says: "By the edicts of toleration, he [Constantine], removed the temporal disadvantages which had hitherto retarded the progress of Christianity; and its active and numerous ministers received a free permission, a liberal encouragement, to recommend the salutary truths of revelation by every argument which could affect the reason or piety of mankind. The exact balance of the two religions [Christian and Pagan], continued but a moment. . . . The cities which signalized a forward zeal by the voluntary destruction of their temples [the Pagan's] were distinguished by municipal privileges, and rewarded with popular donatives. . . . The salvation of the common people was purchased at an easy rate, if it be true that, in one year, twelve thousand men were baptized at Rome, besides a proportionable number of women and children, and that a white garment, with twenty pieces of gold, had been promised by the emperor to every convert. . . . This was a law of Constantine, which gave freedom to all the slaves who should embrace Christianity."

In this manner, Rome paganized the church, and what persecution failed to do, donatives and privileges accomplished. As

the victorious Christians were pressing forward against the impregnable persecuting wall which was supported by the devil, he suddenly drew back, allowing
it to collapse. Thus, as the persecution ceased, it caused them to fall as it were,
by their own force. So what the satanic power failed to do by persecution, he
accomplished by a sudden retreat. When the old dragon saw that he could not
overthrow that spiritual house by persecution, he reversed the scheme and employed his power to undermine the apostolic foundation by donatives and various inducements to the pagans in favor of the Christians. As the pagans rushed
to join the church, the current of apostasy turned against the Christians. Instead
of the church Christianizing the world, the world paganized the church. In this
way the Christians fell under the power of the "dragon" and thereby were swallowed by his heads (paganized). But as satan designed to fully insure his plan,
he turned the persecution toward the pagans, fearing that the true Christian spirit
would revive if the two sects, Christian and Pagan, were in existence.

Gibbon says: "Under his [Athanasius'] reign, Christianity obtained an easy
and lasting victory; and as soon as the smile of royal patronage was withdrawn,
the genius of Paganism, which had been fondly raised and cherished by the arts
of Julian, sunk irrevocably in the dust."—Id., p. 521.

"A special commission was granted to Cynegius, the Preatorian prefect of
the east, and afterwards to the Counts Jovius and Gaudentius, two officers of
distinguished rank in the West; by which they were directed to shut the temples,
to seize or destroy the instruments of idolatry, to abolish the privileges of the
priests, and to confiscate the consecrated property for the benefit of the emperor,
of the church, or the army. . . . Many of those temples were the most splendid
and beautiful monuments of Grecian architecture; and the emperor himself was
interested not to deface the splendor of his own cities, or to diminish the value
of his own possessions. . . . In Syria, the divine and excellent Marcellus, as he is
styled by Theodoret, a bishop animated with apostolic fervor, resolved to level
with the ground the stately temples. . . . But when a sentence of destruction
against the idols of Alexandria was pronounced, the Christians set up a shout
of joy and exultation whilst the unfortunate Pagans, whose fury had given way
to consternation, retired with hasty silent steps. . . . Theophilus proceeded to
demolish the temple of Serapis, . . . and to content himself with reducing the
edifice itself to a heap of rubbish, a part of which was soon afterwards cleared
away, to make room for a church, created in honor of the Christian martyrs."—
Id., Vol. 3, pp. 140-146.

Thus the Pagans joined the Christian church through force and bribery instead of conviction of sin, and thereby Christianity gave way to idolatry. Says Gibbon: "Both religions had been alternately disgraced by the seeming acquisition of worthless proselytes, of those votaries of the reigning purple, who could pass, without a reason, without a blush, from the church to the temple, and from the altars of Jupiter to the sacred table of the Christians."—Id., Vol 2, p. 522.

The church in her purity, filled with the spirit of the meek and lowly Jesus, battled against oppression and torture. They prayed for those who would take their lives, saying, "Lord, forgive them, for they know not what they do." They, like Stephen, kneeled down under a rain of stones, pleading, "Lord, lay not this sin to their charge." But the Christians who were once zealous for the pure standard of the church, took the crown of civil authority, and compelled the Pagans to join their ranks.

As the Pagans and the Christians became one, the dragon wielded his power and great authority into the papacy. By this concentrated ecclesiastical monarchy he erased the Seventh-day Sabbath from the law of God, and in its stead he inserted the pagan Sunday. At this point he directed his power against disloyalty to the demands of the papacy. This pontifical authority continued to wear out the saints of the Most High, as in Daniel 7:25. As Shadrach, Meshach, and Abednego in Babylon, and Daniel in Medo-Persia, prevented the establishment of an ecclesiastical government, and brought to naught the king's decree, just so Luther abolished the pontifical monarchy, and brought to an end the papal authority. As Luther's blow weakened his power, and Protestantism continually irritated his wound, the pope, by the hand of Berthier, was put behind prison bars.

How Idol Worship Crept Into the Church

Just a few more lines from the pen of Gibbons describing how idol and saint worship crept into the Christian church: "The bodies of St. Andrew, St. Luke, and St. Timothy, had reposed near three hundred years in the obscure graves, from whence they were transported, in solemn pomp, to the church of the apostles, which the magnificence of Constantine had founded on the banks of the Thracian Bosphorus. About fifty years afterwards, the same banks were honored by the presence of Samuel, the judge and prophet of the people of Israel. His ashes, deposited in a golden vase, and covered with a silken veil, were delivered by the bishops into each other's hands. . . . In the long period of twelve hundred years, which elapsed between the reign of Constantine and the reformation of Luther, the worship of saints and relics corrupted the pure and perfect simplicity of the Christian model: and some symptoms of degeneracy may be observed even in the first generations which adopted and cherished this pernicious innovation. . . . The Christians frequented the tombs of the martyrs, in the hope of obtaining, from their powerful intercession, every sort of spiritual, but more especially of temporal, blessings. They implored the preservation of their health, or the cure of their infirmities; the fruitfulness of their barren wives, or the safety and happiness of their children."—Id; Vol. 3, pp. 156, 157, 162.

Both classes were unlawfully urged, the Christians to forget the spirit of the gospel, and the Pagans to embody the spirit of the church. The sublime and simple theology of the primitive Christians was gradually corrupted. The demon power was retarded. Although he could not defeat the operations of the Christian engineers by persecution, he succeeded by flattery.

As the unjust persecution against the Christians had ceased, the church took the downward step. Though a few respected the sacredness of the Sabbath, they were not disturbed until after the ecclesiastical monarchy was set up in 538. The dragon had carefully determined to obtain the perpetuity of the combined national religion, Christian in name but Pagan in practice. Satan designed to set up the papacy, and to "wear out the saints of the Most High." The persecution, first against the early Christian church, and second, against paganism in favor of Christianity, was reversed under papal rule. The few Christians who reverenced the Seventh-day Sabbath were, in some respects hunted like rabbits, and there was demanded of them strict obedience to the legal but unchristian religion of the popes.

To come back to our subject,—"The exceeding great horn." Rome in her divided state cast down the truth and stamped upon it. But it was not accomplished in a sudden or arbitrary manner. Sunday observance gradually crept into the Christian church. At first the morning hours were considered somewhat sacred, because the Lord had risen early on that day. After it had become formal, more sacredness was attached to it, and the hours were extended till noon. Finally the entire day was set aside as a day of worship.

While Sunday was growing more and more sacred, the Seventh-day Sabbath was on the decline, and becoming less and less holy. Here we see an example that should be marked carefully by all Christians. To add anything to the religion of Christ, though it may seem good on the surface, results in a deadly sting from beneath. Our God has devised a religion sufficient to save the church, if carefully followed. He needs no man's help, neither can He accept man-made devices.

"For I testify unto every man that heareth the words of the prophecy of this book, If any man shall add unto these things, God shall add unto him the plagues that are written in this book: And if any man shall take away from the words of the book of this prophecy, God shall take away his part out of the book of life, and out of the holy city, and from the things which are written in this book." (Rev. 22:18,19.)

The Roman church displaced the simplicity of the truth with human wisdom and traditions of man. Or, as Daniel puts it: "An host [Pagan flood] was given him against the daily by reason of **transgression,** and it cast down the truth to the ground; and it practiced, and prospered." (Dan. 8:12.) The "host" against the "daily" were the unconverted Pagans brought into the church; therefore, "by reason of transgression." How different from the method employed by John the Baptist! "But when he saw many of the Pharisees and Sadducees come to his baptism, he said unto them, O generation of vipers, who hath warned you to flee from the wrath to come? Bring forth therefore fruits meet for repentance." (Matt. 3:7, 8.)

It may be profitable to ask: is the church at the present time imitating John or the Romans? Are her members Christians or Pagans? The Lord charged His servant to warn ancient Israel against a similar disastrous practice. He said: "And thou shall say to the rebellious, even to the house of Israel, Thus saith the Lord God; O ye house of Israel, let it suffice you of all your abominations, in that ye have brought into My **sanctuary strangers, uncircumcised** in **heart,** and uncircumcised in flesh, to be in My sanctuary, **to pollute it,** even **My house."** (Eze. 44:6, 7.)

Truly, are people working for God or for themselves? The angel, in giving instruction to Daniel, calls the Sabbath and the sanctuary truth, **"The Truth."** (See Daniel 8:12.) Indeed, it is the truth. In keeping the Sabbath we honor God by recognizing Christ's holy memorial of creation.

"God, who at sundry times and in divers manners spake in time past unto the fathers by the prophets, Hath in these last days spoken unto us by His Son, whom He hath appointed heir of all things, **by whom also He made** the **worlds."** (Heb. 1:1, 2.)

Because sin entered the human family, the Lord instituted the sanctuary truth, which typically illustrates His sacrifice, death and resurrection—the revelation of our redemption. Thus, in keeping the Sabbath and sanctuary truth, we openly confess that

Christ is both Creator and Redeemer. "Therefore the Son of man is Lord also of the Sabbath day." (Mark 2:28.)

The Bible is the revelation of creation and redemption in Christ—Creator and Redeemer. Therefore, the Sabbath and the Sanctuary constitute **"The Truth."** (See Hebrews 9:10; 4:4-10.) Thus these two doctrines are coupled together, cannot be separated, and bear the whole truth.

How do we keep the Sanctuary truth? It is kept, not in type, but in anti-type. By faith we believe that Christ, our High Priest, in the heavenly sanctuary is officiating in our behalf, as it was taught in type by the earthly sanctuary, built by Moses. As Israel complied with the requirements of its service in the type, so we must in the anti-type. Thus we "proclaim the truth [Sabbath and Sanctuary] more fully."

SUMMARY
The Horn "Bears Rule Over All the Earth"

In order to fully comprehend what is being taught in this chapter, we again call attention to the chart on page 128. Now let us follow the chart along with the reading. In the foregoing study it is proven that the "exceeding great horn" of the "goat" does not represent imperial Rome only, but also papal Rome, and the present world as well; for the "horn" first persecuted Christ and His followers under the jurisdiction of the Roman monarchy. The truth expressed by the "Daily" and the "Sanctuary" were trodden down "by reason of transgression" in the period of the broken state of Rome up to 508 A.D.; for the imperial government came to an end in the year 476. Furthermore, the papal power "treads" God's truth on the ground up to the termination of the prophetic 1260 years, and ended with the imprisonment of the pope in 1798. But the **"Sanctuary"** and the **"Daily"** were held to the ground by the **"Great Horn"** up to 1844. At that time he lost control of them, and the power of the "THREE ANGELS' MESSAGES" raised the truth from the ground, or from "underfoot" and placed it in the church. Therefore, the "Great Horn" is a symbol of the entire New Testament period to the second coming of Christ—corresponding with the legs of iron, and the feet and toes of the great image of Daniel 2.

These are facts which cannot be denied. However, there is another proof that bears evidence of the same. Said the prophet: "And after thee [king of Babylon] shall arise another kingdom inferior to thee, and another third kingdom of brass, which shall bear rule over **all** the earth." (Daniel 2:39.)

The "brass" kingdom is accepted to represent Grecia, but the fact is that Grecia never did bear rule over **all** the earth. The most distant point of the compass reached by Alexander the Great was a portion of India. Neither did imperial Rome bear rule over **all** the earth. What then? Is Daniel wrong in the interpretation of the dream? If there is any error, Daniel cannot be at fault. The responsibility would naturally fall on God who was the overseer of all the writings, and the interpretations of the Scriptures. If Daniel had made a mistake it was God's duty to have him correct it. But as God is perfect in all His work, He cannot allow error in His Holy Word. Daniel is correct in his interpretation and the "brass" kingdom must bear rule over **all** the earth, for **all** else may fail, but God's Word shall stand forever.

When the goat's notable horn between his eyes (Alexander) was broken off, four others came up in its stead (the four divisions of Grecia). After this another little horn came up from one of the four, and it "waxed exceedingly great, toward the south, and toward the east, and toward the pleasant land." (Daniel 8:9.) Note that this horn waxed **exceedingly** great. That is to say, he was greater than the one "between his eyes" (Alexander). The exceeding great horn went toward the south, and toward the east, and toward the pleasant land (Jerusalem) as in Psalms 106:24 and Zechariah 7:14. Geographically, Babylon, where Daniel had the vision, lies east of Jerusalem. Thus, in the vision the "goat" stood in Babylon. To make the circle, the horn consequently went toward the four corners of the compass, or, as Daniel puts it, "toward the south, and toward the east, and toward the pleasant land." The symbol denotes that the exceeding great horn would extend its dominion over all the earth—the four corners of the compass. The fact is, the horn represents Rome in its three divisions—Imperial, Papal, and the present **unstable world.**

The Bible is correct in making the statement concerning the kingdom of brass, "that it shall bear rule over all the earth," for the brass represents the "goat." Thus the prophet stated: "An he goat came from the west on the face of the whole earth." (Daniel 8:5.)

Had Daniel said of the non-descript beast, symbol of imperial and papal Rome, that it would bear rule over all the earth, the claim would prove incorrect. The non-descript beast, in its first stage, represents imperial Rome, and in his second stage, papal Rome up to 1798, at which time the beast came to its end with the imprisonment of pope Pius VI, and gave place to the "leopard like beast" of Revelation 13:1-3.

Note the accuracy of inspiration. Had the prophet said, "the kingdom of iron shall bear rule over all the earth," it would have been true as far as the iron **bearing rule,** but such affirmation would have discredited this wonderful lesson taught by the symbolic goat. What is true of the iron and clay, is true of the goat; and one corresponds with the other.

The horn extends beyond 1798, and to the second coming of Christ, corresponding with the iron (legs, feet and toes) of the great image in Daniel 2. Of the "horn" we read, "it shall be broken without hand." (Daniel 8:25.) The same terms of speech is used of the feet and toes of the great image in Daniel 2:45. "In the days of these kings," Daniel says, "shall the God of Heaven set up a kingdom, which shall never be destroyed." (Daniel 2:44.) Therefore, the present civilization is the product of the goat, or the kingdom of brass. Had inspiration said the kingdom of iron shall bear rule over all the earth, it would have marred the picture, for the gold, silver and brass (Old Testament time), stands on the legs of iron (New Testament time). Thus the symbol proves that the **Old Testament** period **stands** on the Christian dispensation (Christ); and the **New Testament** period feeds on the **Old Testament** dispensation.

The trunk of the great image, depicting a living being containing all the living organs, corresponds to the Bible, for the **Old Testament** is the great store house of the **Word of God,** and the **New** feeds from the Old. In the Old dispensation, the Lord gathered the **Word of God** into the Bible to feed the world in the New dispensation. The New Testament is the fulfillment of the Old. God's Word spells perfection in every way.

The Sabbath "Trodden" Only Once

We again call your attention to the "woman" (church) of Revelation 12, where we are told she was given **"Two** wings of a **great eagle,** that she might fly into the wilderness . . . that they should feed her there a thousand two hundred and three score days." (Verses 14, 6.) As the **wings** of the lion (Babylon) and the four-headed leopard (Grecian four divisions, Dan. 7:4, 6) represent periods of world history, (see pages 33-42), so the **wings** of the **woman** also must denote **two** great periods of church history. The **eagle** being the king of birds, his wings must stand for chief, head or first. Therefore, each **wing** must be a symbol of **one** of these **two** great periods from their very beginning.

Had not inspiration emphasized the fact that the wings were of a **great** eagle, we could possibly conclude that one of them may stand for the Old Testament period, and the other for the Christian era. But the word, **great**, does not allow such conclusions. Thus, **one** of the wings must apprehend the church history from creation to the crucifixion of Christ, and the other from the resurrection to the end of this present world. Here, too, it would be possible for us to conclude that **one** wing may stand for the period before the Bible came, and the other for the Biblical period after the exodus. But the words of the Revelator overrule that thought, for he says: "And to the woman were given two wings of a great eagle, that she might fly into the wilderness, into her place, where she is nourished for a time, and times, and a half a time, from the face of the serpent." (Rev. 12:14.) Therefore, she was given the wings to fly into the wilderness in the New Testament time.

The symbol reveals that God has had only one church (truth) in all ages, and that the cross of Christ is the only center of attraction. The lesson teaches that the church of God fled into the wilderness only once in her entire history, and that was from 538 to 1798 A.D. During this time the Sabbath and the Sanctuary truths were "cast down to the ground," or "underfoot." Therefore, the continuity of these truths have never before the year 538 been interrupted by the church leadership. Although these divine truths may not always have been respected by members or leaders in the church, they were there for those who wanted them. Thus, God's eternal truth could have been kept by His people, openly, in all ages save the period under papal rule.

Again note, that the truth was cast down, and the "woman" (church) had fled into the wilderness. Inspiration says: "She hath a place prepared of God, that they should feed her there." (See verses 6, 14.) So, while the truth was "cast down" by the church leadership in that period, and the "abomination set up," God had some in obscurity who kept His Sabbath and had knowledge of the Sanctuary truth through the entire 1260 years of wilderness journey. Thus she was nourished (fed), revealing that she was to return.

Double Worship In All Ages

By observing the chart, the history of Sabbath and Sunday observance, or true and false worship, will be noticed. In the beginning the Lord created Adam and Eve, and placed the holy couple in the garden of God, but our first parents transgressed the counsel of the Most High, and sin entered the Eden home. In order to preserve His original plan for the human family, He was compelled to remove our parents from their Edenic abode. To them were born sons and daughters; see Genesis 5:4. Their first two sons are brought to our attention by the Scriptures in a contrast that is most striking, and one that should be carefully considered by every professor of religion.

The sacrifice and religious worship of the two first born in the human family, reveals that the Saviour of the world had made known the divine plan of salvation to the family of Adam. Their system of worship being devised by the Creator Himself, was perfect, and able to save the sinner from his sin. Abel's careful religious observance, according to the instruction of the Deity whom he worshipped, shows that only such worship, honor and praise, can be acceptable to God. Cain was not mindful of the commandment, and thus by presenting that which God had not required went about to establish a religion of his own. As he immediately afterwards slew his brother it should be an object lesson to all: that a worship according to the inclination of men, however good and innocent it may seem, cannot sanctify and save the worshiper. But instead it takes him deeper into sin, and final ruin. Those who are inclined to persecute the ones who do not worship as they do, are bowing down with Cain at the altar made of bricks. Such altars are the product of man by converting the form of the original; and though more attractive than the altar of stone may seem, there is no sanctifying power in them, and their worship is as deadly as poison. The evidence cannot be denied that both forms of worship (true and false) were introduced at about the same time, and ran side by side. Both seem innocent and were conducted about the same way with the distinction that the one is in harmony with God's book and law, and the other is **not.**

The two tracks on the chart, by the side of Abel, represent God's eternal truth, Sabbath and Sanctuary. The Sabbath originated in the garden of God. "And on the **seventh day God** ended **His work** which He had made; and He **rested** on the **seventh day** from **all** His work which He had made. And **God blessed** the **seventh day** and **sanctified** it: because that in it He had rested from **all** His work which God **created and made."** (Genesis 2:2, 3.)

Because of sin, the sanctuary truth was added after the fall of Adam. Both truths are of vital importance. The Sabbath we keep to avoid sinning, but the Sanctuary truth is to save us after we have sinned. The one is to keep us from falling, and the other is the remedy if we fall! If, after receiving the knowledge of the truth, we break the Sabbath, we have sinned and denied the Creator, which is far worse than the sin of Adam. By noncompliance with the Sanctuary truth, we refuse the plan (or remedy), and reject the Saviour of our Salvation. Read "The Desire of Ages," page 165. The Sabbath is a part of the Ten Commandment Law. (Exodus 20:1-17.) The Sanctuary truth is the law of our salvation, after we have sinned. Adam sinned by eating the forbidden fruit. Lucifer sinned by setting himself up as a god. Said he, "I will ascend into heaven, I will exalt my throne above the stars of God: I will sit also upon the mount of the congregation, in the sides of the north: I will ascend above the heights of the clouds; I will be like the most High." (Isaiah 14:13, 14.)

By eating of the forbidden fruit, Adam broke the health (food) law, and by so doing he also, indirectly, broke the Ten Commandment Law; for by transgressing God's Word he dishonored Him as a son would dishonor his earthly father by disobedience, and thereby breaking the fifth commandment. (Exodus 20:12.) Therefore, Adam is guilty of violating two laws, while Lucifer broke only one, the Ten Commandment Law, for he ate nothing that God had forbidden.

Adam's transgression brought him to the grave (dust); for, after eating of the forbidden fruit, it reacted on his physical being, and thus the evil passed from father to son. But as Lucifer had not transgressed the law of health, natural death had no power over him. Adam, by obedience to the provision made for his redemption—accepting the remedy—shall be made alive by resurrection. To Lucifer, for rejecting the same privilege and deceiving the human family, God said: "Thou shalt be brought down to hell, to the sides of the pit." (Isaiah 14:15.) "Thou wast perfect in thy ways from the day that thou wast created, till iniquity was found in thee. . . . I will destroy thee, O covering cherub, from the midst of stones of fire. . . . Thou hast defiled thy sanctuaries by the multitude of thine iniquities, by the iniquity of thy traffick; therefore will I bring forth a fire from the midst of thee, it shall devour thee, and I will bring thee to ashes upon the earth in the sight of all them that behold thee. All they that know thee among the people shall be astonished at thee: thou shalt be a terror, and **never shalt thou be any more."** (Ezek. 28:15, 16, 18, 19.)

There is a lesson here that is worth our consideration. Let the sinner place his finger on his sin. By disobeying God's word in any form, you are breaking one or more of His eternal laws. This is your final opportunity to either accept or reject salvation. Mercy is knocking at the door for the last time. Will you brother, will you sister, give your heart to God?

The readers attention is again called to the chart. The double track passing by Abel and around the cross, shows that the Sabbath and the Sanctuary truths are eternal and divine, and that the recognition of their sacredness had never been thrown out from the church of God until after 508 A.D.; at which time the "goat" with his great horn "cast down the truth to the ground." But in the year 1844, God's truth by the power of the "Three Angels' Messages," was again brought to light. It is evident that the Sabbath and the Sanctuary, (the law and the gospel) are inseparable. If you have been disobedient to God's word in any form, will you now, at the last call, say, "Lord, here I am. Take my stony heart and give me a heart of flesh?" Will you plead that He write His law in your heart? The angel is waiting to seal you with the seal of God. Will you choose darkness rather than light? As the angel is lightening the earth with his glory, will you let him lighten your heart? Yet a little while and God's truth shall triumph, why should you remain behind? Will you stubbornly worship, like Cain, with a religion that cannot save? Will you dishonor the Saviour who died for you, and honor the adversary and enemy of your soul? Why should you perish in just a little while, in the dark millennium? (Follow the chart.) Will you be ready when Jesus comes to take His saints to the mansions above? Take notice that the keeping of the truth is the train to the city of God. "Let us hear the conclusion of the whole matter: Fear God, and keep His commandments: for this is the whole duty of man." (Eccl. 12:13.)

The 1290 and 1335 "days" (years), relative to the "daily" and the "sanctuary" of Daniel 12:11, 12, are now understood for the first time. This being the time in which they are revealed, it is evident that we are dealing with present truth. Therefore, the Scripture must be speaking directly to us at this very time. Thus, both the **cursings** and the **blessings** of this chapter apply to this generation, and we are granted the privilege of choosing either the one or the other.

It is necessary that we comment first on the 10th verse of Daniel 12, for it brings out the fact that at the time this Scripture is revealed, "Many shall be purified and made white, and tried; but the wicked shall do wickedly and none of the wicked shall understand; but the wise shall understand." Therefore, it is necessary that we repent from all sin and separate ourselves from every false way, thus having our vision clear, so that we can understand.

"And at that time shall Michael stand up, the great prince which standeth for the children of thy people: and there shall be a time of trouble, such as never was since there was a nation even to that same time: and at that time thy people shall be delivered, every one that shall be found written in the book." (Daniel 12:1.) The name "Michael," means "who is like God." "Christ is the express image of the Father," and the great Prince of His people.

Thus the title signifies Christ. At this time, Christ (Michael) shall stand up for His people, and every one shall be delivered who is found written in "The Book." Thus God's people **need not fear** in the time of trouble.

"And many of them that sleep in the dust of the earth shall awake, some to everlasting life, and some to shame and everlasting contempt." (Daniel 12:2.) It will be noticed that the resurrection foretold in this Scripture is mixed—some are of the righteous, while others are of the wicked. Therefore, this is a special resurrection, and independent of the one referred to in 1 Thessalonians 4:16, 17, for it plainly says: "The Lord himself shall **descend** from heaven with a shout, with the voice of the archangel, and with the trump of God: and the dead in Christ shall rise first: Then we which are alive and remain shall be caught up together with them in the clouds, to meet the Lord in the air: and so shall we ever be with the Lord."

John also makes it clear that the righteous only are called forth at the coming of the Lord, for he says: "Blessed and holy is he that hath part in the **first** resurrection: **on such the second death hath no power.**" (Rev. 20:6.) Consequently, the mixed resurrection must precede the one at the coming of Christ in the clouds. Those who awake to "everlasting contempt" must be those who pierced Christ, thus fulfilling the following Scripture: "Behold, He cometh with clouds; and **every eye shall see Him,** and they also which **pierced him.**" (Rev. 1:7.)

"And they that be wise shall shine as the brightness of the firmament; and they that turn many to righteousness as the stars forever and ever." (Daniel 12:3.) They who are "wise" are the ones who shall "understand," and **they** shall turn many to **righteousness;** thus they shall **shine as stars** "forever and ever." These are not those who were resurrected in the special resurrection, for it would be after the close of probation, and about the end of the seventh plague, just shortly before the coming of the Lord. Thus the resurrected ones would have no chance to turn **any** to righteousness. Therefore, those who shall **shine as stars** are the 144,000, and all who shall have a part in the closing work of the gospel. Think of the glorious promise! Is there anything like it in all the world? What can you compare with celestial bliss in the presence of God? Life everlasting, without pain or tears! See Revelation 7:17, and Isaiah 11:6, 7; 65:25.

"But thou, O Daniel, shut up the words, and seal the book, even to the time of the end: many shall run to and fro, and knowledge shall be increased." (Daniel 12:4.) What plainer evidence could we ask to convince us that **this** is the time of the end? Has knowledge been increase? Are many running to and fro? While Daniel does not tell how the running is accomplished, Nahum does: "The chariots shall be with flaming torches in the day of His preparation. . . . The chariots [automobiles] shall rage in the streets, they shall justle one against another in the broad ways: they shall seem like torches, they shall run like lightnings." (Nahum 2:3, 4.) The prophecy being understood, it is evident that "the book" is unsealed, and that the time of the end is upon us.

"Then I Daniel looked, and, behold, there stood other two, the one on this side of the bank of the river, and the other on that side of the bank of the river. And one said to the man clothed in linen, which was upon the waters of the river, How long shall it be to the **end** of these wonders? And I heard the man clothed in linen, which was upon the waters of the river, when he held up his right hand and his left hand unto heaven, and sware by Him that liveth forever that it shall be for a time, and times, and an half; and **when** he shall have accomplished to scatter the power of the holy people, **all these things shall be finished."** (Daniel 12:5-7.)

The question was asked, "How long shall it be to the end of these wonders?" The answer is, that it "shall be for a **time** [one year], **times** [two years] and an **half time** [half year]." Thirty days to a month, twelve months to a year, equals 1260 prophetic days (years).

The prophetic period points back to papal supremacy, and the persecution of God's people from 538 to 1798 A.D. (See Dan. 7:25, and Rev. 12:6, 14; 13:5.) The end of the long prophetic period in which the papacy scattered the power of the holy people, is in the past by a hundred and thirty years. The angel declared, **in this time "all** these things shall be finished." Does not all this prove that we are on the verge of eternity?

Will you, brother, will you sister, adorn yourself with the righteousness of Christ? Or will you wait a little longer, until after the harvest is past? Someone shall utter the following words in great disappointment: "The harvest is past, the summer is ended, and we are not saved.' (Jeremiah 8:20.) Shall you, or shall I?

"And I heard, but understood not: then I said, O my Lord, what shall be the end of these things? And He said, Go thy way, Daniel: for the words are closed up and sealed till the time of the end." (Daniel 12:8, 9.) Are they closed now? If not, then is not this the time to which the prophet refers? "Blessed is he that waiteth, and cometh to the thousand three hundred and five and thirty days." (Daniel 12:12.)

THE BEAST (666), FALSE PROPHET, MOTHER OF HARLOTS, MAN OF SIN, WHO ARE THEY?

The mystical number "666" of the beast in Revelation 13:18, as applied to the papacy, proves to be unscriptural as well as unreasonable. While the numerical letters of the title of the pope bears the number 666, there are many other titles, as well as names of individuals, who bear the same number. By simply computing the numerical value of letters in a title, or name, we find it fits many, hence we must look for Biblical proof to make the application. Except we thus prove the idea it would be improper and unfair to apply the symbol to any one individual.

The idea concerning the symbolical application of the false prophet of Revelation 19:20, the woman on the scarlet colored beast of Revelation 17, the leopard-like beast of Revelation 13, the scarlet colored beast of Revelation 17, and the non-descript beast of Daniel 7, as being symbols of the papacy, is unbiblical and also illogical.

"And I beheld another beast coming up out of the earth; and he had two horns like a lamb, and he spake as a dragon. And he exerciseth all the power of the first beast before him, and causeth the earth and them which dwell therein to worship the first beast, whose deadly wound was healed. And he doeth great wonders, so that he maketh fire come down from heaven on the earth in the sight of men, And deceiveth them that dwell on the earth by means of those miracles which he had power to do in the sight of the beast; saying to them that dwell on the earth, that they should make an image to the beast, which had the wound by the sword and did live. And he had power to give life unto the image of the beast, that the image of the beast should both speak, and cause that as many as would not worship the image of the beast should be killed. And he causeth all, both small and great, rich and poor, free and bond, to receive a mark in their right hand, or in their foreheads: And that no man might buy or sell, save he that had the mark, or the name of the beast, or the number of his name. Here is wisdom. Let him that hath understanding count the number of the beast: for it is the number of a man; and his number is six hundred three score and six." (Rev. 13:11-18.)

"And deceiveth them that dwell on the earth by means of those miracles which **he** had power to do in the **sight** of the

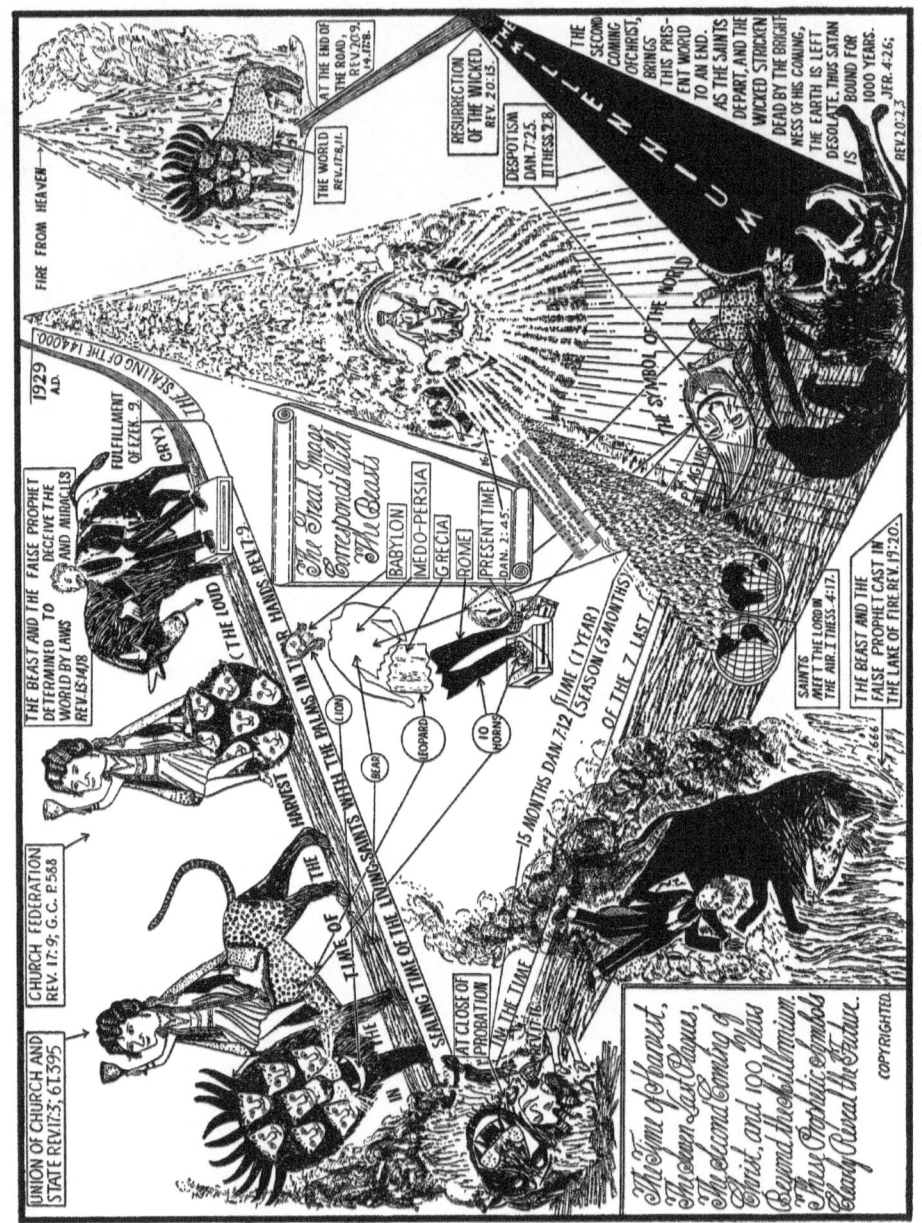

beast." (Verse 14.) The beast spoken of here is the one with lamb-like horns. But some one else is introduced by the pronoun "he," who "had power to do miracles in the sight of the beast" (the lamb-like). The following Scripture will make clear who it is that performs the miracles: "And the **beast** was taken, and with him the **false prophet** that wrought **miracles before him,** [before the two horned beast] with which he deceived them that had received the mark of the beast, and them that worshipped his image. **These both** were cast alive into a lake of fire burning with brimstone." (Rev. 19:20.) Therefore, the miracles are wrought by the false prophet **in the sight** of the two-horned beast.

There are many beasts spoken of in the Bible, but this **two-horned** beast is the only one that can be termed "a man." It will be noticed that from the 11th verse on, of the 13th chapter of Revelation, the Scripture speaks of the two-horned beast and closes with the words: "For it is the number of a man; and his number is six hundred threescore and six." Therefore, the mystical number "666," belongs to the two-horned beast and none other. However, we may not conclude that no one before it could have such a number.

The idea that the papacy is called the beast is altogether wrong. The papacy is represented by symbols on two different beasts. First, on the "non-descript" of Daniel 7, by the "little horn having eyes like the eyes of a man, and a mouth speaking great things"; second, on the "leopard-like" of Revelation 13, by the head that was "wounded to death." These beasts are universal, representing the entire world in their time, both civil and religious. Therefore, it could not be said of either beast, "it is . . . **a man.**" The papacy being only a part of both beasts (horn-head on one, and simply a wounded head on the other) cannot be called **"the beast."** The **two-horned beast** is the only one representing a local religio-political government. Therefore, of him alone can it be said, it is **"a man."** Thus whosoever shall stand at the head of that persecuting power as described in this chapter, and represented by the beast, is the one who shall bear the mystical number 666. The Spirit of Prophecy also states that the "King of the North" brought to view in Daniel 11:45, and the two-horned beast of Revelation 13, is the same power and that **it** shall bear this mystical number 666. We quote: "This power is the last that treads down the true church of God: and as the true church is still trodden down, and cast out by all Christendom, it follows that the last oppressive power has not 'come to his end'; and Michael has not stood up. This last power that treads down the saints is brought to view in Rev. 13:11-18.

His number is 666."—"A Word to the Little Flock," pp. 8, 9. We have proved the truth of the number one way, now we shall prove it in another.

The Destruction of the Beast and the Prophet

The destruction of both the "false prophet" and the "beast" is clearly foretold: "And the beast was taken, and with him the false prophet that wrought miracles **before him** . . . These both were cast **alive** into a lake of fire . . . And the remnant were slain with the sword of him that sat upon the horse, which sword proceeded out of his mouth: and all the fowls were filled with their flesh." (Rev. 19:20, 21.) Their final end is accomplished by being cast alive into a lake of fire. But the rest of the world **("the remnant")** were all slain with the "sword which proceeded out of His mouth: and the fowls were filled with their flesh."

The lake of fire into which the beasts and the false prophet are cast, cannot be at the coming of Christ in the clouds, for the wicked are not destroyed by fire at that time, but "With the spirit of his mouth, and shall destroy with the brightness of his coming." (2 Thess. 2:8.) The beast and the false prophet are cast into a lake of fire after the sixth plague and before the end of the world. This destruction of the "remnant," those that were left after the destruction of the beast and the prophet, is not after the **millennium,** for the wicked at that time are not destroyed by the sword that "proceeded out of His mouth," but by fire that came "down from God out of heaven and devoured them." (Rev. 20:9.) After the millennium and the destruction of the wicked no living creature will eat another. (See Isaiah 11:6-9.) Hence, the beast and false prophet are cast into a lake of fire before the millennium; and that lake of fire becomes a type of the destruction of the wicked on the other side of the millennium—the second death—for the final destruction of the entire multitude is described in the following words: "And death and hell were cast **into a lake of fire.** This is the **second** death. And whosoever was not found written in the book of life was cast into the lake of fire." (Rev. 20:14,15.) Thus the world would be given an ensample before the millennium, of the destruction after the thousand years had ended. The example of the beast and the false prophet is to show that all the wicked will be thrown alive into a lake of fire, and that is the second death. Speaking of the everlasting ruin of the devil, the Word says: "And the devil that deceived them was cast into a lake of fire and brimstone, where the beast and the false prophet are." (Rev. 20:10.) That is, the beast and the false prophet do not come up in the second resurrection, exemplifying that there is no resurrection from the second death. Again, we see there is a type for every event, and let none despise types, for where there is no type, there is no truth. The number 666 is further proven by

The Destruction of the "Man of Sin"

Mark carefully, according to the following testimony, the destruction of the papacy is at another time and by a different process. "Paul states plainly that the man of sin will continue until the second advent. To the very close of time he will carry forward his work of deception."—"The Great Controversy," p. 579. Thus the papacy is to remain to the second coming of Christ, at which time the wicked are to be destroyed by the brightness of His coming. Therefore, the papacy is one thing, and the false prophet another, and the beast still another. The beast "666" and the false prophet, who are to be cast alive into the lake of fire, are the ones who develop the image of the beast —a likeness of the worship in the period of the 1260 years.

The time of that wholesale deception is at hand. It will take more than great knowledge of theology to escape the most powerful trap his Satanic majesty has ever devised. The wonderful miracles will be convincing and the apparently genuine spirit of worship will bring deep conviction upon those who are subject to be misled. As the great men of the world declare its worship true, multitudes will accept their decisions without personal investigation. Add to all of these the following declaration of civil authorities: "As many as would not worship the image of the beast should be killed," and we have an overwhelming power which human strength cannot resist for a moment. Only by a prophetic knowledge of the truth, with confidence in a "thus saith the Lord," and in the power of His Spirit, can one escape the wily snares of the devil.

The Mother of Harlots Not the Beast

It has been explained that the papacy would remain to the last. If the woman on the scarlet colored beast **(Babylon the Great)** comes to her end at a different time and in another way, she cannot be a symbol of the papacy as some have thought. Revelation 17:16, speaking of the woman and the horns of the scarlet colored beast, says: "And the ten horns which thou sawest on the beast, these shall hate the whore, and shall make her desolate and naked, and shall eat her flesh, and burn her with fire."

Note, she is not cast into a lake of fire like the beast and the false prophet, but they (the horns) "shall make her desolate and naked and shall eat her flesh." Thus the **woman's** destruction is at a different time, and in another way than that of the **papacy,** the **false prophet,** and the **beast.** Since what has been said cannot be contradicted, it is evident the **"beast"** is one thing, the **"false prophet"** another, and the **papacy** another, and the **"woman"** still another. It is of great importance that these things be correctly understood, for by the knowledge of the truth only, can God lead His people on to victory.

The Time of the Woman's Destruction

To determine the time of **Babylon's** (woman's) destruction, it will be necessary to refer to Daniel 7:11, 12, "I beheld then because of the voice of the great words which the horn spake: I beheld even till the beast was **slain,** and his **body destroyed,** and given to the **burning flame.** As concerning the rest of the beasts, they had their **dominion taken away:** yet their **lives** were **prolonged** for a **season** and **time."** Concerning the rest of the beasts —the lion, bear, and the leopard, their dominion was taken away, but they remained alive, while the non-descript beast came to his end. The beasts that remain alive, represent the descendants of the three ancient empires. While their dominion is taken away, the inhabitants (beasts) are here at the present time. The end of these beasts would mean the end of the world.

The non-descript beast is not the last beast of this world's history, for he is followed by the leopard-like beast of Revelation 13:1, and the scarlet colored beast of Revelation 17:3. The latter is the last symbol of historical events, by which this present world and the one after the millennium shall be brought to an end, as previously explained. Therefore, the destruction of the **non-descript beast** is before the second coming of Christ. If the lives of the three beasts before it were "prolonged," their time cannot be extended beyond the second coming of Christ. Says Daniel: "Their lives were prolonged for a **season** and a **time."** Therefore, from the time the body of the **non-descript beast** is **destroyed,** there will be **"a season** and **a time,"** to the end of this present world.

If Daniel means year by **"time,"** and a half year by **"dividing of time,"** in the 25th verse of the same chapter, then he must mean the same in the 12th verse. If the interpretation holds good in one verse it must in the other. Therefore, **"time"** would be **one year,** and a **"season"** a fourth part of a year, thus making a total of **one year** and **three months.** However, the period in the

25th verse has a prophetic term of 1260 days (years), but the "time" in the twelfth verse cannot be prophetic, for then it would mean 450 literal years. It is evident that from the time the beast is destroyed, to the end, there will be **fifteen literal months.**

It shall be noticed that the destruction of the "beast" is prophetic of the destruction of the "woman." We quote the scriptures referring to both: "I beheld even till the beast was slain, and his body destroyed, and given to the burning flame." (Daniel 7:11.) "And the ten horns which thou sawest upon the beast, these shall hate the whore, and shall make her desolate and naked, and shall eat her flesh, and burn her with fire." (Rev. 17:16.) The destruction is alike of both (beast and woman). Furthermore, it is the period under the symbol of the woman riding on the beast that **makes** an image of the leopard-like in his first stage (before wounded) or of the **non-descript beast** in his second stage; for, the 1260 year period was represented by both beasts. The image is a false religion internationally set up. Therefore, **one** is the likeness of the **other.** Thus the destruction of the original (non-descript beast) is a prophecy of the destruction of the "woman," and the destruction of the one, is the destruction of the other. It prophetically signifies that the **"image"** (woman riding on the beast—the union of that religio-political system), shall perish **fifteen months** ("season and a time") before the **"remnant"** (rest of the world). Let it be remembered that Daniel's vision is a prophecy, and the vision by John is a revelation. Therefore, the destruction of the non-descript beast is the prophecy, and the destruction of the woman is the fulfillment of the prophecy.

The following scripture referring to the time the "woman" was destroyed, says: "And after these things I heard a great voice of much people in heaven, saying, Alleluia; Salvation, and glory, and honour, and power, unto the Lord our God: For true and righteous are his judgments: for he hath judged the great whore, which did corrupt the earth with her fornication, and hath avenged the blood of His servants at her hand. And again they said, Alleluia. And her smoke rose up for ever and ever. And the **four** and **twenty elders** and the **four beasts** fell down and worshipped God that **sat** on the throne, saying, Amen, Alleluia. And a voice came out of the throne, saying, Praise our God, all ye his servants, and ye that fear him, both small and great." (Rev. 19:1-5.)

The woman was destroyed and her smoke ascended up "for ever and ever," while the **"elders"** and the **"beasts"** were **before the throne.** This proves that the judgment in the **Most Holy** apartment had not ceased, or at least the tribunal had not yet vacated the place of judgment, (explained in another chapter) for after the saints are numbered and sealed, their sins blotted out in the aforesaid judgment, probation shall close, and the sanctuary where the judgment is held shall be vacated of the **elders,** and the **beasts,** as well as the "Lamb," and of the entire angelic host. After which "no man was able to enter the **temple,** till the **seven last plagues** . . . were **fulfilled."** (See Rev. 15:5-8.) Thus it is clear that the woman was destroyed before the seven last plagues were poured out.

Quoting Revelation 19:6, "And I heard as it were the voice of a great multitude, and as the voice of many waters, and as the voice of mighty thunderings, saying, Alleluia: for the Lord God omnipotent **reigneth."** While Christ is in the sanctuary and the judgment in progress, He does not reign, but is a Priest and an Advocate, blotting out the sins of the righteous. But when He is through with the investigative judgment, then He is crowned King of kings and Lord of lords. (See verse 16.)

After the "smoke of the woman rose up for ever and ever," the heavenly host shouted, "Alleluia: for the Lord God omnipotent **reigneth."** Therefore, all the saints were judged prior to the destruction of the "woman," and after she is burned with fire, Christ is crowned King of kings and Lord of lords; then the temple will be vacated and the **seven last plagues** poured out.

The following scriptures bear further evidence. Said the heavenly host: "Let us be glad and rejoice, and give honor to him: for the marriage of the Lamb is come, and his wife hath made herself ready. And to her was granted that she should be arrayed in fine linen, clean and white: for **the fine linen** is the **righteousness of saints.** And he saith unto me, Write, Blessed are they which are called unto the marriage supper of the Lamb." Continued the Angel, "Come hither, I will shew thee the **Bride,** the **Lamb's wife . . .** and shewed me that great city, the holy Jerusalem, descending out of heaven from God." (Rev. 19:7-9; 21:9, 10.) Therefore, the Lamb's wife is the **Holy City** and not the church, and those called to the marriage supper (the saints) are the guests. (See "The Great Controversy," page 427.) They who were before the throne, said of the **New Jerusalem:** "His wife hath made herself ready. And to her was granted [to the city] that she should be arrayed in fine linen, clean and white . . . for the **fine linen** is the righteousness of **saints."** (Rev. 19:7, 8.) Therefore, the Lamb's wife will be ready at the close of probation when the saints are numbered, for they are her "linen." As at the time the woman (Babylon) was burned, the **saints** (linen) were ready. Her destruction shall be a signal that probation has closed. Then some shall be conscious of their doom and shall say, "The harvest is past, the summer is ended, and we are not saved." (Jer. 8:20.) Others shall "wander from sea to sea, and from the north even to the east, they shall run to and fro to seek the words of the Lord, and shall not find it." (Amos 8:12.) When God's people shall have ceased from their God given work, their answer will be: "We have nothing for you, the harvest is past, salvation has ceased, you are too late."

Who Is the False Prophet?

As previously explained the false prophet is not the papacy or the two-horned beast, neither is he the devil, for we read: "And the devil that deceived them was cast into a lake of fire and brimstone, where the **beast** and the **false prophet are.**" (Rev. 20:10.) Therefore, the false prophet is the one who shall precede the manifestation of Satan himself. Said the apostle, "And no marvel; for Satan himself is transformed into an angel of light." (2 Cor. 11:14.)

As the doctrines held by the false prophet cannot be fully supported by the Scriptures, miracles are performed to secure the confidence of the people. As the **great men** and **religious leaders declare** to the public that the so-called true religion is the **truth of Christ,** and that the false **prophet** is **His servant,** multitudes will fall into Satan's snare. His false prediction of the coming of the Lord, will be fulfilled by Satan himself as he appears as an angel of light. His dazzling brightness, and the false fulfillment of the prophet's prediction, in addition to the already overwhelming delusion, will ensnare a multitude greater than the first. "While appearing to the children of men as a great physician who can heal all their maladies, he will bring disease and disaster, until populous cities are reduced to ruin and desolation."—"The Great Controversy," p. 589.

The Woman Sitting On the Heads

Said the angel: "The seven heads are seven mountains, on which the woman sitteth." (Rev. 17:9.) It has been previously explained that the heads represent the present day apostate Christendom, (See pages 88-96). They are called "mountains" (denominations), seven in number, meaning all. As the prostitute sits on **all** seven, the symbol with unmistakable evidence reveals that so-called Christendom will submit itself to be governed by one head, of which the woman is a symbol. (See "The Great Controversy," page 588.)

Preliminary to that miracle working power, Protestantism, Catholicism, and Spiritualism, will have grasped each other's hand by means of a church federation. The difference of opinion in doctrinal points will be considered of no vital importance to salvation. They will see in that apparently innocent union a great movement for the settlement of differences as well as for the conversion of the world. At the appearance of the false prophet, and of Satan himself, their expectations would be realized, and the ushering in of the long expected millennial time of peace shall be proclaimed to be at hand. Thus on the surface it will bear evidence that the world's crises arc about to end. But as God's people have been warned of it all, they refuse to worship the image of the beast, which is a false international religion, and will be charged as rebellious, disturbers of the peace, and trouble makers. This will bring the great persecution of Revelation 12:17.

To them it will be said: "Art thou he that troubleth Israel?" As the saints answer them in the manner of the prophet Elijah: "Nay but . . . in that ye have forsaken the commandment of the Lord, and thou hast followed Baalam," it will incur the displeasure of the wicked and cause them to enrage against the innocent.

The Woman Sitting On the Beast

While the Revelator saw in vision the beast who bears the number 666, and the false prophet, enforcing a false religion by law and miracles within the borders of the government represented by the two-horned beast, he was shown another interesting sight: "And I saw," he says, "a woman sit upon a scarlet colored beast, full of names of blasphemy, having seven heads and ten horns. And the woman was arrayed in purple and scarlet colour, and decked with gold and precious stones and pearls, having a golden cup in her hand full of abominations and filthiness of her fornication." (Rev. 17:3, 4.) This symbol reveals that after the woman had sat on the "heads" (united the churches) she also succeeded to sit on the beast. The beast is a symbol of the entire present world—both civil (ten horns) and religious (seven heads). As the woman sitting on the heads denotes union of churches, just so, **sitting** on the beast represents internationally the church and the state governed by the same head (woman). Therefore, an international system of religion and a combination of church and state. In such a system the great men of earth will see a vision of settling the troubles of the world, welding the people and the nations into a world-wide brotherhood, fulfilling by a medium of religion, 1 Thess. 5:3,

"For when they shall say, Peace and safety; then sudden destruction cometh upon them, . . . and they shall not escape." Though their intention is to reduce crime as well as wars, their hope will be in vain.

The Cup, Jewels, and the Loud Colors

The cup in the hand of the woman being of the most precious metal, and as she is decked with gold and precious stones, it denotes a most overwhelming temptation—fully realized in the miracle working power by the false prophet and Satan himself. Her cup (books) contains false doctrines, and being "golden," it shows that they are plated with Christianity. Thus the following prophetic words shall meet their fulfillment: "And he had power to give life unto the image of the beast, that the image of the beast should both speak, and cause that as many as would not worship the image of the beast should be killed. And he causeth all, both small and great, rich and poor, free and bond, to receive a mark in their right hand, or in their foreheads: And that no man might buy or sell, save he that had the mark, or the name of the beast, or the number of his name." (Rev. 13:15-17.)

"Such will be the experiences of God's people in their final struggle with the powers of evil . . . Satan leads many to believe that God will overlook their unfaithfulness in the **minor** affairs of life; but the Lord shows in His dealings with Jacob that He can in no wise sanction or tolerate evil. All who endeavor to excuse or conceal their sins, and permit them to remain upon the books of heaven unconfessed and unforgiven, will be overcome by Satan."—"Patriarchs and Prophets," p. 202. "Those who are without God's protection will find no safety in any place or position."—"Testimonies for the Church," Vol. 8, p. 50. Of that troublous time said Christ: "He that findeth his life" to gain the favor of men "shall lose it: and he that loseth his life for my sake shall find it." (Matt. 10:39.) That time shall reveal him that serveth God and him that serveth Him not. Then, shall the world be divided into two great classes—"The sheep on the right and the goats on the left." (Matt. 25:33.) Apparently it will seem that God's people must either perish or yield to the demands of the wicked, but mighty angels who excel in strength will reverse the current of destruction.

"And a mighty angel took up a stone like a great millstone, and cast it into the sea, saying, Thus with violence shall that great city Babylon be thrown down, and shall be found no more at all. And the voice of harpers, and musicians, and of pipers, and trumpeters, shall be heard no more at all in thee; and no craftsman, of whatsoever craft he be, shall be found any more in thee; and the sound of a millstone shall be heard no more at all in thee; And the light of a candle shall shine no more at all in thee; and the voice of the bridegroom and of the bride shall be heard no more at all in thee: for thy merchants were the great men of the earth; for by thy sorceries were all nations deceived!" (Rev. 18:21-23.)

While multitudes are falling into the snares of the devil, and as he is endeavoring to wipe out the church, the "Third Angel's Message" breaks through with mighty power and a **"loud cry,"** saying, "Come out of her, my people, that ye be not partakers of her sins, and that ye receive not of her plagues." (Rev. 18:4.) And as the "Cry" of the angel (messenger) rings through the earth a great multitude of all nations leave the false, but popular system of worship, and against all earthly favor take their stand with the saints under the protection of divine power. This will incur the wrath of the dragon.

SUMMARY
(Follow Chart On Page 150)

The tabulation of events in this chapter fully illustrate the great prophetic occurrences that are to transpire in rapid succession as shown in the chart. The union of the churches represented by the "woman" sitting on the "heads" must take place before the combined power of the "beast" and the "false prophet" is fully realized. The symbols ("false prophet" and the "beast") reveal that there shall be a **national** alliance of church and state. But the woman riding on the beast, denotes an **international** system of church and state, enforced by civil law, and miraculous power. At the close of probation, the union represented by the symbol of the "scarlet colored beast," shall be dissolved with the destruction of the "woman" or head of that union as pictured at the turning point of the chart. The world at that time, as represented **by the horns of the beast,** shall "hate" the harlot, dethrone her, and "burn her with fire;" which can be nothing less than by revolution against the head of that religio-political system. Then the prophecy of Revelation 16:19, will meet its fulfillment: "And the great city [Babylon] was divided into three parts." That is, the **union** of Protestantism, Catholicism, and Spiritualism was **dissolved.** Note the verb, **"was",** being in past tense, shows that the great city Babylon was divided before the seven plagues were poured out; that is, at close of probation, when the woman was dethroned. "And the cities of the nations fell: and great Babylon [in her divided state] came in remembrance before God, to give unto her the cup of the wine of the fierceness of His wrath." (Verse 19, last part.) The fierceness of God's wrath is poured out upon Babylon in her divided state in the time of the seventh plague.

The **head** of the **non-descript beast** of Daniel seven, in the burning fire with the "woman" as depicted in the chart, represents the same event. The "beast" is a **prophecy,** and the "woman" is the **revelation** of that prophecy. Then the four angels of Revelation seven, who were "holding the four winds of the earth [the nations in check], that the wind should not blow on the earth, nor on the sea, nor on any tree," shall let the wind "blow"; and as there would remain nothing to hold the nations and peoples together and to restrain hostilities, the conflict within and without, will result in the final battle of "Armageddon." (Rev. 16:14, 16.) From that point of the chart (close of probation) to the second coming of Christ and the beginning of the millennium, there will be fifteen months—"a season and a time." (Dan. 7:11, 12.)

At about the time of the seventh plague the beast and the false prophet will be cast into the lake of fire. A literal fulfillment, and the same will become a type of the final destruction of the wicked after the millennium, which is the second death. The destruction of the woman riding on the scarlet colored beast, and the false prophet with the two-horned beast being cast alive in the lake of fire, denotes that this religio-political system will be internationally dissolved.

At the appearance of the Lord, the saints shall be gathered (Matt. 24:30), and the wicked destroyed. (2 Thess. 2:8.) The nations are represented by the "beasts," the "man of sin" by the "little horn having eyes of a man and a mouth speaking great things." (Daniel 7:25.)

The great image of Daniel two, corresponds with the beasts of Daniel seven. These beasts are also represented by the leopard-like beast of Revelation thirteen—the mouth of a lion, feet of a bear, body of a leopard, and the ten horns. The scarlet colored beast of Revelation seventeen is a continuation of the leopard-like after his deadly wound was healed. Thus he is pictured on the chart showing that he has the characteristics of all the beasts before him. Therefore, the destruction of the beasts of Daniel seven, is also the destruction of the beasts that were shown to John in vision; and the end of all the beasts, mean the end of the world.

The great stone of Daniel two, that smote the image on the

feet, is a symbol of the coming of Christ; and the breaking of the image denotes the breaking of the nations. As the scarlet colored beast brings this present world to an end, he also represents the world on the other side of the millennium, after the second resurrection.

The fire coming down out of heaven upon the beast, denotes the second death of the wicked, one-hundred years after the second resurrection. Then the prophecy of Enoch shall meet its complete fulfillment: "Behold, the Lord cometh, . . . to execute judgment upon **"all,"** and to convince **all** that are ungodly . . . of all their ungodly deeds which they have ungodly committed, and of all their hard speeches which ungodly sinners have spoken against Him." (Jude 14, 15.) While the 14th verse of Jude applies to Christ's coming to the Most Holy apartment in the heavenly sanctuary, and the 15th verse to His second advent, the completeness of the words find their fulfillment after the millennium, for at that time only can He **execute** the final "judgment upon **all** the ungodly," from Cain to the end of this present world.

The first part of the chart, dated 1929, to the curve, marked Ezekiel 9, is the period in which the 144,000 are sealed—the separation of the tares from the wheat—the purification of the church. As the 144,000 are the "first fruits," the fulfillment of Ezekiel 9 and the sealing of the servants of God (the 144,000), marks the commencement of the final harvest, or as it is also called, "The Loud Cry." At that time the great multitude of Revelation 7:9, will be gathered in the church by the servants of God (the 144,000). (See Isaiah 66:19, 20.)

The cases of all who are sealed from 1929 to the final close of probation will be investigated before the throne in the heavenly sanctuary while living. The investigation commences after the fulfillment of Ezekiel 9. Those who are sealed from 1929 to the fulfillment of Ezekiel 9 (close of probation for the church), are living saints, 144,000 in number, who shall never die—translated without tasting death. The class which neglected their opportunity were left without the seal to perish under the ruin of Ezekiel 9; Isaiah 63; and Isaiah 66:15-17.) This example of the destruction of the sinners in the church, is a type of the destruction of the sinners in the world after the close of probation. The great multitude of Revelation 7:9, living at the time of the close of probation for the world, shall also never die, of whom the 144,000 were a type. But all the wicked being left without the seal, shall perish. "Hitherto is the end of the matter;" "Fear God [not man] and keep His commandments: for this is the whole duty of man." (Eccl. 12:13.)

THE ONE HUNDRED AND FORTY-FOUR THOUSAND
REVELATION SEVEN AND FOURTEEN

The ground of this most vital subject has been extensively covered in "The Shepherd's Rod," Vol. 1. Therefore, we intend to bring out only that phase which does not appear in the first volume. The following questions will be answered in this chapter: At the time the Lord commands the angel to seal them (the 144,000) are they found by that message in the world or in the church? At what time are they sealed? Why are they "virgins"? Why is there "no guile" in their mouth? Are they men only or of both sexes? Why are they called "servants of God"? Why are they Israel?

We quote from the writings of the "Spirit of Prophecy": "This was the time of Jacob's trouble. Then **all** the saints cried out with anguish of spirit, and were delivered by the voice of God. The **one hundred and forty-four thousand** triumphed. Their faces were lighted up with the glory of God."—"Life Sketches," page 117. Note that the 144,000 in number, were present in "the time of Jacob's trouble." According to the following quotation, that time of trouble commences immediately after the close of probation: "When Christ shall cease His work as mediator in man's behalf, **then** this time of trouble will begin."—"Patriarchs and Prophets," page 201. That time of trouble is before any of the sleeping saints are resurrected, therefore the 144,000 are not resurrected, but are living saints who have never tasted death and are to be translated at the second coming of Christ.

The 144,000 Sealed While in the Church

To make this clear we must comment on the typical day of atonement. That notable day in the ceremonial system was a day of cleansing, judgment, and covering. The command was given that in the seventh month and on the tenth day of the month (day of atonement), every Israelite was to afflict his soul, confess his sin, and bring a sacrifice. He who failed to respond to the divine call was cut off (perished) from among God's people. Therefore, it was a day of judgment and purification of the camp of Israel. While the sinner perished, the godly were preserved. This living example was set forth for our benefit at this present time, upon whom the anti-typical day of atonement is come. This picture in the earthly tabernacle is intended to point out the work in the heavenly.

When the judgment opened in 1844, as previously explained, the investigation began with the dead, and when that part of the work is finished, then commences the judgment of the living. While the investigation for the congregation of the dead is in progress, there can be no separation among the congregation of the living. But when our High Priest shall begin the atonement for the living, there must be a message of present truth—sounding of the trumpet—urging every one to lay hold on the Lamb of God (Christ) by which only, can he in figure, come to the sanctuary, confess his sin and secure his life. Unless the close of the judgment for the dead and the commencement for the living be made known to us, we would have no present truth while the judgment for the living is in session. Neither would such judgment be legal or just. He who fails to respond to the heavenly summons, will be left without the seal or covering of God, and therefore must be cut off from among His people, as prefigured by the services in the typical day of atonement.

Says the apostle: "For the time is come that judgment must begin at the house of God." (1 Peter 4:17.) The fact that to the "Seventh-day Adventist" church alone has come just such a message as the one mentioned, presented to them in "The Shepherd's Rod," Vol. 1, is an additional proof that this particular church is the house of God. This time of judgment is also called the "time of harvest." "Let both grow together until the harvest," said Christ, "and in the time of harvest I will say to the reapers, Gather ye together first the tares, and bind them in bundles to burn them: but gather the wheat into my barn." (Matt. 13:30.) The words of our Master are in perfect harmony with the typical day of atonement, foretelling that it is a day of separating the tares from the wheat, or cutting off of the unrepentant sinners from among God's people (purification of the church). Therefore, the harvest commences with the closing work for the church. Said Christ: "Let both grow together **until** the harvest." In Revelation 14:4, speaking of the 144,000 we read, "These are the **first fruits** unto God and to the Lamb." Therefore, it is evident that in the purification or separation of the tares from the wheat in the church of God, there shall be 144,000 who have confessed their sins; and are thus made white and clean by the precious blood of Christ, for they are "the **first fruits.**" This is also proven by the "Spirit of Prophecy," for we read: "This sealing of the servants of God is the same that was shown to Ezekiel in vision."—"Testimonies to Ministers," page 445. We quote from "Testimonies for the Church," Vol. 3, p. 266: "The true people of God, who have the spirit of the work of the Lord, and the salvation of souls at heart, will ever view sin in its real, sinful character. They will always be on the side of faithful and plain deal-ing with sins which easily beset the people of God. Especially in the **closing work for** the **church,** in the **sealing time** of the 144,000."

Again on page 267: "Mark this point with care: Those who receive the pure mark of truth, wrought in them by the power of the Holy Ghost, represented by a mark by the man in linen, are those 'that sigh and that cry for **all** the abomina-tions that be done' in the **church.** . . . Read the ninth chapter of Ezekiel. But the general slaughter of **all** those who do not thus see the wide contrast between sin and righteousness, and do not feel as those do who stand in the counsel of God and receive the mark, is described in the order to the five men with the slaughter weapons: 'Go ye after him through the city, and smite; let not your eye spare, neither have ye pity; slay utterly old and young, both maids, and little children, and women; but come not near any man upon whom is the mark; and begin at my sanctuary.'"

The definition of "general" is: "extensive but not universal." Therefore it does not mean the destruction of the world at the appearance of the Lord; but it has reference to the wicked in the church. This slaughter is literal; it is to separate and release God's people from sin and sinners; otherwise the marking would be of no value. The same subject is again brought to view in "Testimonies for the Church," Vol. 5, page 211: "Here we **see** that **the church**—the Lord's sanc-tuary—was the first to feel the stroke of the wrath of God." The wrath of God cannot, and never has been spiritual. We are again reminded that the 144,000 are the **remnant: "Now** indeed are the **remnant** 'men wondered at' . . . 'In that day shall the branch of the Lord be beautiful and glorious, and the fruit of the earth shall be excellent and comely **for them** that are **escaped** of **Israel.** And it shall come to pass, That he that is **left in Zion,** and he that **remaineth in Jerusalem,** shall be called holy, even every one that is written among the living **in** Jerusa-lem.'"—Id., page 476. Thus the 144,000 are those who are sealed in the **judg-ment for** the **church,** and with them the judgment for the living commenced. Therefore, they are the first fruits.

When this number is sealed, probation will close for the church, and the judgment for those who are in the world will commence. As the "tares" perish at the time when probation is closing for the church, just so at the close of the judgment for the world the sinners shall come to their end; the one is a figure of the other. It is said of the 144,000: "These are they which are not defiled with women for they are virgins." (Rev. 14:4.) The "women" mentioned in this Scripture are symbols of impure churches. These "women" are brought to view in Revelation 17, under the figure of the woman sitting on the scarlet colored beast. We quote verse 5: "And upon her forehead was a name written, mystery, Babylon the great, the **mother of harlots** and abomination of the earth." This mother and her daughters are the "women" with whom the 144,000 are not defiled, for the message of the sealing found them in the church. Thus being in the church of God when sealed, they are **"virgins"**—"not **defiled** with women" (with fallen churches).

The Servants of God in the Time of the Harvest

In Revelation 7:3, the 144,000 are called "The **servants** of our God." If servants, then they must have duties to perform. They are again brought to view by the prophet Isaiah in connection with the purification of the church and the destruction of the wicked: "And I will set a sign among them, and I will send those that **escape** (the 144,000) of them into the nations. . . . And they shall bring all your brethren for an offering unto the Lord out of **all** nations, . . . in a clean vessel into the **house** of the Lord"—the church. (Isa. 66:19, 20.) "And the fruit of the earth shall be excellent and comely **for them** that are **escaped of Israel."** (Isa. 4:2.) Therefore, the 144,000 are called **"servants."** (For further study of Isa. 66, see "The Shepherd's Rod," Vol. 1, pp. 165-172.)

It is also said of this wonderful company: "And in their mouth was found no guile." (Rev. 14:5.) This Scripture makes it clear that the gospel they proclaim is altogether the true Word of God. Therefore, the message they present to the world cannot be questioned as to its purity. The prophet of Patmos after speaking of the sealing of the 144,000 says: "After this I beheld, and, lo, a great multitude, which no man could number, of all nations, and kindreds, and people, and tongues, stood before the throne, and before the Lamb, clothed with white robes, and palms in their hand." (Rev. 7:9.) Therefore, this great multitude is gathered from all nations, after the closing work for the church, and in the time of the great harvest. The palms in their hands signify victory over the beast and his image, death and the grave. One of the elders before the throne said of them: "These are they which came out of great tribulation" (the time of Jacob's trouble). (Verse 14.) The servant of the Lord also bears witness in the following quotations: "'And the heaven departed as a scroll when it is rolled together; and every mountain and island were moved out of their places. And the kings of the earth, and the great men, and the rich men, and the chief captains, and the mighty men, and every bondman, and every free man, hid themselves in the dens and in the rocks of the mountains; and said to the mountains and rocks, Fall on us, and hide us from the face of Him that sitteth on the throne, and from the wrath of the Lamb: for the great day of His wrath is come; and who shall be able to stand?' Rev. 6:14-17.

"'After this I beheld, and, lo, a great multitude, which no man could number, of all nations, and kindreds, and people, and tongues, stood before the throne, and before the Lamb, clothed with white robes, and palms in their hands; and cried with a loud voice, saying, Salvation to our God which sitteth upon the throne, and unto the Lamb. . . . These are they which came out of great tribulation, and have washed their robes, and made them white in the blood of the Lamb'. . . . Rev. 7:9, 17.

"In these Scriptures **two** parties are brought to view. One party permitted themselves to be deceived, and took sides with those with whom the Lord has a controversy."—"Testimonies for the Church," Vol. 9, pp. 267, 268. As the Spirit of Prophecy points out these **two** companies (those who cried for the rocks, and those with the palms) both living in the time of the great tribulation and the wrath of God, it is evident that the great multitude with the palms in their hands are living saints won to the gospel in the time of the harvest by the work of the 144,000.

Are the 144,000 of Both Sexes?

The command to mark this company so that they fall not under the slaughter weapons by the figure of the five men, reads as follows: "And the Lord said unto him, Go through the midst of the city, through the midst of Jerusalem, and set a mark upon the foreheads of the **men** that sigh and that cry for all the abominations that be done in the midst thereof." (Ezekiel 9:4.) Because the Word says: "Set a mark upon the foreheads of the **men,**" therefore some have held the position that the entire company is made up of men only. The second reason given for this erroneous idea is that they are to be kings and priests and therefore they must be men. The idea carried by these passages cannot be sustained by other portions of Scripture. Thus we are compelled to study deeper into the subject.

While Ezekiel calls them "men," John says they are "virgins." (Rev. 14:4.) Now, if we should take the position that Ezekiel means men only, then we can as well say, John means women only. Can it be possible that one writer should contradict the other? No indeed. We conclude by the following Scriptures that the 144,000 are of both sexes: "The same came for a witness, to bear witness of the light, that all **men** through him might believe." (John 1:7.) **"All men,"** must include both men and women, otherwise salvation would be for men only. "And I, if I be lifted up from the earth, will draw all **men** unto me." (John 12:32.) If the word all **men** in this text does not include both sexes, then the women are lost. "And the time of this ignorance God winked at; but now commandeth all **men** everywhere to repent." (The Acts 17:30.) Again, if **"all men"** include not both male and female, then women are not commanded to repent. It is evident that the noun, **men,** is a collective Biblical term of both men and women. The same is true by creation, for, God made the woman of the man. Therefore, she is a **wo-man.** Again in Gal. 3:28, we read: "There is neither male nor female: for ye are **all one** in Christ Jesus."

Since there is no difference between either sex in Christ, then we see that women as well as men can be kings and priests. The same thought can be carried out by the experience of the Jewish nation: "And Deborah, a prophetess, the wife of Lapidoth, she **judged** Israel at that time. . . . And the children of Israel came up to her for judgment." (Judges 4:4, 5.) This woman held a man's position, being a **judge** of God's people, which is equivalent to a king. Not only a king, but she was a prophetess as well. Again we read in Luke 2:36, 37, "And there was one **Anna,** a prophetess, the daughter of Phanuel, of the tribe of Aser: she was of a great age, and had lived with an husband seven years from her virginity; and she was a widow of about fourscore and four years, which departed not from the temple, but served God with fastings and prayers night and day." Also the wife of Shallum being a prophetess taught Israel and controlled the college. (See 2 Kings 22:14-16.) Phillip the evangelist had four daughters who also did prophesy. (See The Acts 21:8, 9.)

From Paul's statement in 1 Timothy 2:12, "I suffer not a woman to teach, nor to usurp authority over the man, but to be in silence," you will note the meaning here is, that the woman is to be in subjection to the man as God had ordained, and not that she is forbidden to hold the office of a teacher. Again we quote, "Let your women keep silence in the churches: for it is not permitted unto them to speak; but they are commanded to be under **obedience,** as also saith the law." (1 Cor. 14:34.) Read the chapter and you will see that Paul wishes to establish order in the churches, for there was great confusion by speaking in unknown tongues. Therefore, to silence the confusion, he says: "Let your women keep silence in the churches." He is not forbidding them to speak if they have a duty to perform. If this lesson was heeded in this age there would be a great change for the better in the house of God.

In the beginning God created both the man and the woman equal, as king and queen. "And God blessed **them,** and God said unto **them,** Be fruitful, and multiply, and replenish the earth, and subdue it: and have dominion over the fish of the sea, and over the fowl of the air, and over every living thing that moveth upon the earth." (Gen. 1:28.) Note that the dominion was given to them both. However, after they sinned a change was made: "Unto the woman He said, . . . thy desire shall be to thy husband, and He shall **rule over thee."** (Gen. 3:16.) So, after the woman sinned she fell under the government of man. But that which Eve lost by deception, shall be restored by redemption. Thus again the equality of both shall be established as kings and queens. Therefore, "There is neither male nor female in Christ Jesus." Christ himself confirms the idea in the following expression: "For when they shall rise from the dead, they neither marry, nor are given in marriage, but are as the angels which are in heaven." (Mark 12:25.)

Thus the noun **"men"** used by Ezekiel, and the noun **"virgins"** by John is a collective Biblical term comprehending both. Furthermore, the denomination numbers a little over 300,000 at present time. Only about a third of them are men. If every man was sealed and numbered as one of the 144,000, we still would be far short of reaching the total. Again we note at the time of the passover in Egypt the blood on the door-post was a type of the marking or sealing. ("The Shepherd's Rod," Vol. 1, pp. 96-98.)

In that night wherever the blood appeared on the door-post, the first born whether male or female, perished not; just so now, those who receive the seal, have applied the blood on the doorpost (forehead), and as the first born of both classes, those who died and those who did not, were a type of the present priesthood (ministry), evidently, the type points forward to a ministry in the anti-type made up of both sexes—the first born who died represent the class that shall fall under the slaughter weapons of the five men; and the first born who escaped from death, represent the class that shall receive the mark of the man with the writer's inkhorn and pass from death to life. Thus the first born who lived and passed through the red sea, are a type of the 144,000. The first fruits of the harvest, are the servants of God in the time of the **"loud cry"** of the Third Angel's Message.

After the purification of the church and the sealing of the servants of God, then the message in the 18th chapter of Revelation shall culminate in a **"loud cry"**: "Come out of her, my people, that ye be not partakers of her sins, and that ye receive not of her plagues." (Verse 4.) As the saints hear the voice of the good Shepherd in the gospel message, they separate themselves from the world and join the 144,000. While this sifting process in the fallen churches is in progress, the man with the

Writer's inkhorn seals those who come out. When all the saints shall come out of Babylon into the church, then the work of the man with the writer's inkhorn shall cease and probation will close. (See "Early Writings," p. 279.) Therefore, the activity of the five men with the slaughter weapons shall continue and their work will cease when Christ comes to take His saints, for it is they who have charge of the city—church. (See Ezek. 9:1; "The Great Controversy," p. 656.) Then the present world will come to an end and the millennium of desolation commence; during which time the saints shall judge the wicked.

The 144,000 are called Israel because their experience is a duplication of that of Ancient Israel going out of Egypt to possess the promised land. Ancient Egypt is a symbol of the world. The Egyptian bondage is a symbol of the bondage of sin. The exodus movement is a type of the church separating from sin and sinners. The destruction of the first born in Egypt and the drowning in the red sea, denotes the destruction of the wicked in the separation of the saints. The wilderness is a symbol of the church being apart from the world. The destruction of the disobedient in the wilderness, is an illustration of keeping the church clean after being purified. The possession of the promised land is a type of Israel (the saints) possessing the world. The war against the heathen in the promised land denotes the destruction of the wicked in the world. We are going over the same road once again, and in so doing, we must avoid the mistakes that were made in the former experience.

AT PROBATION'S END, GRAVES CEASE
REVELATION 14 AND 15

Chapter 14:1, "And I looked, and, lo, a Lamb stood on the mount Sion, and with him an hundred forty and four thousand, having his Father's name written in their foreheads." The "Lamb" denotes Christ, signifying the position He occupies before the close of probation, while yet interceding for His people; therefore, the specific number of saints stand with Him on earth while He is yet in the Most Holy place. Mount Zion in old Jerusalem was an ancient spot of that city, and the place of the royal residence of David and his successors. Therefore, from that viewpoint we must present the meaning of the "Lamb" that stood on the mount Zion. We are told by the following Scriptures the Lord had made a promise that the house of David (Mount Zion) was a light to him and to his sons forever. "Howbeit the Lord would not destroy the house of David, because of the covenant that he had made with David, and as he promised to give a light to him and to his sons **forever.**" (2 Chron. 21:7.) The promise was not to Mount Zion (house of David) in ancient Jerusalem, for the existence of the Jewish nation was conditional.

"Now to Abraham and his seed were the promises made: He saith not, And to seeds, as of many; but as of one, And to thy seed, which is Christ"—"the son of David." (Gal. 3:16.) Therefore, mount Zion, as in Revelation 14:1, is the eminent royal spot in the heavenly Jerusalem, as David himself says: "For there are set thrones of judgment, the thrones of the house of David." (Psa. 122:5.) David looked forward to the time when the judgment in heaven would be set up: "In that day there shall be a fountain opened to the house of David and to the inhabitants of Jerusalem for sin and for uncleanness." (Zech. 13:1.)

Therefore, John's vision of the 144,000 as they stood on Mount Zion with the Lamb, is an incident after this special company of saints had been sealed, and some time before the close of probation. The sealing of the 144,000 is at the closing of the judgment of the dead, and at the beginning of the judgment of the living. Therefore, they have a great duty to perform upon the earth in connection with the judgment. Their service was typified by ancient Israel when they were obliged to possess the Promised Land. The prophet Zechariah has well described the time: "In that day shall the Lord defend the inhabitants of Jerusalem; and he that is feeble among them at that day shall be as David; and the house of David shall be as God, as the angel of the Lord before them. And it shall come to pass in that day, that I will seek to destroy all the nations that come against Jerusalem [the church]. And I will pour upon the house of David, and upon the inhabitants of Jerusalem, the spirit of grace and of supplications: and they shall look upon me whom they have pierced, [because He died for their sins] and they shall mourn for him, as one mourneth for his only son, and shall be in bitterness for him, as one that is in bitterness for his first born." (Zech. 12:8-11.) What a wonderful experience it will be when we fully comprehend the love of God and the price paid for our redemption!

The prophet Micah calls the 144,000, the "remnant of Jacob." (See "The Shepherd's Rod," Vol. 1, p. 102.) "And they shall waste the land of Assyria with the sword, and the land of Nimrod in the entrances thereof: thus shall he deliver us from the Assyrian, when he cometh into our land, and when he treadeth within our borders. And the remnant of Jacob shall be in the midst of many people as a dew from the Lord, as the showers upon the grass, that tarrieth not for man, nor waiteth for the sons of men. And the remnant of Jacob shall be among the Gentiles in the midst of many people as a lion among the beasts of the forest, as a young lion among the flocks of sheep: who, if he go through, both treadeth down, and teareth in pieces, and none can deliver. Thine hand shall be lifted up upon thine adversaries, and all thine enemies shall be cut off. . . . And I will execute vengeance in anger and fury upon the heathen, such as they have not heard." (Micah 5:6-9, 15.)

"The portion of Jacob is not like them; for he is the former of all things: and Israel is the rod of his inheritance: the Lord of hosts is his name. Thou art my battle axe and weapons of war [144,000]: for with thee will I break in pieces the nations, and with thee will I destroy kingdoms; and with thee will I break in pieces the horse and his rider; and with thee will I break in pieces the chariot and his rider; with thee also will I break in pieces man and woman; and with thee will I break in pieces old and young; and with thee will I break in pieces the young man and the maid; I will also break in pieces with thee the shepherd and his flock; and with thee will I break in pieces the husbandman and his yoke of oxen; and with thee will I break in pieces captains and rulers." (Jer. 51:19-23.) Therefore, at the fulfillment of John's vision, the 144,000 "Stand on Mount Zion," not bodily, but in the sense of the position they occupy. In the same way as the five virgins who went in with Him to the marriage. (See "The Great Controversy," p. 427.) As ancient Israel was a terror to the heathen in the promised land, just so the Israel of God at this time will be a terror to the sinner in the world, and as ancient Israel had to fight with the sword to possess the land, just so Israel now must battle with the "sword of the Spirit" to possess the world (promised land).

"And I heard a voice from heaven, as the voice of many waters, and as the voice of a great thunder: and I heard the voice of harpers harping with their harps: And they sung as it were a new song before the throne, and before the four beasts, and the elders: and no man could learn that song but the hundred and forty and four thousand, which were redeemed from the earth." (Rev. 14:2, 3.)

The song was sung in heaven by heavenly beings before the throne, and before the beasts, and the elders. Therefore, it is evident that the judgment was in progress. (Further explanation to follow.) Note that the 144,000 did not sing, but they only could learn the "song" as it was sung in heaven; that is, they alone understood the heavenly truth in that particular time and their position in connection with the message they must bear.

"And I heard a voice from heaven saying unto me, Write,

Blessed are the dead which die in the Lord from henceforth: Yea, saith the Spirit, that they may rest from their labours; and their works do follow them." (Rev. 14:13.) "Which die from henceforth," that is, from the commencement of the **"loud cry."** Thus the word declares that some of the saints will be laid in the grave even during the time of the harvest **(loud cry).** We quote from "Counsels on Health", p. 375 "Many will be laid away to sleep before the fiery ordeal of the time of trouble shall come upon the world."

While some of the saints shall be laid to sleep in the time of the **"loud cry,"** it is made clear by Revelation 15:1, 2, that all who are alive after probation has closed and before the commencement of the pouring out of the plagues will be translated without tasting death: "And I saw another sign in heaven, great, and marvelous, seven angels having the seven last plagues; for in them is filled up the wrath of God. And I saw as it were a **sea of glass** mingled with fire: and them that had gotten the victory over the beast, and over his image, and over his mark, and over the number of his name, **stand on the sea of glass,** having the harps of God." The **"sea of glass"** is a symbol of **life eternal.** (Explained in another chapter.) In as much as all who had gotten the victory stand on the **sea,** it denotes that they have passed from death to life, and their destination **now** is **"God, new Jerusalem."**

Verses 5-8: "And after that I looked, and, behold, the temple of the tabernacle of the testimony in heaven was opened: And the seven angels came out of the temple, having the seven plagues, clothed in pure and white linen, and having their breasts girded with golden girdles. And one of the four beasts gave unto the seven angels seven golden vials full of the wrath of God, who liveth for ever and ever. And the temple was filled with smoke from the glory of God, and from His power; and no man was able to enter into the temple, till the seven plagues of the seven angels were fulfilled." After the investigation is completed and every case decided, the temple of the testimony will open similar to when the typical opened at the close of the sacrificial system: and the vail which divided the two apartments rent in twain from the top to the bottom." (See Matt. 27:51.)

The door that is opened after the close of probation is the entrance to **the holy place** which was closed in 1844. After the close of probation the temple is to be filled with the power and glory of God so that **no** man shall be able to enter in till after the seven plagues are fulfilled. Showing that all God's people stood on the **sea** of **glass** (eternal life) and then probation closed. Thus after Jesus leaves the **most holy** place, God's servants shall have no funeral sermons to preach and no gospels for sinners.

THE TWENTY-FOURTH CHAPTER OF MATTHEW, AND THE SIGNS OF CHRIST'S COMING

"And as He sat upon the mount of Olives, the disciples came unto Him privately, saying, Tell us, when shall these things be? and what shall be the sign of thy coming, and of the end of the world? And Jesus answered and said unto them, Take heed that no man deceive you. For many shall come in my name, saying, I am Christ; and shall deceive many. And ye shall hear of wars and rumors of wars: see that ye be not troubled: for all these things must come to pass, but the end is not yet. For nation shall rise against nation, and kingdom against kingdom: and there shall be famines, and pestilences, and earthquakes, in divers places. All these are the beginning of sorrows. Then shall they deliver you up to be afflicted, and shall kill you: and ye shall be hated of all nations for my name's sake. And then shall many be offended, and shall betray one another, and shall hate one another. And many false prophets shall rise, and shall deceive many. And because iniquity shall abound, the love of many shall wax cold. But he that shall endure unto the end, the same shall be saved. And this gospel of the kingdom shall be preached in all the world for a witness unto all nations; and then shall the end come." (Verses 3-14.)

The direct question put to Christ and His answer as to the assurance of His second coming, and the end of this present world, is too plain and self explanatory to leave room for doubt. He did not say that the end of the present sinful world was not to come, but He plainly stated that it **will** come. However He said before the end shall come, "This gospel of the kingdom [the signs of His second coming as foretold in this chapter] shall be preached in all the world for a witness unto **all** nations [not that all nations shall be converted, but for a witness] and **then shall the end come."** Those who teach contrary to this plain statement of the Master, are they of whom He says: "Many false prophets shall arise and shall deceive many." Furthermore, the Lord says: "For as the lightning cometh out of the east, and shineth even unto the west; **so shall** also the **coming** of the Son of man be." (Verse 27.)

While some of these false prophets make a complete denial of His coming, others dare say, "He is already come." Still others claim that no one shall see Him when He comes, but, He shall establish His kingdom on earth, and this world will never come to an end, etc. We ask the question: Is Christ telling an untrue story, or are these false prophets fulfilling His prediction by trying to deceive the saints concerning His coming, and overthrow their faith in the Master's Word, and thus defraud them of a crown of life? If these are not the deceivers of whom He speaks, then who are they?

If such workers of iniquity dare try to contradict His plain language as in this instance, may it not be expected that they shall attempt to overthrow the entire truth of the Bible?

When Christ **shall come** "as lightning cometh out of the east, and shineth even unto the west," these false prophets shall be ashamed. The Revelator also declares: "Behold, He cometh **with clouds;** and **every** eye shall **see Him,** and they also which **pierced Him:** [that is, they that pierced him shall be resurrected prior to His coming. See Dan. 12:2] and all kindreds of the earth shall wail because of Him. Even so, Amen." (Rev. 1:7.) Yes, our Christ shall come and we shall see Him as He is, "And it shall be said in that day, Lo this is our God: **we have waited** for **Him,** and He will save us: this is the Lord; we have waited for **Him,** we will be **glad** and rejoice in **his salvation."** (Isa. 25:9.)

Though these false prophets and sinners do not want to see Him come, they must: "And the kings of the earth, and the great men, and the rich men, and the chief captains, and the mighty men, and every bondman, and every free man, hid themselves in the dens and in the rocks of the mountains; And said to the mountains and the rocks, Fall on us, and hide us from the face of Him that sitteth on the throne, and from the wrath of the lamb: For the great day of His wrath is come; and **who** shall be **able** to stand?" (Rev. 6:15-17.) And so shall the end come to the sinners, but not to God's people: "For the Lord himself shall descend from heaven with a shout, with the voice of the archangel, and with the trump of God: and the **dead in Christ** shall **rise** first: Then we which are alive and remain shall **be caught up together** with them **in the clouds, to meet** the **Lord** in the **air:** and so shall **we** ever be **with the Lord."** (1 Thess. 4:16, 17.)

To the sinners that day shall be a fearful day, and to them shall He come "as a thief in the night," but not so to those who wait for Him. For, speaking of the great persecution that overtook His people in the dark ages during the 1260 years of Daniel 7:25, He says: "Immediately after the tribulation of those days shall the sun be darkened, and the moon shall not give her light, and the stars shall fall from heaven, and the powers of the heavens shall be shaken: And then shall **appear** the sign of the Son of man in heaven: and then shall all the tribes of the earth mourn, and they shall **see** the Son of man coming in the clouds of heaven with power and great glory. And He shall send His angels with a great sound of a trumpet, and they shall gather together His elect from the four winds, from one end of heaven to the other." (Matt. 24:29-31.)

The Master looking forward to this generation, says, "there shall be signs in the sun, and in the moon, and in the stars." (Luke 21:25.) Thus, "immediately after the tribulation" (the great persecution) the sun was to be darkened. On the 19th of May, 1780, this prophecy was fulfilled. Quoting from "The Great Controversy": "'Almost if not altogether alone, as the most mysterious and as yet unexplained phenomenon of its kind, . . . stands the dark day of May 19, 1780—a most unaccountable darkening of the whole visible heavens and atmosphere in New England'." An eye-witness living in Massachusetts describes the event as follows:

'In the morning the sun rose clear, but was soon overcast. The clouds became lowery, and from them, black and ominous, as they soon appeared, lightening flashed, thunder rolled, and a little rain fell. Toward nine o'clock, the clouds became thinner, and assumed a brassy or coppery appearance, and earth, rocks, trees, buildings, water, and persons were changed by this strange, unearthly light. A few minutes later, a heavy black cloud spread over the entire sky except a narrow rim at the horizon, and it was as dark as it usually is at nine o'clock on a summer evening. . . .

'Fear, anxiety, and awe gradually filled the minds of the people. Women stood at the door, looking out upon the dark landscape; men returned from their labor in the fields; the carpenter left his tools; the blacksmith his forge, the tradesman his counter. Schools were dismissed, and tremblingly the children fled homeward. Travelers put up at the nearest farmhouse. 'What is coming?' queried every lip and heart. It seems as if a hurricane was about to dash across the land, or as if it was the day of the consummation of all things.

'The extent of this darkness was extraordinary. It was observed as far east as Falmouth. To the westward it reached to the farthest part of Connecticut, and to Albany. To the southward, it was observed along the seacoast; and to the north as far as American settlements extend.'

"The intense darkness of the day was succeeded, an hour or two before evening, by a partially clear sky, and the sun appeared, though it was still obscured by the black, heavy mist. 'After sundown, the cloud came again overhead, and it grew dark very fast.' 'Nor was the darkness of the night less uncommon and terrifying than that of the day; not withstanding there was almost a full moon, no object was discernible but by the help of some artificial light, which, when seen from the neighboring houses and other places at a distance, appeared through a kind of Egyptian darkness which seemed almost impervious to the rays.' Said an eye-witness of the scene: 'I could not help conceiving at the time, that if every luminous body in the universe had been shrouded in impenetrable shades, or struck out of existence, the darkness could not have been more complete.' Though at nine o'clock that night the moon rose to the full, 'it had not the least effect to dispel the death-like shadows.' After midnight the darkness disappeared, and the moon, when first visible, had the appearance of blood.

"May 19, 1780, stands in history as 'The Dark Day.' Since the time of Moses, no period of darkness of equal density, extent, and duration, has ever been recorded. The description of this event, as given by eye-witnesses, is but an echo of the words of the Lord, recorded by the prophet Joel, twenty-five hundred years previous to their fulfillment: 'The sun shall be turned into darkness, and the moon into blood, before the great and terrible day of the Lord come.'

"In 1833, two years after Miller began to present in public the evidences of Christ's soon coming, the **last** of the signs appeared which were promised by the Saviour as tokens of His second advent. Said Jesus, 'The stars shall fall from heaven.' And John in the Revelation declared, as he beheld in vision the scenes that should herald the day of God, 'The stars of heaven fell unto the earth, even as a fig-tree casteth her untimely figs, when she is shaken of a mighty wind.' This prophecy received a striking and impressive fulfillment in the great meteoric shower of November 13, 1833. That was the most extensive and wonderful display of falling stars which has ever been recorded; 'The whole firmament, over all the United States, being then, for hours, in fiery commotion! No celestial phenomenon has ever occurred in this country, since its first settlement, which was viewed with such intense admiration by one class in the community, or with so much dread and alarm by another.' 'It's sublimity and awful beauty still linger in many minds. . . . Never did rain fall much thicker than the meteors fell toward the earth; east, west, north, and south, it was the same. In a word, the whole heavens seemed in motion. . . . The display, as described in Professor Silliman's journal, was seen all over North America. . . . From two o'clock until broad daylight, the sky being perfectly serene and cloudless, an incessant play of dazzling brilliant luminosities was kept up in the whole heavens.'

'No language, indeed, can come up to the splendor of that magnificent display; . . . no one who did not witness it can form an adequate conception of its glory. It seemed as if the whole starry heavens had congregated at one point near the zenith, and were simultaneously shooting forth, with the velocity of lightning, to every part of the horizon; and yet they were not exhausted—thousands swiftly followed in the tracks of thousands, as if created for the occasion.'

"In the New York **Journal of Commerce** of Nov. 14, 1833, appeared a long article regarding this wonderful phenomenon, containing this statement: 'No philosopher or scholar has told or recorded an event, I suppose, like that of yesterday morning. A prophet eighteen hundred years ago foretold it exactly, if we will be at the trouble of understanding stars falling to mean falling stars . . . in the only sense in which it is possible to be literally true.'

"Thus was displayed the **last of those signs** of His **coming,** concerning which Jesus bade His disciples, 'When ye shall see all these things, know that it is near, even at the doors.' After these things, John beheld, as the great event next impending, the heavens departing as a scroll, while the earth quaked, mountains and islands removed out of their places, and the wicked in terror sought to flee from the presence of the Son of man."—pp. 306-308, 333, 334.

Christ had bidden His people watch for the signs of His advent, and rejoice as they should behold the tokens of their coming King. "And when these things begin to come to pass," He said, "then look up, and lift up your heads; for your redemption draweth nigh." (Luke 21:28.) He pointed His followers to the budding trees of spring, and said: "Now learn a parable of the fig tree; When his branch is yet tender, and putteth forth leaves, ye know that summer is nigh: So likewise ye, when ye shall see all these things, know that it is near, even at the doors." (Matt. 24:32, 33.) While the Saviour has clearly pointed out the nearness of His coming to the generation that shall witness **all** these signs, He has not left us in darkness as to how long it will be from the time of the fulfillment of these signs to that great and glorious event, for He added: "This generation [the one that has seen the signs] shall not pass, till all these things be fulfilled." (Verse 34.) As the generation spoken of by the Master is about to pass away, and the kingdom of everlasting life ushered in, the searcher of truth should not neglect his opportunity by allowing things of lesser importance to occupy his mind, or time.

Committed to S. D. A. Denomination

The gospel of the coming of Christ in this generation, and the signs of the times as in Matthew 24, was committed to the

Seventh-day Adventist denomination since 1844. No other body of people has had the burden of the message that is taught in this chapter (the signs and the end of the world), and the urgency of its speedy delivery in this generation. Therefore, whatever commendation, or condemnation is written to the "servant" in Matthew 24, cannot be applied to another people. Furthermore, as the rest of Christendom had fallen by 1844 because they rejected the messages that were sent to them, and thus God would not let light shine through them since that time, it is evident that the gospel of the 24th chapter of Matthew could not have been preached by any other people. Therefore, the statement concerning the **servant** in the following verse is applicable only to the foregoing denomination.

"Who then is a faithful and wise servant, whom his Lord hath made ruler over His household, to give them [to the world] meat in due season"—present truth? (Verse 45.) Note, that there is a question as to whom this faithful servant could be. If that people to whom primarily this gospel was committed had been faithful, then the following promise would have been theirs: "Blessed is that servant, whom his Lord when He cometh shall find so doing. Verily I say unto you, That He shall make him ruler over **all** His goods." (Verses 46, 47.) The significance of **"all His goods"** is the finishing of the gospel, bringing everlasting righteousness, and ushering in the kingdom of Christ! What a wonderful promise! But, observe the danger of loosing this everlasting glory: "But and if that evil servant shall say in his heart, My Lord **delayeth** His coming; and shall begin to smite his fellowservants, and to **eat** and **drink** with the drunken." (Verses 48, 49.) The "servant" (singular) that shall "begin to smite his fellow servants" (plural) signifies the leadership—the "angel" of the church of the Laodiceans—those who have charge of the "household." But the "servants" (plural) apply to the ministry under that leadership. By the unfaithfulness of "that servant," the gospel has been delayed; the generation is about to pass, and the work is years behind. The result is, that the **delay** has not been expressed by action only, but it is even said by words, "My Lord **delayeth** His coming." And as one sin leads to another, the doctrine of "Health Reform," eating foods that have been devitalized by modern inventions, the "dainties" of Babylon, etc.—indulging fleshly lusts, has been largely disregarded, thus fulfilling the words, "eat and drink with the drunken."

The doctrine of health reform is said to be "the **right** hand and arm of the **Third Angel's** Message," and that the medical work is "the **right hand** of the message." The idea of health reform is a thing of the past so far as the church as a body is concerned, and the leadership cares little. But that is not the worst; this unfaithful servant of God has even dared stretch his hand over the gulf to form an unlawful alliance of the denominational medical institutions with those of the world, who are bitterly opposed to the idea of health reform—right hand and arm of the "Third Angel's Message." The very channel which was instituted to uphold and carry that part of the work, is being bound by a confederacy; and now in order to maintain this alliance it has been compelled to sacrifice the very principle for which it was organized. Thereby God's agency for treating the sick and preventing disease by healthful living and divine healing through obedience of the truth, has been substituted by drugs.

Thus the devil has cut off the right hand and arm of the "Third Angel's Message," and by this cunning device has robbed the church of God of its medical institutions! What a calamity! What a loss! Would not God's faithful people at such a time as this come up to the help of the Lord against the mighty? How a body of people with so much light can become so blind is beyond human understanding; it is a mystery!

Had they (those who were charged with this great responsibility) been faithful to the trust committed to them, the everlasting blessings found in the following verse would have been their's: "That He shall make him ruler over all his goods." But to him who neglects his Master's commission: "The Lord of that servant shall come in a day when he looketh not for Him, and in an hour that he is not aware of, and shall cut him asunder, and appoint him his portion with the hypocrites: there shall be weeping and gnashing of teeth." (Verses 50, 51.) Had they taken heed to the last urgent message sent them, calling for decided changes in these things, the following chapter (Matthew 25) would have been prophetically different.

The Ten Virgins—Matthew 25

"Then shall the kingdom of heaven be likened unto ten virgins, which took their lamps, and went forth to meet the bridegroom. And five of them were wise, and five were foolish. They that were foolish took their lamps, and took no oil with them: But the wise took oil in their vessels with their lamps. While the bridegroom tarried, they all slumbered and slept. And at midnight there was a cry made, Behold, the bridegroom cometh; go ye out to meet him. Then all those virgins arose, and trimmed their lamps. And the foolish said unto the wise, Give us of your oil; for our lamps are gone out. But the wise answered, saying, Not so; lest there be not enough for us and you: but go ye rather to them that sell, and buy for yourselves. And while they went to buy, the bridegroom came; and they that were ready went in with him to the marriage: and the door was shut. Afterward came also the other virgins, saying, Lord, Lord, open unto us. But he answered and said, Verily I say unto you, I know you not. Watch therefore, for ye know neither the day nor the hour wherein the Son of man cometh." (Verses 1-13.)

Observe that the 25th chapter is a continuation of the 24th. Mark the word, "then," meaning the time they fulfilled the prophetic words contained in verses 48-51. The virgins are a figure of the church. Number "ten," has the symbolic meaning of universal (the church as a body). Note that they are **all** "virgins." The 144,000 are designated by the same word. (See Rev. 14:4.) The word "virgins," signify that the class represented by them (ten), are not those who are called **out** from Babylon (fallen churches) at the time the "cry" is made. For, if they were to come out of Babylon by the call "Come out of **her,** my people" (Rev. 18:4), they would have been **defiled** with **"women"** (fallen churches), and therefore, could not be called "virgins." Thus, the message of the "Midnight Cry" must find them in the house of God—virgins.

The "Midnight Cry" was first proclaimed prior to 1844, and the coming of the "Bridegroom" was Christ's coming to the Most Holy place in the heavenly sanctuary for the investigative judgment of the saints. The **investigation** being in **two** sections; first, the judgment for the **dead,** and the second for the **living,** the **"cry"** must be repeated, otherwise we would have no present truth for the time of the judgment of the **living.** The **"cry"** for the **living** being of a greater importance to the world than the one for the dead, and as the "virgins" are a figure of the living church, the parable must have a direct application to the church at this present time,—the coming of the bridegroom for the judgment of the living. But indirectly it points back to the commencement of the "Midnight Cry" (the first angel's message—the judgment for the dead). The messages being of the same event, "judgment," both (for the living and for the dead) are called the **"midnight cry."** The same is proven by the parable itself.

"While the bridegroom tarried, they all slumbered and slept. And at midnight there was a cry made, Behold, the bridegroom cometh; go ye out to meet him. Then all those virgins arose, and trimmed their lamps." Note that they "slumbered and slept" **before** the cry was made. In the summer of 1844, midway between the time when it was first thought that the 2300 days would end (on March 21), and the second date (October 22 of the same year), this period they applied as being the "tarrying time." But mark that the **"cry"** had been going on for some years (the message by Miller), and the tarrying time was applied at its close, after they had discovered their miscalculation; which is contrary to a proper application of the parable; for according to the parable they tarried before the cry was made. Therefore, the tarrying time must be the judgment for the dead, before the bridegroom came to the investigation of the living; in which time the "ten virgins" developed. So, that is the time in which they all slumbered and slept. This application is also in perfect harmony with the message to the Laodiceans. (See Rev. 3:14-19; Isa. 52:1, 2.)

If the foregoing application is correct, then at the end of the tarrying period, or just prior to the commencement of the judgment of the living, there must be a message—"cry"; and if the "virgins" are a figure of the church as a body in the time of the "cry," then, that message must be for the church only. This is also proven in "The Great Controversy," page 425. In as much as there is just such a "cry" presented in "The Shepherd's Rod," Vol. 1, it not only shows that the application of the parable is correct, but it also proves that church to be the "House of God."

"They **all** slumbered and slept." This statement by the Master proves that the church as a body has been asleep—being in perfect harmony with the previous explanation of the 24th chapter of Matthew. Five were foolish and five wise. Number "ten" being a symbol of the church as a body, the number **five** and **five,** mean half and half. The denomination numbers at the present time a little over 300,000; half of this number would be about 150,000. If we should subtract the dead material (backsliders, but still on the church record), the number derived after such deduction, would be about 144,000. Thus again it proves that the 144,000 are the **five wise virgins;** and the foolish ones are they who shall fall under the destroying weapons in the hand of the "five men."

"But the wise took oil in their vessels with their lamps." The "oil" is a symbol of the Spirit of God in the form of a message (truth); for, it is the substance that gives the light (the prophetic Word of God). The lamp must be a symbol of the **heart** into which the Word (oil) is being retained. The trimming of their lamps, is the "trimming" of their hearts; that is, their conscience being aroused they began to show interest. But only five of them had an extra supply of oil in their vessels. As they started out to meet the bridegroom, the lamps of the foolish ones went out; and as they found themselves in darkness, it made their progress impossible. Now, the question arises: What made their lamps go out, and why could they go backward, but not forward? As the message of the judgment for the dead was the present truth since 1844, at the beginning of the judgment for the living (when the cry was made), it became present truth no longer. Consequently their lamps went out. They could not move forward because they were **foolish;** that is, they did not accept the light—the judgment for the living. Was the "oil" beyond their reach? The words in the parable prove that they **all** heard the "cry," "arose, and trimmed their lamps." Five of them failed to get the supply of oil because they were **"foolish,"**—they did not study for themselves. Allowed others to think for them; they chose the easy, popular side, and accepted the decisions of the leaders, copies the mistakes of others, and were thus left without a supply of oil,—robbed of the truth, cheated of glory, and left in darkness!

"And the foolish said unto the wise, Give us of your oil; for our lamps are gone out." At last the foolish virgins saw themselves in darkness. Then they went to the wise and asked for oil as a gift; "But the wise answered, saying, Not so; lest there be not enough for us and you: but go ye rather to them that sell, and buy for yourselves." The oil is sold and there must be something given in exchange to obtain the supply. The price they had to pay was to "sigh and cry for the abominations done in the midst thereof," give up sinning and obey the truth. Their receipt for the value of exchange would have been the seal of the living God in their foreheads.

"And while they went to buy, the bridegroom came; and they that were ready went in with him to the marriage: and the door was shut. Afterward came also the other virgins, saying, Lord, Lord, open unto us. But he answered and said, Verily I say unto you, I know you not." As the foolish virgins at last came to the door, it is evident that they obtained the oil (learned of the message), but there had been a delay—the door was shut, and they were left out. Now, why were they unconcerned at first, and very zealous at last? The experience in this instance is about the same as that of the deluge. While Noah preached the coming of the flood, the world paid little attention to his message; but those who believed, went into the ark at a given time and the door was closed. But not long afterwards, signs of Noah's prediction appeared; and as drops of rain began to fall the wicked multitude became alarmed and rushed for the ark, but the door was closed and they were left out. The door that "was shut," is a symbol showing that probation for the church had closed just shortly after the foolish virgins became alarmed. At last they were willing to pay the price and buy the oil; but it was not a change of heart, only the fear of losing out. Their course of action had left them without the seal—"the man with the writer's inkhorn" had passed them by. What a terrible mistake! What a disappointment! Almost saved, but entirely lost!

"The coming of Christ as our high priest to the most holy place, for the cleansing of the sanctuary, brought to view in Daniel 8:14; the coming of the Son of man to the Ancient of days, as presented in Daniel 7:13; and the coming of the Lord to His temple, foretold by Malachi, are descriptions of the same event; and this is also represented by the coming of the bridegroom to the marriage, described by Christ, in the parable of the ten virgins, of Matthew 25."—"The Great Controversy," p. 426.

The description by Daniel applies to the commencement of the judgment for the dead; but the one by Malachi 3:1-3, is applicable to the judgment for the living—all of the same event—day of atonement—cleansing of the sanctuary.

"The coming of the bridegroom, here brought to view, takes place before the marriage. The marriage represents the reception by Christ of His kingdom. The holy city, the New Jerusalem, which is the capitol and representative of the kingdom, is called 'the bride, the lamb's wife.' Said the angel to John, 'Come hither, I will show thee the bride, the Lamb's wife.' 'He carried me away in the spirit,' says the prophet, 'and showed me that great city, the holy Jerusalem, descending out of heaven from God.' Clearly, then, the bride represents the holy city, and the virgins that go out to meet the bridegroom are a symbol of the church. In the Revelation the people of God are said to be the guests at the marriage supper. If **guests,** they cannot be represented also as the **bride.** Christ, as stated by the prophet Daniel, will receive from the Ancient of days in heaven; 'dominion, and glory, and a kingdom'; He will receive the New Jerusalem, the capitol of His kingdom, 'prepared as a bride adorned for her husband.' Having received the kingdom, He will come in His glory, as King of kings and Lord of lords, for the redemption of His people, who are to 'sit down with Abraham, and Isaac, and Jacob,' at His table in His kingdom, to partake of the marriage supper of the Lamb." —Id., pp. 426, 427.

The virgins were called to meet Him, and thus by faith go in with Him to appear before the Father—the Great Judge. The seal is the permit; it places their names in the Lamb's book of Life, and thus it grants to them the right to appear before the Father in the judgment; not in person, but in figure; thus having their sins blotted out. Matthew 24:36, 50, are descriptions of the same event. "Watch therefore, for ye know neither the day nor the hour wherein the Son of man cometh." (Matt. 25:13.) This has reference to the time of the judgment, and not of His coming to earth; for, the saints shall know the day and the hour of Christ's coming in the clouds to receive the redeemed, as it shall be an-nounced by the Father shortly before His coming. (See "The Great Controver-sy," p. 640.)

Summary of the Ten Virgins

The number, "ten", being a symbol of universal, it represents the church as a body prior to the commencement of the judgment of the living—in the sealing period of the 144,000, and before the "Loud Cry" of the Third Angel's Message; being the period of the **first** fruits of the harvest. The five wise virgins were they who trusted in God and His word only; having no confidence in man, and were hungry for truth, searching for light, and gladly accepting it when it came. Thus they received the seal of God's approval, their sins were blotted out, and their lives made sure—they passed from condemnation and death into glory and life eternal. They are God's servants, kings and priests—144,000 in number.

The five foolish virgins are they who had confidence in men; they were willing that others should think and study for them. Their love for this world and the things of it, exceeded their love for Christ and the world to come. They had no true sense of the awful result of sin. Their zeal for self, drowned their zeal for the house of God and His honor. They were satisfied with their lamps trimmed and but little oil in them. They saw no necessity for more light—prophets, truth or message. They said in their hearts, we are rich and increased with goods and have need of nothing. They were prejudiced against light upon the word of God, and accepted not the truth because the channel through which it came was not of their choice.

The knowledge of present truth, which the five foolish virgins possessed since 1844 is the judgment of the dead, and was the only oil in their lamps. When the judgment of the living commenced, and the "cry was made," they were found without this extra oil in their vessels; they had neglected their Lord's command: "Watch therefore, for ye know neither the day nor the hour wherein the Son of man cometh." Thus when the wise ones started out to meet the bridegroom the lamps of the foolish went out, for, the judgment of the dead had passed. There-fore, it was present truth no more, and thus they were left in darkness. At the beginning of the judgments of God they saw their mistake and rushed for the ark of safety, but it was beyond their reach for they knew nothing of the message, and by the time they ac-quired it (filled their lamps with oil), there had been a delay, the angel had passed "through the city, through Jerusalem," the church—the sealing was finished, and probation for the church had closed—the door was shut. Thus they were left out. Then they came with these words: "Lord, Lord, open unto us, But He answered and said, Verily I say unto you, I know you not." "Appoint his portion with the hypocrites: there shall be weeping and gnashing of teeth." **What** a disappointment that will be!

It will be noticed that the close of probation for the church and the one for the world are two different events. The former is a miniature representation of the latter. The Scripture for the preceding one is found in Matthew 25:11, 12; but of the final one we read: "He that is unjust, let him be unjust still: and he which is filthy, let him be filthy still: and he that is righteous, let him be righteous still: and he that is holy, let him be holy still. And, behold, I come quickly; and my reward is with me, to give every man according as his work shall be." (Rev. 22:11, 12.) At this time those who were like the five foolish virgins, will say, "The harvest is past, the summer is ended, and we are not saved." (Jer. 8:20.) "And they shall wander from sea to sea, and from the north even to the east, they shall run to and fro to seek the word of the Lord, and shall not find it." (Amos 8:12.)

THE SEVEN SEALS AND THE SANCTUARY

In order to make a proper application of the seven seals, we must have a better understanding of the heavenly sanctuary service, its origin, and the object of its existence as taught by the earthly sanctuary built by Moses. (Heb. 8:5.)

In the sanctuary construction and service, is revealed the plan of salvation. The first apartment, called the holy place, in which the high priest officiated daily with sacrifices and divers manners of gifts and washings, was a place for confession of sin. All of which was a shadow of heavenly things, clearly revealing the plan of salvation. The second apartment, within the vail, called the "most holy," or the "holiest of all," was open only in the seventh month, and tenth day of the month, in each year; there redemption from the condemnation of the law was assured. (Lev. 23:27-30; 16:34.) It was called the day of atonement, judgment, or cleansing of the Sanctuary. (Lev. 16:33; Dan. 7:10; 8:14.) This was a day for the blotting out of sins accumulated during the year, and was a symbol of the great day of atonement; not in figure, but in reality. (See Lev. 16:19. Also "The Great Controversy," page 485.) The seat overshadowed by the cherubims being called the mercy seat, proves that it is a throne of mercy, and therefore a throne of judgment, where sinners can obtain mercy.

The entire system—priest, sacrifice, and service—was a type of Christ and His administration in the heavenly sanctuary, which the Lord pitched and not man. (See Heb. 8:2, and "The Acts of the Apostles," page 14.) The holy place was for the confession of sin, but the most holy for blotting out sin.

While the services in the earthly sanctuary were in operation, there could have been no services in the heavenly until after Christ ascended and became our High Priest. (See Hebrews 8.) Therefore, when the services in the heavenly began, the services in the earthly ceased. The true worshippers in the earthly, who by faith looked forward to the administration of the heavenly, were credited in the books of heaven as worthy of life eternal. Their records were to be investigated when Christ our High Priest entered within the vail into the holiest of all to blot out sin. (See Dan. 7:10.)

Says the Spirit of God: "It is impossible that the sins of men should be blotted out until after the judgment at which time their cases are to be investigated."—"The Great Controversy," page 485. While the services in the earthly sanctuary were in force, the heavenly served as a depository for confessed sins. The same is true even under Christ's administration while in the holy apartment, until He entered into the most holy.

The Plan of Salvation Preceded the Fall

The heavenly sanctuary being for confession and the blotting out of sin, it could not have existed before sin entered and brought about the necessity for such a structure. Although the sanctuary service was originated after Adam sinned, the plan of salvation had always existed, and was revealed in, and by, the sanctuary service. Thus the plan that preceded the fall is found in Christ, in whom there was and is redeeming power for all.

Is the Sanctuary the Eternal Place of God's Throne?

While the earthly sanctuary existed, God met His people in the most holy place, where His presence was manifested between the cherubims on the mercy seat. Therefore, some have taken the position that the eternal place of God's throne is in "the holiest of all" of the heavenly sanctuary, but such an idea is contrary to both type and antitype. The first reason is, that the sanctuary did not always exist, as previously explained; second, the most holy was closed while Christ ministered in the holy. Says Paul: "We have such an high priest, who is set on the right hand of the **throne** of the Majesty in the heavens." (Heb. 8:1.) If God's throne was in the "most holy" place when Christ ascended on high, then He must have immediately entered the "holiest of all," instead of the "holy place." Such a position is contrary to both Scripture and service. God met His ancient people in the holiest of all, where, in figure, their sins were blotted out. Thus, symbolically showing, that He cannot meet His saints face to face until after He has met them in the "most holy"—blotted out their sins, not in figure, but in reality—in the anti-typical day of atonement. We shall prove this again from another angle.

The Revelator, in a vision about 96 A.D., was permitted to look into both apartments. A voice from heaven said to him: "Come up hither, and I will shew thee things which **must be hereafter.**" Then he saw a throne set, and one sat on the throne, and before the throne there was a sea of glass like unto a crystal. (See Rev. 4:1-6.) The voice told him that the things which he saw were to be **"hereafter"**; that is, in the future from the time of the vision. Hence, it is evident that there was no throne there at that time—about 62 years after Christ had ascended to the

Father. Therefore, Christ sat on the right hand of God, but not on the throne in the sanctuary. What, then? Has God more than one throne? "Throne" is a seat, and wherever **God** sits, there His throne is. Note that "around and before the throne" **in the sanctuary,** is the **"sea of glass."**

Now we read of another throne: "And he shewed me a pure **river of water of life,** clear as crystal, **proceeding out of the throne** of God and the Lamb." (Rev. 22:1.) Again, note that from one of the thrones proceeds the **"river of life,"** but from the other, the **"sea of glass."** Therefore, there are two thrones. Christ sat at the right hand of God on the throne from which proceeds the "river of life," for this is the one called, **"the throne of God and the lamb."** This is God's eternal place of abode; but the one in the sanctuary was set for the time being, (See Dan. 7:9, 10), during Christ's ministration in the holiest of all, which is a throne of judgment—of blotting out sins and granting of rewards. The one from which proceeds the river of **life** is a throne of life and of eternity.

Where is the Throne Seen By John?

Revelation 4:1, 2, 4-6: "After this I looked, and, behold, a door was opened in heaven: and the first voice which I heard was as it were of a trumpet talking with me; which said, Come up hither, and I will shew thee things which must be hereafter. And immediately I was in the spirit; and, behold, a throne was set in heaven, and one sat on the throne. . . . And round about the throne were four and twenty seats: and upon the seats I saw four and twenty elders sitting, clothed in white raiment; and they had on their heads crowns of gold. And out of the throne proceeded lightnings and thunderings and voices: and there were seven lamps of fire burning before the throne, which are the seven spirits of God. And before the throne there was a sea of glass like unto crystal: and in the midst of the throne, and round about the throne, were four beasts full of eyes before and behind."

The description of the place is such that it bears evidence of being in the heavenly sanctuary. The same is supported by the Spirit of Prophecy: "As in vision the apostle John was granted a view of the **Temple** of God in heaven, he beheld there 'seven lamps of fire burning before the throne.' He saw an angel 'having a golden censer; and there was given unto him much incense, that he should offer it with the prayers of all saints upon the golden altar which was before the throne.' Here the prophet was permitted to behold the first apartment of the **sanctuary** in heaven; and he saw there the 'seven lamps of fire' and the 'golden altar' represented by the golden candlestick and the altar of incense in the sanctuary on earth. Again, 'the temple of God was **opened'**, and he looked **within the inner vail,** upon the holy of holies. Here he beheld 'the ark of His testament,' represented by the sacred chest constructed by Moses to contain the law of God."—"Patriarchs and Prophets," page 356.

In the earthly sanctuary, the high priest alone was permitted to officiate in the second apartment, within the vail, and it has been understood by some that the throne seen by John could not have been in the most holy, because the twenty-four elders are before the throne. That thought is incorrect, for it would be unreasonable to take the position that God would move His throne **from** the "holiest of all," **to** the "holy place," rather than for the elders to enter in the most holy before the throne. Furthermore, it is the throne of the Eternal One that makes the second apartment **most holy.** Therefore, if we take the position that the throne of God was moved into the first apartment, then **it** would become the "most holy." Thus, if the elders and the beasts, or creatures, were not permitted in the second apartment before the throne, neither would they be permitted in the first apartment before the throne. Taking any other stand than this would be saying that the **apartment is holier** than the **Creator** and His throne.

According to Paul, the services within the vail of the earthly tabernacle cannot clear all that takes place in the heavenly. Said he: "The Holy Ghost this signifying, that the way into the holiest of all was **not** yet made manifest, while as the first tabernacle was yet standing." (Heb. 9:8.) Therefore, we must find the truth of the services in the heavenly sanctuary from another angle. We quote Daniel 7:9, 10: "I beheld till the thrones were cast down, and the Ancient of days did sit, whose garment was white as snow, and the hair of his head like the pure wool: his throne was like the fiery flame, and his wheels as burning fire. A fiery stream issued and came forth from before him: thousand thousands ministered unto him, and ten thousand times ten thousand stood before him: the judgment was set, and the books were opened."

The prophet was shown the commencement of the judgment (atonement), or as it is also called, the cleansing of the sanctuary, which takes place in the most holy apartment; for he says, "the judgment was set, and the books were opened." Now note that, "Thousand thousands ministered unto him and ten thousand times ten thousand stood before him." Thus we see that Paul is right, that the service of the heavenly was not fully manifested by the service in the earthly. Though the high priest alone was permitted to enter the most holy place in the earthly, an innumerable company entered into the heavenly. Therefore, where is the evidence that the elders cannot be in the holiest of all? It is impossible to apply the fulfillment of the 2300 prophetic days—years—of Daniel's vision in chapter 8, verse 14, at any other time than the judgment in 1844.

This prophetic period commenced at the going forth of the commandment to restore and to build Jerusalem. (Dan. 9:25.) The decree made by the king of Persia was carried out in 457 B.C. (See Ezra 7.) Therefore it terminated in 1844; at which time Christ passed from the "holy" into the "most holy" place. For further study, see "The Great Controversy," page 486.

We shall endeavor to prove that the vision of Daniel is of the same event as that of John. Daniel speaks of **thrones** (plural), then he makes a distinction of the throne of God (Ancient of days) by the "fiery stream" coming from before Him. The book of Daniel is a **prophecy,** but the vision of John is a **revelation.** Daniel says he saw "thrones," but John gives us the number of them—twenty-five in all. (Rev. 4:2, 4.) Daniel says, "a fiery stream came forth from before him;" John tells us what the stream is: The "sea of glass mingled with fire." (Rev. 4:6; 15:2.) Daniel says: "Thousand thousands . . . and ten thousand times ten thousand stood before him." John tells us who they are: "And I beheld, and I heard the voice of many **angels** round about the throne and the **beasts** and the **elders:** and the number of them was ten thousand times ten thousand, and thousands of thousands." (Rev. 5:11.) Daniel says, "the judgment was set and the books were opened." John adds that one of the books was in the hand of Him that sat on the throne and was sealed with seven seals. (Rev. 5:1.) Thus John gives us more explicit revelation of the same event.

The door he saw "open" is the vail between the "holy" and the "most holy," for there is no other that had been kept closed. Therefore, the word "hereafter" in chapter 4, verse 1, means from the time of the vision—pointing forward to 1844.

Though the priest of the earthly sanctuary entered the "most holy" place but once a year, according to Paul, Christ entered the "holy" place once forever. (See Heb. 9:12.) And of that time the apostle says, He is "to appear in the presence of God for us," in the "holiest of all." (Verse 24.) Therefore, Christ could not enter the first apartment as a priest before His resurrection from the dead, at which time He became our High Priest; neither could He enter into the most holy in that capacity before the day of judgment, for Paul says, He "entered in **once.**" Then the prophecy by Daniel and the revelation by John, **can be** of no other event than the commencement of the judgment at the date stated (1844).

Only those whose names are written in the Lamb's book of life are brought into the presence of God—in the "most holy" place. Says the apostle: "Having therefore, brethren, boldness to enter into the **holiest** by the blood of Jesus." (Heb. 10:19.) As the same vision continues, we pass to the fifth and sixth chapters of Revelation.

Quoting 5:1, 3, 5-7; 6:1, "And I saw in the right hand of Him that sat on the throne a book written within and on the backside, sealed with seven seals. . . . And no man in heaven, nor in earth, neither under the earth, was able to open the book, neither to look thereon. . . . And one of the elders saith unto me, Weep not: behold, the Lion of the tribe of Juda, the Root of David, hath prevailed to open the book, and to loose the seven seals thereof. And I beheld, and, lo, in the midst of the throne and of the four beasts, and in the midst of the elders, stood a Lamb as it had been slain, having seven horns and seven eyes, which are the seven Spirits of God sent forth into all the earth. And he came and took the book out of the right hand of him that sat upon the throne. . . . And I saw when the Lamb opened one of the seals."

The book sealed with seven seals, in the right hand of the Great Judge, must contain the names of those whose sins are to be blotted out. Inasmuch as this is the only book that **"no man** in heaven nor in earth . . . was able to open, neither to look thereon," save the Lamb which was before the throne (See chapter 5:1-9), it is unquestionably clear that the book with the seven seals is the one called "The Lamb's book of Life." And with it the judgment opened. The same is repeated in Revelation 20:12, "And I saw the dead, small and great, stand before God; and the books were opened: and **another book** was opened, **which is the book of life:** and the dead were judged out of those things which were written in the books, according to their works." (See "The Great Controversy," page 480.) Since this cannot be refuted, it is evident that a foundation for the application of the seals is established.

We quote the scripture of the first four seals: "And I saw, and behold a white horse: and he that sat on him had a bow; and a crown was given unto him: and he went forth conquering, and to conquer. And when he had opened the second seal, I heard the second beast say, Come and see. And there went out another horse that was red: and power was given to him that sat thereon to take peace from the earth, and that they should kill one another: and there was given unto him a great sword. And when he had opened the third seal, I heard the third beast say, Come and see. And I beheld, and lo a black horse; and he that sat on him had a pair of balances in his hand. . . . And when he had opened the fourth seal, I heard the voice of the fourth beast say, Come and see. And I looked, and behold a pale horse: and his name that sat on him was Death, and Hell followed with him. And power was given unto them over the fourth part of the earth, to kill with sword, and with hunger, and with death, and with the beasts of the earth." (Rev. 6:2-5, 7, 8.)

Some have applied the seven seals of the sixth chapter of Revelation to the church in the New Testament time, but the symbols are contrary to the application. In both **Old** and New Testament time, God's church has been symbolized by a chaste woman. (See Jer. 6:2; Rev. 12:1.) Inspiration makes no change in the rule for a symbol of an impure church, for in Revelation 17:1, 4, 5, an harlot is used to point out a church, or churches, that are fallen or untrue. The change of this rule, (from "woman" to "man" or "horses") cannot be found anywhere within the Bible.

It is not only unscriptural to apply men and horses as symbols of the church, but it is altogether unfitting as well. Neither can any proof be presented to show that the seals apply only to the New Testament time. Therefore, the application of the symbols must be sought elsewhere. Thus we are confronted with the necessity of deeper study on the subject. According to the counsel of the servant of the Lord, we are admonished to study this, for it holds out an important truth for those who shall have a part in the closing of the gospel work. Quoting "Testimonies For the Church," Vol. 9, page 267: "The fifth chapter of Revelation needs to be closely studied. It is of **great importance** to those who shall act a part in the work of God **for these last days.**"

Had the chapter been properly understood, explained, and published before the above testimony was written, there would have been no need for this urgency. Furthermore, if it had been explained in the past, where is the lesson of such great importance, and who is bearing the responsibility of its deliverance to the world? But the fifth chapter, separated from the fourth and sixth, cannot be comprehended, for these chapters contain one subject; namely, the seven seals. The fifth chapter is mentioned because it is the heart and key of the subject.

It would be impossible to correctly understand the lesson of the seals in the sixth chapter, unless we know something about the "elders," the "book," and the "beasts" of the fourth chapter, where the vision begins. When we acquire some knowledge of their duties before the throne, and the purpose of the assembly, as well as the occasion, then only can we make a proper application that can stand the test.

Unless the meaning of every symbol is fittingly explained so that it cannot be contradicted, and a present truth lesson with special significance derived, the interpretation cannot be dependable and there can be no truth in it. God does not make vain repetitions, neither would He waste the time of His servants to write them. Therefore, every little symbol has its meaning, and reveals a great truth.

The Judgment and the Seals—Revelation Chapter 4

Verse 1: "After this I looked, and, behold, a **door was opened** in heaven: and the first voice which I heard was as it were of a trumpet talking with me; which said, Come up hither, and I will shew thee things which must be hereafter." The door that was opened cannot be any other than the one separating the two apartments; namely, the holy from the most holy, in the heavenly sanctuary, as shown by the earthly sanctuary built by Moses. That apartment was to be opened at the beginning of the judgment, typified by the day of atonement as previously explained. Then we make no mistake in concluding that the scene is the judgment in session, and as the voice said to John, "I will shew thee things which must be hereafter," it is evident that he looked forward in vision to the opening of the judgment in 1844.

If these conclusions are correct, and the vision describes the judgment in progress, then the same must be proven by the things seen in vision. A judgment in session requires a judge, an advocate, a jury, and representatives of those who are to be judged, for they cannot be there (in heaven) in person. There must be books containing the names, and records of the deeds, of those who are to be judged; also the time of the judgment, and the reward. We quote the scripture describing the Great Judge: "And immediately I was in the spirit: and, behold, a throne was set in heaven, and one sat on the throne. And he that sat was to look upon like a jasper and a sardine stone: and there was a rainbow round about the throne, in sight like unto an emerald." (Verses 2 and 3.)

The glory of God is represented by the likeness of precious stones. The rainbow reveals God's never failing promise and great mercy. God said to Noah: "This the token of the covenant which I make between me and you and every living creature that is with you, for perpetual generations: I do set my **bow** in the cloud, and it shall be for a **token of a covenant** between me and the earth." (Gen. 9:12, 13.)

The following verse depicts the jury: "And round about the

throne were four and twenty seats: and upon the seats I saw four and twenty elders sitting, clothed in white raiment; and they had on their heads crowns of gold." (Revelation 4:4.) The crowns of gold denote their kingly authority to act upon the case. The white robes show that they are men from earth, redeemed by the blood of Christ. "And round about the throne, were four beasts full of eyes before and behind." (Verse 6.) "And when he had taken the book, the four beasts and four and twenty elders fell down before the Lamb, having every one of them harps, and golden vials full of odours, which are the prayers of saints. And they sung a new song, saying, Thou art worthy to take the book, and to open the seals thereof: for thou wast slain, and hast redeemed us to God by thy blood out of every kindred, and tongue, and people, and nation." (Revelation 5:8, 9.) Note the beasts and elders all sang, saying: "For thou hast redeemed us out of **every kindred, and tongue, and people, and nation.**" Thus, the beasts, as well as the elders, are redeemed from the earth.

Again, note that the beasts and elders make a total of twenty-eight. It would be impossible for only twenty-eight persons to be redeemed out of **every** kindred, tongue, and people, and nation: for if there were only one redeemed out of every nation, the number would run into thousands, instead of twenty-eight. Therefore, it is evident that the **"four beasts"** are symbols which represent four groups of saints gathered from all ages, and out of every kindred, tongue, people, and nation. In a similar way the world empires after the flood are symbolically represented by beasts. Thus by the beasts are represented those that shall be judged.

"And the four beasts had each of them six wings about him; and they were full of eyes within: and they rest not day and night, saying, Holy, Holy, Holy, Lord God Almighty, which was, and is, and is to come." (Revelation 4:8.) "Full of eyes." Eyes are to give light to the body. Therefore, they stand as a symbol, signifying that God's people have had sufficient light in every age. "Before and behind" denotes prophetic light, revealing to them the past, present and future; this being made possible by the Spirit of God and by holy angels. The number "four" shows that there are four classes of saints to be considered in the judgment. Two of these classes are to be resurrected; namely, those who died naturally, and those who were martyred. The other two are they who shall be translated at the coming of Christ; namely, the 144,000 of Revelation 7:1-8, and the great multitude with palms in their hands, as shown in verse 9. (See "The Shepherd's Rod," Vol. 1, pp. 41-51.) As the wings of the lion, and also of the four-headed leopard beast (Babylon and Grecia) represent numbers of periods as previously explained (on pages 33-42), then they must stand for the same on these beasts. They are to point out the seal under which the judgment began—the sixth seal—therefore six wings. "Lord God Almighty, which was, and is, and is to come." That is, God before the judgment, in the time of the judgment, and after the judgment.

Verse 7: "And the first beast was like a lion, and the second beast like a calf, and the third beast had a face as a man, and the fourth beast was like a flying eagle." The beasts by nature also represent the four periods of the church. The first beast is like a lion. "Lion" is the king of beasts, and is intended to point out the first period of the church before the ceremonial section, with which the judgment began. (See chart in "The Shepherd's Rod," Vol. 1, p. 224.) The second beast being "like a calf," it is evident that he represents the sacrificial, or typical section. Thus the beast with the "face of a man" must represent the anti-typical period after the crucifixion. And the fourth beast was like a "flying eagle." He represents the period in the time of the harvest. The last period is symbolized by the flying eagle to denote the church that shall be translated. A "flying eagle" is **king** of **birds,** as the lion is **king of beasts,** which is a sign of victory, thus making a perfect symbol. As the judgment of the dead began with the beast like a **lion,**—king of beasts,—just so the judgment of the living begins with the beast like an **eagle,**—king of birds. The entire truth of these "four beasts" is not yet revealed.

As the beasts and the elders praise and worship God, it is sufficient testimony that creation is satisfied that He is just, and true, and the Creator of all. Those whose names are written within the book of the "seven seals" are the ones whose sins are to be blotted out with the precious blood of Christ. Thus praise, and honor, and glory, is due to our God forever and ever.

"I, even I, am he that blotteth out thy transgressions for mine own sake, and will not remember thy sins." (Isa. 43:25.) "I will bear the indignation of the Lord, because I have sinned against him, until he **plead** my cause, and execute **judgment** for me: he will bring me forth to the light, and I shall behold his righteousness. He will turn again, he will have compassion upon us; he will subdue our iniquities; and thou will cast **all** their sins into the depths of the sea." (Micah 7:9,19.) Shall we with the great apostle say: "For I am persuaded, that neither death, nor life, nor angels, nor principalities, nor powers, nor things present, nor things to come, nor height, nor depth, nor any other creature, shall be able to separate us from the love of God, which is in Christ Jesus our Lord?" (Romans 8:38, 39.)

Thus far our attention has been called to the Great Judge, the jury of twenty-four elders, the four beasts representing those who shall be judged, and the book containing the names—sealed with seven seals. Now our attention is turned to the advocate.

"And I beheld, and, lo, in the midst of the throne and of the four beasts, and in the midst of the elders, stood a Lamb as it had been slain, having seven horns and seven eyes, which are the seven Spirits of God sent forth into all the earth. And he came and took the book out of the right hand of him that sat upon the throne. And when he had taken the book, the four beasts and the four and twenty elders fell down before the Lamb, having every one of them harps, and golden vials full of odours, which are the prayers of saints." (Rev. 5:6-8.)

The "Lamb" is a symbol of Christ, our defender. Said John: "My little children, these things write I unto you, that ye sin not. And if any man sin, we have an **advocate** with the Father, Jesus Christ the righteous." (1 John 2:1.)

The seven horns on the Lamb signifies completeness of power and authority, verifying the words spoken by Christ: "All power is given unto me in heaven and in earth. (Matt. 28:18.) This immeasurable power is for our good, and is freely offered to us. Said Jesus: "If ye have faith as a grain of mustard seed, ye shall say unto this mountain, remove hence to yonder place; and it shall remove; and nothing shall be impossible unto you." (Matt. 17:20.) Dear friend, these words are either true or untrue. There can be no middle ground. As Christ cannot lie, will you try His never failing word, and let Him fulfill His promise?

The **seven eyes** of the Lamb denote completeness of vision; evidence that there is nothing hid from our Advocate, and that all things are open and naked unto Him; equally so with God the Father. The Psalmist describes God's power in vision in the following words: "Whither shall I go from thy Spirit? or whither shall I flee from thy presence? If I ascend up into heaven, thou art there: If I make my bed in hell, behold, thou art there. If I take the wings of the morning, and dwell in the uttermost parts of the sea; even there shall thy hand lead me, and thy right hand shall hold me. If I say, surely the darkness shall cover me; even the night shall be light about me. Yea, the darkness hideth not from thee; but the night shineth as the day: the darkness and the light are both alike to thee." (Psa. 139:7-12.)

The Revelator says the horns and the eyes of the Lamb "are the seven Spirits of God **sent** forth into **all** the earth." **All** of this power, both in might and in vision, is embodied and demonstrated by the Spirit of God. Said Jesus, "It is expedient for you that I go away: for if I go not away, the Comforter will not come unto you; but if I depart, I will send him unto you." (John 16:7.) "But the Comforter, which is the Holy Ghost, whom the Father will send in my name, he shall teach you all things, and bring all things to your remembrance, whatsoever I have said unto you." (John 14:26.)

"**The seven lamps** of fire burning before the throne, which are the seven Spirits of God." (Rev. 4:5.) The lamps of fire, seven in number, present before the throne, represent completeness of the truth of God—present truth revealed to every generation since the world began—by which we are judged. Those who are obedient to all the light and truth given them, have come up to the requirements—they are sealed, and cleared from the condemnation of the law of God.

"The seven lamps . . . which are the seven Spirits of God." (Rev. 4:5.) This Scripture proves the fact that light and truth are revealed by the Spirit of God only. "But the Comforter, which is the Holy Ghost, whom the Father will send in my name, he shall teach you all things, and bring all things to your remembrance, whatsoever I have said unto you." (John 14:26.) The rejecting of light and present truth is the sin against the Holy Ghost. "And whosoever speaketh a word against the Son of man, it shall be forgiven him: but whosoever speaketh against the Holy Ghost [present truth] it shall not be forgiven him, neither in this world, neither in the world to come." (Matt. 12:32.) Our attitude towards present truth would "Either make a tree good, and his fruit good; or else make the tree corrupt, and his fruit corrupt: for the tree is known by his fruit." (Verse 33.) Thus, present truth has the power to change the individual and fit him for eternal life, which is the seal of the living God. Said Jesus: "Verily, verily, I say unto thee, Except a man be born of **water** and of the **Spirit,** he cannot enter into the kingdom of God." (John 3:5.)

Sea of Glass

"And before the throne there was a sea of glass like unto crystal: and in the midst of the throne, and round about the throne, were four beasts full of eyes before and behind." (Rev. 4:6.) According to the punctuation in the verse just quoted, it means that the beasts are in the midst of the throne and round about the throne. It would be impossible for them to be in the midst, and also round about the throne—mercy seat. If they were in the midst of the throne, they would be taking the place of God, the Judge, and His Son, the Lamb. Thus, we conclude that the first clause of the verse is mispunctuated. By omitting the colon the Scripture would read as follows: "And

before the throne there was a sea of glass like unto crystal **and in the midst** of the throne." Thus, it is the sea of glass in the midst, and before the throne; and not the beasts. "The sea of glass" proceeds from the throne, and is a symbol of life eternal in the same manner as the "Lamb" is a symbol of Christ, our Advocate.

The sea is the most extensive body upon the earth; thus it is used to represent eternity. "Clear as crystal" denotes perfection, freedom from sin and defects. In Revelation 15:2, we read: "And I saw as it were a sea of glass mingled with fire." Fire would be the only perfect symbol that could be used to represent life. Therefore, the sea of glass proceeds from God's throne, and represents life eternal, which is the reward of those whose names are in the Lamb's book of life, within the seven seals. "And there shall in nowise enter into it anything that defileth, neither whatsoever worketh abominations, or maketh a lie: but they which are written in the Lamb's book of life." (Rev. 21:27.) In the judgment it is granted to the saints "that had gotten the victory over the beast, and over his image, and over his mark, and over the number of his name," to stand on the sea of glass—life eternal. (Rev. 15:2.)

The arrangement and the scene, as described by John, proves that it is the judgment in session; for it is held in the "Holy of Holies"—typified by the earthly sanctuary and its service, in which Aaron, the high priest, officiated in the seventh month, on the tenth day of the month. It was called the day of atonement—judgment, the cleansing of the sanctuary or purification of the church—the separation of the tares from the wheat. There we behold the Great Judge (God the Father), the Advocate (the Lamb—Jesus Christ the righteous), a jury (the twenty-four elders—clothed with the righteousness of Christ—white robes); a representation of those who are to be judged (the four beasts); the light and truth which they have kept (the seven lamps); the reward which is to be granted to those who are judged (sea of glass); and the book containing the names of all the righteous, beginning with Adam and on to the close of probation—the end of the gospel (seven seals). "And I saw in the right hand of him that sat on the throne a book written within and on the backside, sealed with seven seals." (Rev. 5:1.) Because the book contains the names of all who are sealed with the seal of God (His truth) it is called the book of seals, also the Lamb's book of life.

In the following scripture we behold the entire universe watching with intense interest the affairs of the human family as the scroll unrolls, revealing to them the mystery of God: "And to make all men see what is the fellowship of the mystery, which from the beginning of the world hath been hid in God, who created all things by Jesus Christ." (Eph. 3:9.) Quoting Revelation 5:11-14, "And I beheld, and I heard the voice of many angels round about the throne and the beasts and the elders: and the number of them was ten thousand times ten thousand, and thousands of thousands; Saying with a loud voice, Worthy is the Lamb that was slain, to receive power, and riches, and wisdom, and strength, and honour, and glory, and blessing. And every creature which is in heaven, and on the earth, and under the earth, and such as are in the sea, and all that are in them, heard I saying, Blessing, and honour, and glory, and power, be unto him that sitteth upon the throne, and unto the Lamb for ever and ever. And the four beasts said, Amen. And the four and twenty elders fell down and worshipped him that liveth for ever and ever." The Scripture quoted proves that the entire universe is satisfied with the love of God, and the righteousness of Christ. We repeat verse 13: "And **every** creature which is **in heaven,** and on the **earth,** and **under** the earth, and such as are in the sea, and **all** that are in **them,** heard I saying, Blessing, and honour, and glory, and power, be unto him that sitteth upon the throne, and unto the Lamb for ever and ever."

The Opening of the Book

"And I saw a strong angel proclaiming with a loud voice, Who is worthy to open the book, and to loose the seals thereof? And no man in heaven, nor in earth, neither under the earth, was able to open the book, neither to look thereon. And I wept much, because no man was found worthy to open and to read the book, neither to look thereon. And one of the elders saith unto me, Weep not: behold, the Lion of the tribe of Juda, the Root of David, hath prevailed to open the book, and to loose the seven seals thereof. And I beheld, and, lo, in the midst of the throne and of the four beasts, and in the midst of the elders, stood a Lamb as it had been slain, having seven horns and seven eyes, which are the seven Spirits of God sent forth into all the earth. And he came and took the book out of the right hand of him that sat upon the throne. And when he had taken the book, the four beasts and four and twenty elders fell down before the Lamb, having every one of them harps, and golden vials full of odours, which are the prayers of the saints." (Rev. 5:2-8.)

This scripture reveals that there is not another in the vast universe of God that is worthy, or that can open the book, for "the Lion of the tribe of Juda, the Root of David, has prevailed." Christ acquired the above title by His birth, and by His victory on the cross for those who would believe in Him as the Saviour of the world. He has prevailed by shedding His blood on Calvary; thus none other can open the book, for He alone has died for the human race. This "book" contains the names of the saints, and the "seven seals" comprise, prophetically, the world's history, during which time the saints are sealed. These seven periods of unfulfilled history sealed the book, and the only one that could open it—see into the future—was the "Lamb." The book was "written within and on the backside"—"written within" is the prophetic word of God; "and on the backside," is the historical fulfillment of prophecies. "And all that dwell upon the earth shall worship Him, whose names are not written in the book of life of the Lamb slain from the foundation of the world." (Rev. 13:8.) "Who hath wrought and done it, **Calling the generation from the beginning?'** (Isa. 41:4.)

It is Christ who has prepared the way for this judicial procedure to plead for His people, and to blot out their sins. "In the typical service, only those who had come before God with confession and repentance, and whose sins, through the blood of the sin offering, were transferred to the sanctuary, had a part in the service in the day of atonement. So in the great day of final atonement and investigative judgment, the only cases considered are those of the professed people of God. The judgment of the wicked is a distinct and separate work, and takes place at a later period. 'Judgment must begin at the house of God: and if it first begin at us, what shall be the end of them that obey not the gospel?' As the books of record are opened in the judgment, the lives of all who have believed on Jesus come in review before God. Beginning with those who first lived upon the earth, our Advocate presents the cases of each successive generation, and closes with the living."—"The Great Controversy," pp. 480, 483.

Besides the book in the hand of the judge, there are other books, but this one which no other being in heaven or in earth was worthy to open, save the "Lamb," is the one called "The Lamb's Book of Life." And the Revelator says that those only shall enter the city of God whose names are written in the Lamb's book of life. "'A book of remembrance' is written before God, in which are recorded the good deeds of 'them that feared the Lord, and that thought upon His name.'"—Id., p. 481.

The Seals By Periods—Revelation Six

As the evidence brought forth cannot be questioned that with the book of seals the judgment opened, and as it began with the righteous who lived upon the earth first, and ends with the last, it is positive that the seven seals spread over the entire world's history. Consequently, they include every saint since the world began. The number "seven" bears the same evidence.

As there are seven seals in consecutive order, it is clear that our world's history is divided into seven different periods. The judgment begins with the first and ends with the last. Evidently the first six seals complete the cases of those who were dead preceding the judgment, and while it is in session; but the seventh sealing period, being the last, must concern the living.

There is sufficient scriptural evidence that all the saved in all ages are sealed with the seal of God; for this reason the seven periods are called "seven seals," and the names of those who are sealed are written in the book; consequently, the book is sealed with seven seals. (See John 6:27; Eph. 4:30; 1:13; 2 Tim. 2:19; 2 Cor. 1:22; Rev. 9:4.)

The Meaning of the Horses and Riders

Revelation 6:1-8, "And I saw when the Lamb opened one of the seals, and I heard, as it were the noise of thunder, one of the four beasts saying, Come and see. And I saw, and behold a white horse: and he that sat on him had a bow; and a crown was given unto him: and he went forth conquering, and to conquer. And when he had opened the second seal, I heard the second beast say, Come and see. And there went out another horse that was red: and power was given to him that sat thereon to take peace from the earth, and that they should kill one another: and there was given unto him a great sword. And when he had opened the third seal, I heard the third beast say, Come and see. And I beheld, and lo a black horse; and he that sat on him had a pair of balances in his hand. And I heard a voice in the midst of the four beasts say, A measure of wheat for a penny, and three measures of barley for a penny; and see thou hurt not the oil and the wine. And when he had opened the fourth seal, I heard the voice of the fourth beast say, Come and see. And I looked, and behold a pale horse: and his name that sat on him was Death, and Hell followed with him. And power was given unto them over the fourth part of the earth, to kill with sword, and with hunger, and with death, and with the beasts of the earth.

The horses are symbols of the earth, revealing four great changes since the world began, and the riders depict the human family under these four great variations; thus making a perfect symbol, for we ride upon the earth as we would upon a horse. Had sin not entered within the human family there would have been but one horse. But since sin entered and marred the plan of God for His children, the earth was cursed, and thus a great

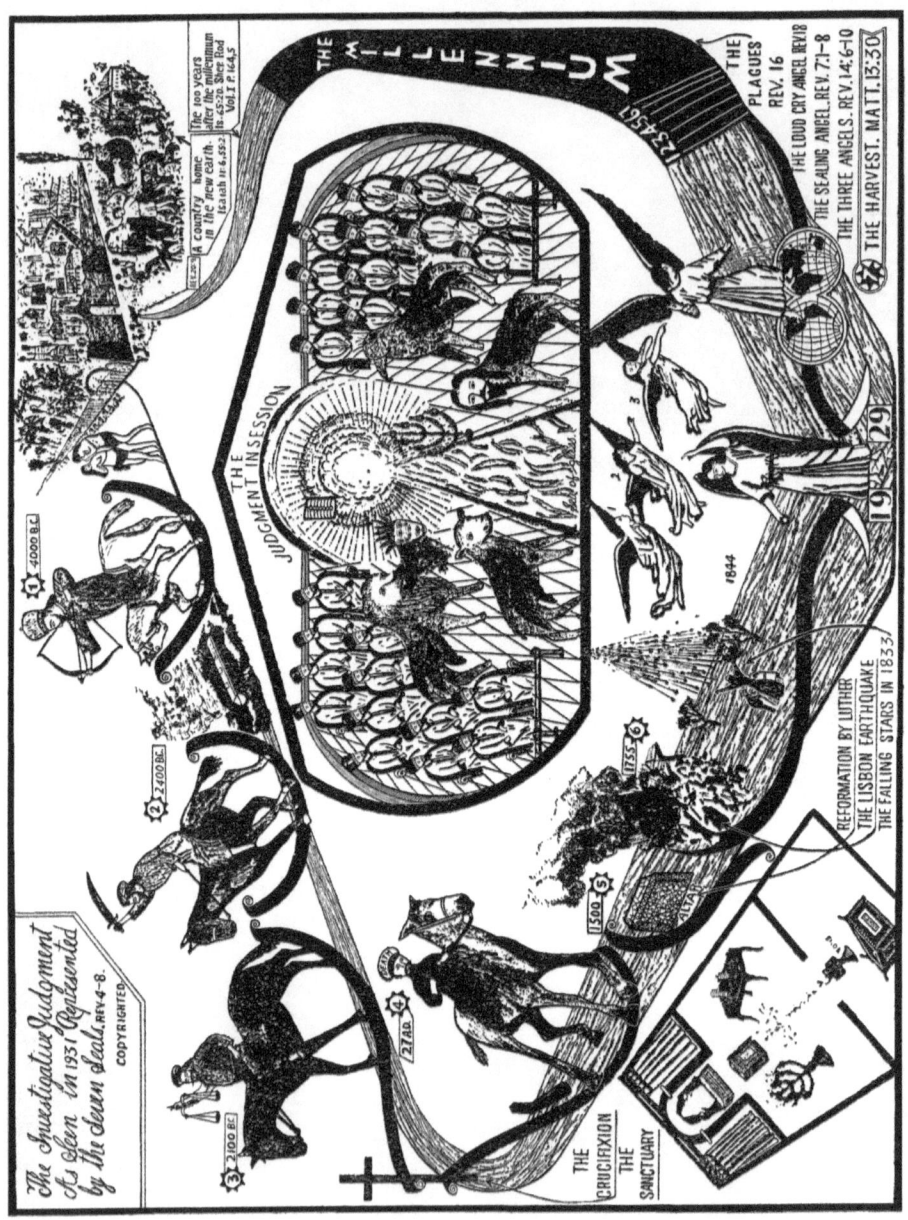

204

change came; and as sin multiplied, curse after curse was added. Therefore, the white horse was succeeded by red, and the red by black, and the black by pale.

The rider on the white horse was given a crown, but after sin entered he lost his crown of kingship and glory. Therefore, the rider on the red horse, instead of having a crown, has a great sword; and to the sword was added a pair of balances, and to the balances, death.

First Seal—White Horse

Revelation 6:2, "And I saw, and behold a white horse: and he that sat on him had a bow; and a crown was given unto him: and he went forth conquering, and to conquer." "White" being a symbol of purity, denotes that the white horse represents the beginning of our world—sinless, as the earth was in her garb of beauty and perfection, with all the wonders on the land and in the sea.

"'And the Lord God planted a garden eastward in Eden;'. . . Everything that God had made was the perfection of beauty, and nothing seemed wanting. . . . In this garden were trees of great variety, many of them laden with fragrant and delicious fruit. There were lovely vines . . . presenting a most graceful appearance, with their branches drooping under their load of tempting fruit, of the richest and most varied hues."—"Patriarchs and Prophets," pp. 46, 47.

The earth with its delicate flowers and carpet of living green, over which the blue heavens spread as its dome, exhibited a natural view of beauty and elegance such as no language can describe. Only the great Master Artist can bring forth such a wonder without flaw.

The First Rider

As the white horse represents the beginning of our earth in her sinless state, the rider can be none other than Adam himself, with whom the judgment began. The crown is a symbol of kingly authority. "And God said, Let us make man in our image, after our likeness: and let them **have dominion** over the fish of the sea, and over the fowl of the air, and over the cattle, and over all the earth, and over every creeping thing that creepeth upon the earth." (Gen. 1:26.) The same is expressed in the words, "And a crown was given **Him.**" Therefore, the Lord set in motion a perfect world, with a king created by the hand of God, and we are the sons of Royalty.

"Behold a white horse: and he that sat on him . . . went forth conquering and to conquer." The symbolical words are the fulfillment of the words spoken by the Creator's lips: "And God blessed them [Adam and Eve], and God said unto them, Be fruitful, and multiply, and replenish the earth, and subdue it." (Gen. 1:28.) It was God's plan to multiply the human family, and to have them subdue the earth. Therefore, Adam went conquering and to conquer. Though sin entered, and death claimed the human family, God's plan has been carried out, and the earth is inhabited. Thus he "went forth conquering and to conquer."

"And I saw, and behold a white horse: and he that sat on him had a **bow**." The bow is an implement used to conquer with (replenish). Therefore, Adam was given a bow (Eve) corresponding with the words: "And the Lord God said, It is not good that man should be alone; I will make him an help meet for him. And the Lord God caused a deep sleep to fall upon Adam, and he slept: and he took one of his ribs, and closed up the flesh instead thereof: And the rib, which the Lord God had taken from man, made he a woman, and brought her unto the man. And Adam said, This is now bone of my bones, and flesh of my flesh: she shall be called Woman, because she was taken out of Man." (Gen. 2:18, 21-23.) "And Adam called his wife's name Eve: because she was the **mother of all living**." (Gen. 3:20.) Thus this sacred institution was originated by the Creator of the universe. "'Marriage is honorable'; it was one of the first gifts of God to man, and it is one of the two institutions that, after the fall, Adam brought with him beyond the gates of Paradise."—"Patriarchs and Prophets," p. 46. Thus Adam conquered (inhabited the earth) with the bow (Eve).

Second Seal—Red Horse

"And when he had opened the second seal, I heard the second beast say, Come and see. And there went out another horse that was red: and power was given to him that sat thereon to take peace from the earth, and that they should kill one another: and there was given unto him a great sword." "And there went out another horse that was red." If the white horse represents the first period, then the red horse must stand for the one that followed. "Red" is the same as scarlet, which is a symbol of sin and condemnation.

After Adam sinned, the earth was cursed, and its perfect beauty marred. Thus the white horse passed away, and a red one took its place. Said God, "Cursed is the ground for thy sake; in sorrow shalt thou eat of it all the days of thy life." But this symbol applies more directly after the flood, for the entire surface of the earth was changed by the deluge. "A third dreadful curse rested upon it in consequence of sin. As the water began to subside, the hills and mountains were surrounded by a vast, turbid sea. . . . The earth presented an appearance of confusion and desolation impossible to describe. The mountains, once so beautiful in their perfect symmetry, had become broken and irregular. Stone, ledges, and ragged rocks were now scattered upon the surface of the earth. In many places, hills and mountains had disappeared, leaving no trace where they once stood; and plains had given place to mountain ranges. These changes were more marked in some places than in others. Where once had been earth's richest treasures of gold, silver, and precious stones, were seen the heaviest marks of the curse. And upon the countries that were not inhabited, and those where there had been the least crime, the curse rested more lightly."—"Patriarchs and Prophets," page 108. Thus the red horse represents the period after the flood.

The Rider on the Red Horse

"And power was given to him that sat thereon to take peace from the earth, and that they should kill one another: and there was given unto him a great sword." As soon as sin entered the human family, it multiplied fast, like a fruitful tree. What a vast difference between the first rider and the second. No longer has he a crown on his head, but instead, a great sword in his hand. Righteous Abel was the first to fall under its edge. But as the symbol has a direct application after the flood, it finds its perfect fulfillment in the tower of Babel.

As the earth's inhabitants began to multiply after the deluge, sin did likewise, and though they had to believe Noah's prediction of the flood, they mistrusted his predictions after the flood. "And God blessed Noah and his sons, and said unto them, Be fruitful, and multiply, and replenish the earth . . . And I will establish my covenant with you; neither shall all flesh be cut off any more by the waters of a flood; **neither shall there any more be a flood** to destroy the earth. And God said, This is a token of the covenant which I make between me and you and every living creature that is with you, for perpetual generations; I do set my bow in the cloud, and it shall be for a token of a covenant between me and the earth." (Gen. 9:1, 11, 13.)

Their disbelief in the word of God spoken by Noah, impelled them, in defiance of God, to engage in building the tower of Babel as a defense against a second flood. (See Gen. 11:3, 4.) God's displeasure over their ignorance of His power, and disbelief in His word, caused Him to destroy the tower and confound their language. "So the Lord scattered them abroad from thence upon the face of all the earth. . . . Therefore is the name of it called Babel; because the Lord did there confound the language of all the earth: and from thence did the Lord scatter them abroad upon the face of all the earth." (Gen. 11:8, 9.) The confusion at the tower of Babel gave birth to the races and languages. As they parted in separated tribes, the neighboring ones began to quarrel one with another. As they grew to nations, their quarrels turned into wars.

Thus the period under the "red horse" gave birth to the existing unrest among the nations. Therefore, power was given him "to take peace from the earth, and that they should kill one another: and there was given unto him a great sword." Thus the evidence proves that the red horse represents the period after the flood; and the rider, its inhabitants, corresponding with the "lion" (Babylon), and later with the "bear" (Medo-Persia). At the commencement of the Persian government, the previous quarrels broke out in bloody wars, thus the words by the ribs in the mouth of the bear, "Arise, devour much flesh" (Dan. 7:5) met a perfect fulfillment. Therefore, peace was taken from the earth by the great sword in the hand of the rider on the red horse.

The Third Seal—Black Horse

Revelation 6:5, "And when he had opened the third seal, I heard the third beast say, Come and see. And I beheld, and lo a black horse; and he that sat on him had a pair of balances in his hand." The white horse is a symbol of purity, being submerged by the red which is a symbol of sin, and the red being succeeded by the "black" denotes spiritual darkness, or mental blindness. Therefore, the color (black), signifies misconception of God's personality.

As man plunged into sin, his moral and spiritual powers were weakened to the extent that his vision of God's invisible presence was blotted out. The sinner's spiritual corruption and immoral inclinations demanded a visible deity to redeem him from everlasting ruin. Thus the worship of the unseen and omnipresent One was forsaken, and the adoration of idols substituted. This state of spiritual darkness had overwhelmed the inhabitants of our world in the days of Abram, only about three hundred years after the flood.

As there is no record of idol-worship before that time, the black horse must represent the period from that date to the Christian era. Evidently Israel after the flesh comes under the period of the black horse. In each instance, when the world reached the climax of Satanic deception, God, in His mercy and love for sinners, was compelled to make certain moves to preserve human probation. At that time He could not destroy the sinners from the face of the earth and yet keep His promise to Noah. To assure the preservation of the covenant He called out Abram from idolatry to the worship of the true God, starting out a separate nation by one family similar to that of Adam and Noah; and the result was that the twelve Patriarchs of Israel came forth, of whom God made one great nation.

The Balances in the Rider's Hand

Verse 5, last part, "And I beheld, and lo a black horse; and he that sat on him had a pair of balances in his hand." As the white horse rider's crown and bow refer to his privileges, and the great sword in the hand of the red horse's rider shows his prerogative, just so the balances in the hand of the rider of the black horse must have reference to the people and their characteristics, in that period.

Balances are used for commercial purposes. Therefore, the symbol denotes the first introduction of a commercialistic idea. Prior to, or about Abram's time, commercial trading between nations was unknown. But in the period represented by the black horse this idea was born. The Phenician-Semitic race are credited with the ever-increasing discovery, with Sidon and Tyre as their chief commercial centers. "Who hath taken this counsel against Tyre, the crowning city, whose **merchants** are princes, whose **traffickers** are the **honourable of the earth?**" (Isa. 23:8.)

"We must mention another 'Little' people of this Semitic race whose influence upon the world has been more potent than that of Egypt, or Babylonia— the Phenicians. Their state also was one of the smallest in antiquity. . . . Their two chief cities were Sidon, and, a short distance away, the queen of Phenician cities, Tyre. But in time they were to spread their trade-colonies all over the Mediterranean, and up into other lands, ever on the search for **new** Trade areas and commercial centers. They were the **bees of the ancient world** carrying the pollen of culture wherever they went. The necessities of trade and commerce drove them to **perfect** the **alphabet.** And from them the western world obtained it. In some respects they were unique in the ancient world, and this distinction was interred with them. For they were not interested in conquests, save **commercial;** and they did not mind paying tribute to military powers, as long as those powers did not interfere with their rights of trade. They had a Greek-like capacity for assimilating to themselves whatever Egypt, Babylonia, Assyria, Persia or any other phase of civilization offered; but their chief genius lay in invention, technical skill, **business activity, and in industry.** In the working of iron, gold, ivory, glass, and purple dyes they stood in the ancient world without a peer.

"We recall from the Old Testament the story of David's wish to build a temple worthy of the worship of the God of Israel. It is intimated to him that the work had better be left to his son Solomon. So we see Solomon making a treaty with Hiram, King of Tyre. Hiram was to furnish cedar and cypress-wood, together with carpenters and stone-masons for the building, and to ship the materials on rafts to Juda. Much of the external splendor of Solomon's brilliant and showy rule should be credited to the technical skill of these **master-craftsmen** of Phenicia. Through their cities flowed the highly profitable trade of Arabia and the East: and their manufacturers were kept busy turning out their products of metals, glass, and purple. By sea and by land they traveled everywhere—missionaries of trade—the **master-bargainers of the Old World.** At the time of Homer the Phenicians were credited with being pirates—robbers—and merchants only by virtue of necessity. Possibly nothing worse than legend, but we are told they brought their trinkets, beads, and cheap baubles, which they sold at high prices and kidnaped boys and girls to be sold in the eastern markets as a side-line."—"Essential Knowledge,—The Phenicians," Vol. 1, pp. 69, 70.

Hurt Not the Oil and the Wine

Verse 6, "And I heard a voice in the midst of the four beasts say, . . . and see thou hurt not the oil and the wine." According to Revelation 4:6, the four beasts are round about the throne. Therefore, the throne is in the midst of the beasts. Says John: "And I heard a voice in the midst of the four beasts." One of the things he heard was, "See thou hurt not the oil and the wine." Therefore, whatever is meant by the symbol, it is not of men, but of God, for it was He who commanded, "Hurt not the oil and the wine."

It is an accepted fact by nearly all Bible students that "oil" is used by the Scriptures as a symbol of the Holy Spirit, as in Psalms 45:7; Isaiah 61:1-3; Zechariah 4:12. "Wine" is used as a symbol of the blood of Christ, and as the "life is in the blood," the wine denotes life eternal, found only in "the Lamb of God which taketh away the sins of the world." Said Jesus, "The words that I speak unto you they are spirit and they are life"—"oil" and "wine." The words in the Bible are the "Spirit" and the "Life." Therefore, the command, "hurt not the oil and the wine," has reference to the Bible—the Spirit and the Life. But why was the command given to this particular rider? Why not to one of the others? The only answer that can be given is that the period under the black horse and his rider gave birth to the Bible. The command was obeyed and the Bible came. In time of idolatry and dense spiritual darkness, God, in His never failing love, blessed the human family by the gift of His written Word for a Light to the world. The voice from the throne "Hurt not the oil and the wine," is the voice in the Bible and the words of Jehovah. The remaining part of verse six will be explained in another study.

The Fourth Seal

Verses 7 and 8: "And when he had opened the fourth seal, I heard the voice of the fourth beast say, Come and see. And I looked, and behold a pale horse: and his name that sat on him was Death, and Hell followed with him. And power was given unto them over the fourth part of the earth, to kill with sword, and with hunger, and with death, and with the beasts of the earth."

As the Old Testament time closes with the third seal, the New begins with the opening of the fourth seal. Consequently, the pale horse and the non-descript beast of Daniel 7:7, 8, occupy the same period. Evidently one beast must resemble the other or the symbol would not be perfect. Rome was symbolized by a non-descript beast because its government was a mixture of civil and religious laws, with Pagan and Christian doctrines. Therefore, it was beyond description as previously explained. The pale horse has the same meaning, for his complexion is faint, wanting, not having a specific or definite color. Pale—non-descript.

The rider represents the ruling heads of government. His name is Death. "Death and Hell [hades or grave as in the revised version] followed with him." This is a perfect description of the unjust, persecuting Roman power, corresponding to the beast as Daniel saw it: "It devoured and brake in pieces, and stamped the residue with the feet of it." In the opening of the fourth seal, Rome, under the symbol of the non-descript beast in both his stages (imperial and papal) persecuted its subjects for their religious belief, and millions lost their lives. Therefore, "Death and Hell [grave] followed with him."

"And power was given unto **them** over the fourth part of the earth: to kill with sword, and with hunger, and with death, and with the beasts of the earth." Here is given the exact time in which imperial and papal Rome would hold sway over the earth, to kill the followers of Christ by means of these various forms of cruelty. Again, note the perfection of the Scriptures using the pronoun "them," meaning both imperial and papal Rome, also civil and religious authority. Note the first part of the sentence. "And power was given unto them over the **fourth part of the earth.**" This present world, from creation to its end or the beginning of the millennium, shall number 6,000 years. The pale horse rider was to have power over a fourth part of the earth. We divide 6,000 into four equal parts, and we have 1500 years. Therefore, the cruel and unjust persecution by Rome was to lose its power at the end of the 1500 years or the fourth part. That is exactly what happened. At that time Martin Luther arose against the papacy and inflicted the deadly wound, by the instrument of truth—"The just shall live by faith." And the result was that Protestantism came on the stage of action in opposition to the papacy. Up to the beginning of the fifteenth century the papacy reigned supreme as a king of kings, by the iron arm of the state in the garb of so-called spiritual authority; but at that time her power was broken.

From the crucifixion of Christ to the "Augsburg Confession," a document compiled by Luther, constituted a period of 1500 years. This document was signed by the protestant states and adopted as their creed, and was a protest against the pope. So at the time appointed, their power, Pagan and Papal, was broken. (See "The Shepherd's Rod," Vol. 1, pp. 209-222.) Thus perfectly fulfilling the symbolical prophecy that "power was given unto them over the fourth part of the earth." Here is a truth that overthrows the idea that the earth has been in existence for longer than 6,000 years. It also proves the application of the seals to be absolutely correct.

Only four horses are introduced instead of seven, or, a horse to a seal. Four is another Biblical number to denote that the representation by the horses is world wide (four points of the compass). (See page 54). While the number of horses represent the universal effect of the curse of sin, the number of seals denote the completeness of the gospel and the sealing of the saints.

The Fifth Seal

Verses 9-11: "And when he had opened the fifth seal, I saw under the altar the souls of them that were slain for the word of God, and for the testimony which they held: And they cried with a loud voice, saying, How long, O Lord, holy and true, dost thou not judge and avenge our blood on them that dwell on the earth? And white robes were given unto every one of them; and it was said unto them, that they should rest yet a little season, until their fellowservants also and their brethren, that should be killed as they were, should be fulfilled."

The closing of one seal and the opening of the other consumed a period of thirty years. Thus the fourth seal closed in 1530 A.D., up to which period the pale horse rider was to have **power.** Therefore, the reformation by Luther falls under the fifth seal; and after it was opened John was shown, "the souls of them that were slain for the word of God," under the fourth seal. "And it was said unto them [the slain], that they should rest yet a little season, until their fellowservants also and their brethren, that should be killed as they were, should be fulfilled." The words show that although despotism had lost its power, the persecution had not altogether ceased, for their fellow servants and their brethren were yet to be killed under the fifth seal. Says John: "And when he had opened the fifth seal, I saw under the **altar** the souls of them that were slain for the word of God." Therefore, it was the Christians who were slain.

The altar is a symbol as well; thus it also must be considered. Altar is used for worship; and as the souls of them that were slain for the **Word of God** were under it, we know that it was an altar of true worship—the reformation by Luther.

The Sixth Seal

Verses 12, 13: "And I beheld when he had opened the sixth seal, and, lo, there was a great earthquake; and the sun became black as sackcloth of hair, and the moon became as blood; and the stars of heaven fell unto the earth, even as a fig tree casteth her untimely figs, when she is shaken of a mighty wind."

The sixth seal opens with the Lisbon earthquake of November 1, 1755. Following the earthquake the sun was darkened, May 19, 1780, and the moon appeared as blood the following night. The "falling of the stars," has reference to the great meteoric shower of November 13, 1833. Jesus, looking forward to the fulfillment of these signs, said: "Immediately **after** the tribulation of those days shall the sun be darkened, and the moon shall not give her light, and the stars shall fall from heaven, and the powers of the heavens shall be shaken." (Matt. 24:29.) Therefore, under the sixth seal came the signs of the time of the end—the great earthquake in 1755, the dark day in 1780, the falling stars in 1833, and the beginning of the judgment in 1844.

On verses 14-17, comment is found in "Testimonies for the Church," Vol. 9, pp. 267, 268: "'And the heaven departed as a scroll when it is rolled together; and every mountain and island were removed out of their places. And the kings of the earth, and the great men, and the rich men, and the chief captains, and the mighty men, and every bond man, and every free man, hid themselves in the dens and in the rocks of the mountains; and said to the mountains and rocks, Fall on us, and hide us from the face of Him that sitteth on the throne, and from the wrath of the Lamb: for the great day of His wrath is come; and who shall be able to stand? (Rev. 6:12-17.) After this I beheld, and, lo, a great multitude, which no man could number, of all nations, and kindreds, and people, and tongues, stood before the throne, and before the Lamb, clothed with white robes, and palms in their hands; and cried with a loud voice, saying, Salvation to our God which sitteth upon the throne, and unto the Lamb. . . . These are they which came out of great tribulation, and have washed their robes and made them white in the blood of the Lamb.' . . . Revelation 7:9-17."

According to the following testimony, Revelation 6:12-17, has a double application; and it is clear that these verses also refer to the time of the purification of God's church, for the servant of the Lord says, "In these scriptures two parties are brought to view. One party permitted themselves to be deceived, and took sides with those with whom the Lord has a controversy. They misinterpreted the message sent them, and clothed themselves in robes of self-righteousness. Sin was not sinful in their eyes. They taught falsehood as truth, and by them many souls were led astray."—Id., page 268. It is inferred, from the testimony just quoted, that they have taught falsehood. We ask the reader to consider what has been taught by the symbols found in the books of Daniel and Revelation. For instance, consider the truth brought to view here, as compared with what has been taught for some years.

The Seventh Seal, Revelation 8:1-5

Verses 1, 3-5: "And when he had opened the seventh seal, there was silence in heaven about the space of half an hour. And another angel came and stood at the altar, having a golden censer; and there was given unto him much incense, that he should offer it with the prayers of all saints upon the golden altar which was before the throne. And the smoke of the incense, which came with the prayers of the saints, ascended up before God out of the angel's hand. And the angel took the censer, and filled it with fire of the altar, and cast it into the earth: and there were voices, and thunderings, and lightnings, and an earthquake."

We have omitted the second verse, for it has reference to the seven trumpets. The **silence** in heaven for **about half an hour** cannot be the second coming of Christ, as some have thought, for afterward the angel with the golden censer and incense, offered the prayers for the saints from the golden altar. The altar is in the holy place, just opposite the throne that is in the most holy. The two apartments were separated by a vail. In the day of atonement, the vail or door of the earthly tabernacle was opened and the high priest went in. But let it be remembered that the door (vail) was left open while the high priest officiated. Thus the two apartments became one. For this reason the congregation were not permitted in the holy place on that day, as they were at other times, for the vail being lifted, the holy place also became most holy. So while the door to the most holy was open, the entrance to the holy was closed. Therefore, the high priest alone used both apartments on the day of atonement. (See Lev. 16:17.) Thus the golden altar before the throne, from which the angel offered the prayers of the saints, was, and is, used in both periods—before, and in the time of the judgment. As the entire judicial tribunal (Judge, Advocate, Elders, etc.) were in the temple after the seventh seal had been opened, it is evident that the judgment was in progress, and probation had not closed at the time of the "silence." For after the judgment has ceased and probation closed, no man can enter the temple. (See Rev. 15:8.)

Had the "silence" of "half an hour" pointed to the coming of Christ, at which time He takes His saints with Him, there would be no necessity for the angel to offer their prayers. Furthermore, it would be unnecessary to "cast" fire, which is the Spirit of God, from the golden altar to the earth. Again, if the opening of the seventh seal means the coming of Christ, then only those under the six seals would have been considered in the judgment, and there could be no seventh seal, which would show lack of perfection and completeness of the judgment, and of the gospel. It would also be contrary to the number of seals on the book. As the six seals have reference to six periods in which the saints were sealed, the seventh must also apply to a sealing period; otherwise it cannot be called, seventh "seal."

Now let us consider the truth as taught by the last seal. Note carefully the order of each act. The seal is opened, and silence follows, for it reads: "and when he **had** opened the seventh seal there was silence." The Revised Version, Weymouth, the Greek, and the Bulgarian Bibles read the same way. The silence was followed by the angel coming to the altar with the censer, after he offered the prayers of the saints. And then he filled the censer with fire, and cast the fire to the earth, and again the voices, and thunderings, and lightnings, and an earthquake. This is the exact order of each event.

What made the silence? As the judgment opened, John states: "And out of the throne proceeded lightnings, and thunderings and voices;" and the four beasts "rest not day and night, saying, Holy, Holy, Holy, Lord God Almighty." (Rev. 4:5, 8.) The voices are continuous day and night while the judgment is going on. But sometime after the seventh seal was opened these voices were silenced for about half an hour. After the angel offered the prayers of the saints, and cast the fire upon the earth, the voices resumed. "And there were voices, and thunderings, and lightnings, and an earthquake." Evidently the judgment, for some reason, had stopped, and half an hour later it resumed. It cannot be otherwise, for, if the judgment was going on, and the beasts and the elders kept silent, it would indicate that there was something wrong—something to which they could not say "amen" and praise God. Therefore, the only proper conclusion is, that for some reason the judgment retired for half an hour.

What made the interruption and brought about the change? Let us first determine the length of the prophetic half hour's time. A day in prophetic time stands for a year. (Ezek. 4:6.) One hour is a twenty-fourth part of a prophetic year, and figuring thirty days to a month, it would be about two weeks. Half an hour would be half of two weeks; therefore, seven literal days. Seven days were used for purification. (See Ex. 29:35, 37; Lev. 12:2; 13:4, 5; 1, 9, 11, 12, 14, 15, 21, etc.) From these references we conclude that the "half an hour" or seven days stand for the **purification** of the church, pointing forward to the fulfillment of Malachi 3:1-6. But we have a more definite proof, which will clear all doubts.

In observance of the Passover, the Lord commanded Israel to celebrate that occasion seven days. (See Lev. 23:5-8.) Surely no one would say that God commanded His people to commemorate that event seven days with no object in view. Israel after the flesh going into Egypt, then out of Egypt to Mount Sinai, the passover in Egypt on the night when the death angel smote the first born of man and beast at the departure of Israel, are types of the church at the present time—the church going out of Egypt—worldliness, the purification of the church, the separation of the tares from the wheat—the fulfillment of Ezekiel 9. (A complete explanation of the subject is given in "The Shepherd's Rod," Vol. 1, pp. 64-113; see also chart on page 224.) The Spirit of Prophecy bears witness of this by the following statement: "The Passover was to be both commemorative and typical, not only pointing back to the deliverance from Egypt, but forward to the greater deliverance which Christ was to accomplish in **freeing** His people from the **bondage** of sin."—"Patriarchs and Prophets," p. 277.

Thus the silence of half an hour points forward to this great event for the church of God. Its fulfillment would bring us to the time of the harvest, or as it is called, the Loud Cry of the Third Angel's Message of Revelation 18—the last message for the world. Thus, while the five men with the slaughter weapons are taking away those represented by the tares within the church, there will be silence in heaven for about half an hour (seven days), after which the judgment will commence again for those who shall be sealed in the time of the great harvest, which is the end of the world. Said Jesus: "Let both grow together until the harvest: and in the time of harvest I will say to the reapers, Gather ye together first the tares, and bind them in bundles to burn them: but gather the wheat into my barn"—the church. (Matt. 13:30.)

They who are to be sealed at that time were seen by John as a great multitude with palms in their hands. (See Rev. 7:9.) Hence the scroll has made a turn, and the sealing for those who shall be judged while living, has begun. As we stated before, the passover night in Egypt is a type of the purification of the church, separating the tares from the wheat. The crossing of the Red Sea by the Israelites pointed forward to the fulfillment of Isaiah 63. (See "The Shepherd's Rod," Vol. 1, pp. 96-103.)

Therefore, the prophet declares the words of the Lord: "For the day of vengeance is in mine heart, and the year of my redeemed is **come.**" (Isa. 63:4.) We quote verses 1-3, also 17, 18: "Who is this that cometh from Edom, with dyed garments from Bozrah? this that is glorious in his apparel, travelling in the greatness of his strength? I that speak in righteousness, mighty to save. Wherefore art thou red in thine apparel, and thy garments like him that treadeth in the winefat? I have trodden the winepress alone; and of the people there was none with me: for I will tread them in mine anger, and trample them in my fury; and their blood shall be sprinkled upon my garments, and I will stain all my raiment. . . . . O Lord, why hast thou made us to err from thy ways, and hardened our heart from thy fear? Return for thy servant's sake, the tribes of thine inheritance. The people of thy holiness have possessed it but a little while: our adversaries have trodden down thy sanctuary."

The prophet saw Christ himself returning from the slaughter of the Edomites— the class who were deceiving God's people in the church, the tares, or adversaries who had trodden down His sanctuary. "Bozrah" means "sheepfold"—the church. He saw His garments stained with the blood of the tares, in delivering His people from their hands. The prophet asked: "Wherefore art thou red in thine apparel, and thy garments like him that treadeth the winefat?" The purification of the church makes it necessary for Christ to leave the place of judgment and descend to deliver His redeemed (the 144,000), and this is what causes the judgment to cease, and the voices to be silenced for about half an hour—seven days. The Spirit of Prophecy bears witness of the same. "The Lord Jesus shall rise up from His mediatorial work in the heavenly sanctuary, and shall clothe himself with the garments of vengeance, and surprise them at their unholy feast; and they will find themselves unprepared for the marriage supper of the Lamb."—"Testimonies for the Church," Vol. 5, p. 690. Peter, looking forward to the purification of God's church, and the commencement of the judgment for the living, says: "For the time is come that judgment must begin at the house of God: and if it first begin at us, what shall be the end of them that obey not the gospel of God?" (1 Peter 4:17.)

Had the church as a body, or at least the leaders of the Seventh-day Adventist denomination accepted the message of reform as presented to them in "The Shepherd's Rod," Vol. 1, there would be no necessity for that class to fall by the figure of the five men with the slaughter weapons. It is the reception or rejection of the message that will fix the destiny of the two classes as described in the following testimony: "I asked the meaning of the shaking I had seen, and was shown that it would be caused by the straight testimony called forth by the counsel of the **true witness to the Laodiceans.** This will have its effect upon the heart of the receiver, and will lead him to exalt the standard and pour forth the straight truth. Some will not bear this straight testimony. They will **rise up against it,** and this is what will **cause a shaking** among God's people."—"Early Writings," p. 270.

In the earthly sanctuary, the high priest entered the most holy apartment once a year, and on that particular day every Israelite was to confess his sin. He who neglected to comply with the divine requirements was cut off from his people. (See Lev. 23:29, 30.) Thus the day of anti-typical atonement, judgment, or cleansing of the sanctuary, as set forth in Daniel 8:14, is a day of purification for the camp of Israel, the church—putting away sin and sinners. The earthly sanctuary was a figure of the heavenly. (See Heb. 9:23, 24.) It was instituted with its ceremonial system to point forward to the work of Christ, our High Priest in the heavenly sanctuary during the anti-typical period—New Testament time. As the sanctuary with all its services, was a figure or type of the true, heavenly, under the administration of Christ, so the typical day of atonement must point out the truth in the anti-typical period—our time.

While the judgment for the living is in progress, every sin must be confessed and put away. He who would neglect this great privilege, will find himself involved in everlasting ruin—cut off from among His people. Ignoring this most vital subject would not profit us in the least.

Reformation in View

The great reformation in view, vividly represented by the angel at the golden altar with the prayers of the saints, and the casting of the fire from the altar to the earth, is foretold, also, in the following testimony: "In visions of the night representations passed before me of a great reformatory movement among God's people. Many were praising God. The sick were healed, and other miracles were wrought. A spirit of intercession was seen; even as was manifested before the great day of Pentecost. Hundreds and thousands were seen visiting families, and opening before them the word of God. Hearts were convicted by the power of the Holy Spirit, and a spirit of genuine conversion was manifest. On every side doors were thrown open to the proclamation of the truth. The world seemed to be lightened with the heavenly influence. Great blessings were received by the true and humble people of God."—"Testimonies for the Church," Vol. 9, p. 126.

My brethren, the Lord is speaking to us. Shall we not heed His voice? Shall we not trim our lamps and act like men who look for their Lord to come? "The time is one that calls for light bearing, and for action." Awake, I beseech you, from the sleep of death. Let not the last day find you destitute of heavenly treasure.

Are all the living judged and sealed under the seventh seal? Or have some been considered before its opening? To answer this question we quote Revelation 8:3, "And another angel came and stood at the altar, having a golden censer; and there was given unto him much incense, that he should offer it with the prayers of all saints upon the golden altar which was before the throne." Note, the prayer is offered for all saints. No one, knowing God's truth, would dare pray for the dead, for it is abomination in God's sight; much less would an angel commit such sin.

The Psalmist declares that prayers for the dead are the invention of the heathen, "They joined themselves also unto Baalpeor, and ate the **sacrifices** of the dead. Thus they provoked him to anger with their inventions: and the plague brake in upon them." (Psa. 106:28, 29.) "The dead praise not the Lord, neither any that go down into silence." (Psa. 115:17.) If the dead praise not God, how can an angel offer a prayer for them before God?

The phrase, "**all** saints," has reference to all the living who are to be judged. Evidently this is done under the seventh seal. If **"all,"** then it is definite that **all** the living saints are counted under the seventh seal. Thus, with the opening of the last seal, commences the judgment for all the living saints. Let nothing confuse you on this point. If we say the prayers of **all** saints had some connection with the dead, then they should have been offered at the commencement of the judgment—the opening of the first seal, for after the judgment the prayers cannot profit them.

Note the words at the opening of the judgment for the dead in 1844: "And when he had **taken the book,** the four beasts and four and twenty elders fell down before the Lamb, having every one of them harps, and **golden vials full of odours, which are the prayers of saints.**" (Rev. 5:8.) Mark that no angel offered a prayer, but the prayers of the saints were presented by the beasts and elders through praise by harps, and **golden vials full of odours;** that is, there was no prayer offered for the dead, but their prayers which they had prayed, being recorded while they were yet alive, were presented before the throne. The 144,000 are sealed before the silence "of half an hour,' or at the opening of the seal, but they are judged in the period of the seventh seal, for the prayer was for **"all"** saints—the living.

Is there any way whereby we can determine the time of the opening of the seal, and the commencement of the judgment for the living? If God so faithfully revealed to the living the commencement of the judgment for the dead, it cannot be possible that He would keep secret the time of the judgment for the living. If He did, we would have no present truth in the time of the last seal; neither could there be justice in such secrecy, nor could such judgment be legal. Therefore, a revelation of the judgment for the living, is of as great importance as the revelation of the gospel itself. For the judgment (blotting out the sins) is the crowning act in the gospel of Christ. Thus we conclude that when the seal is opened, and the judgment for the living begins, we must know it. The day of atonement in its type proves the same, for the Israelites were well informed of the event, their duty, and the consequence.

The date of that most glorious event for the righteous, but exceeding solemn for the wicked, will be made known at the fulfillment of the following verse: "And the angel took the censer, and filled it with fire of the altar, and cast it into the earth: and there were voices, and thunderings, and lightnings and an **earthquake.**" (Rev. 8:5.) The casting of the fire from the altar into the earth is the outpouring of the Spirit of God. We have stated before that the book of Revelation is a revealing of prophecies, and not a prophecy of itself. Therefore, we find the prediction of this glorious event in Joel 2:28, 29. The "voices, and thunderings, and lightnings," denote the opening of the judgment for the living, as they also denote the opening of the judgment for the dead. (See Rev. 4:5.) The earthquake will be the sign of the event.

Summary of Commencement and Termination of Seals

The first seal covers the entire period from Adam to the flood; the second, from the flood to Abraham; the third, from Abraham to Christ; the fourth, from Christ to 1500 A.D.; the fifth, from 1500 A.D. to 1755 A.D.; the sixth, from 1755 A.D. to the fulfillment of Ezekiel 9; the seventh, to the close of probation.

However, the seals, in one sense of the word, do not close. They continue and overlap each other. For instance, the inhabitants of the earth are still multiplying (Adam—"conquering and to conquer"); the wars among the nations are ever on the increase, and peace has departed from the earth. Thus, the "sword" is still in the rider's hand. Commercialism is ever growing (the "balances"), and persecution has not ceased, but is to revive, and to bring about a trouble such as never was, as described by Daniel the prophet. (Dan. 12:1.) The signs of the times under the close of the sixth seal are speaking louder and louder. But shortly after the close of the seventh seal, everything upon earth shall cease for a thousand years.

WHEAT AND BARLEY EACH FOR A PENNY

In our study of the "Seven Seals" we reserved for future explanation the following scripture: "And I heard a voice in the midst of the four beasts say, A measure of wheat for a penny, and three measures of barley for a penny." (Rev. 6:6.) Again we turn the reader's attention to the fact that the voice came from the throne. (See chapter 5, verse 11.) Therefore, the price of the cereals is fixed by the Great Judge.

There must be something of great importance in these symbols, for the Great Jehovah Himself is speaking. What could it be? Weymouth's translation reads as follows: "A whole **days wage** for a loaf of bread, a whole **days wage** for three barley cakes." Weymouth translates the penny as a day's wage. We believe the words of Jesus justify this: "For the kingdom of heaven is like unto a man that is an householder, which went out early in the morning to hire labourers into his vineyard. And when he had agreed with the labourers for a **penny a day,** he sent them into his vineyard." (Matt. 20:1, 2.) The penny is the fixed days wage by the householder of the vineyard.

Note that the barley is but one third the price of the wheat; in other words, one goes into the field and gathers only one measure of wheat and receives a full day's pay, but the other who works all day gathers three measures of barley, and receives no more than a day's wage—"a penny." The symbols have a very close connection with the parable given by Christ. Therefore, let the reader concentrate on the subject, for here is a truth worth our earnest attention.

"And he went out about the third hour, and saw others standing idle in the market place, And said unto them; Go ye also into the vineyard, and whatsoever is right I will give you. And they went their way. And again he went out about the sixth and ninth hour, and did likewise. And about the eleventh hour he went out, and found others standing idle, and saith unto them, Why stand ye here all the day idle? They say unto him, Because no man hath hired us. He said unto them, Go ye also into the vineyard; and whatsoever is right, that shall ye receive." (Matt. 20:3-7.)

The "householder" in the parable has reference to God the Father, for the parable is to reveal the kingdom of heaven.

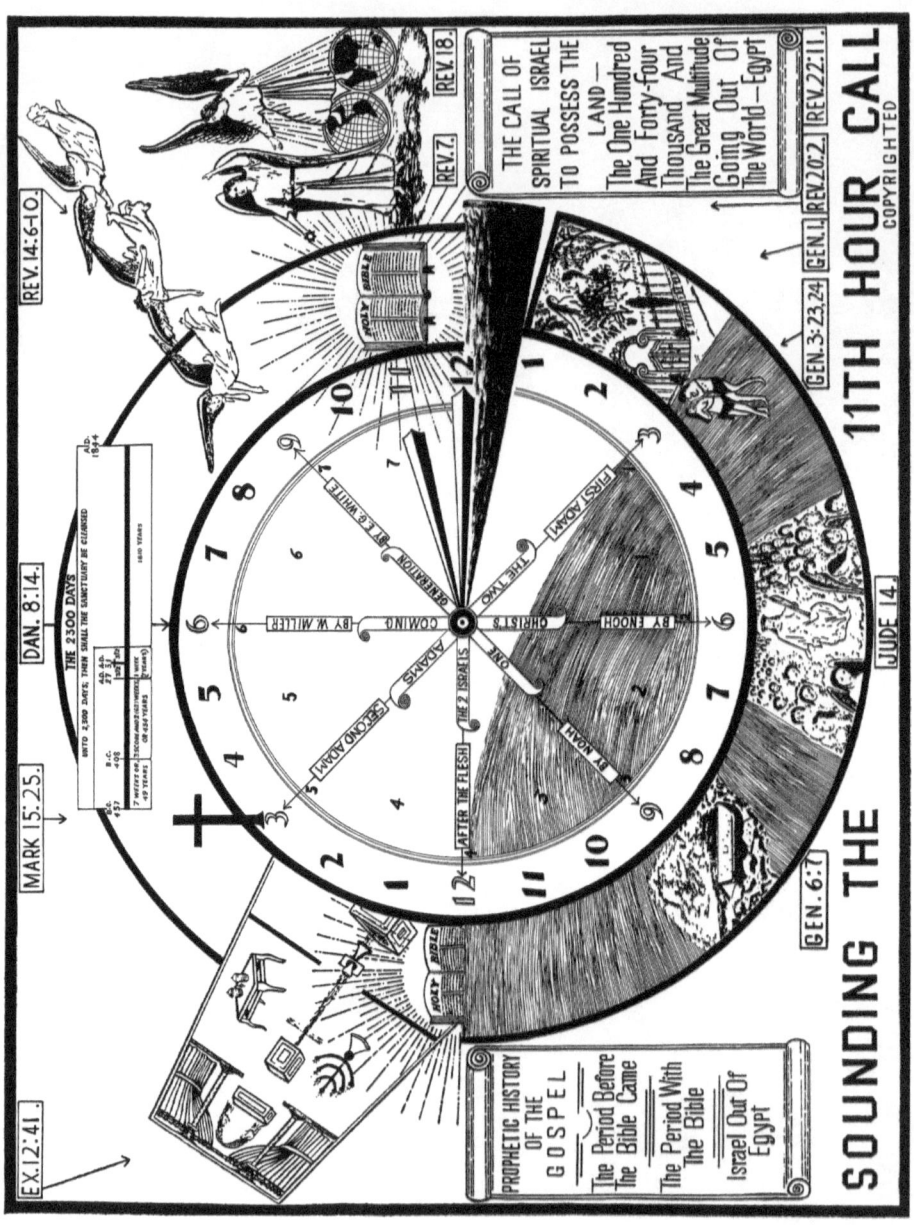

SOUNDING THE 11TH HOUR CALL

224

Therefore, the vineyard is the world and those sent to labor in it are the church. The parable cannot refer to one literal day of twelve hours, into which God has made **five calls** for laborers in the vineyard (world); for there is no record where God raised five church organizations in one day, and had them operating all at the same time. Therefore, the calls in the parable must extend over a period of world history in connection with the church, and that period Jesus allegorically compares to a twelve-hour day into which He hired laborers on five different occasions. If we can locate the time to which each one of these calls refer, then we shall fully comprehend the lesson and the time in which we are living. We shall endeavor to prove that the parable has reference to the "wheat and barley," each for a "penny."

Note that the householder **bargained** only with those he hired first. Also, note that they went to work in the **morning**. He hired the laborers at five intervals. Four of them were **three hours** apart; but the fifth and last call was only **two hours** later than the fourth which was at the eleventh hour—just **one hour** before sunset.

The Ancient Time Clock

Fearing that some may not understand the ancient time clock, we feel a brief explanation may be necessary. To make it more comprehensive we call the reader's attention to the chart, page 22. In the days of Christ, and even now in some countries, time is regulated by sunset at twelve o'clock. Near the equator, where the days and nights are continually equal, the sun sets at twelve and rises at twelve. Therefore, six o'clock would be noon hour in the light part, according to the chart, and at six o'clock in the dark part, would be midnight. This is the kind of time Jesus used in the parable.

Therefore, the first call to the ones with whom the householder agreed for a penny a day, would have been at twelve o'clock A. M.—sunrise. The second call, at the "third hour," is just three hours after sunrise. The third call, at the "sixth hour," would be at noonday. The fourth interval, at "ninth hour," would be three hours after the noon hour, or three o'clock by modern time. The fifth call, two hours later, at the "eleventh hour," would be five o'clock according to present time, and just an hour before sunset.

With the previous explanation of Revelation 6:6, ("A measure of wheat for a penny and three measures of barley for a penny"), we shall endeavor to prove that the symbols point back to the parable of the householder, and Jesus allegorically looked forward to John's vision. If the explanation perfectly fits the parable and the vision, in harmony with God's book and law, and a present truth lesson is derived therefrom, then only must we accept it as truth.

The Morning Call

Matt. 20:1, 2, "For the kingdom of heaven is like unto a man that is an householder, which went out early in the morning to hire laborers into his vineyard. And when he had agreed with the labourers for a penny a day, he sent them into his vineyard." Jesus could have no reference to any other people than Israel after the flesh, for they are the ones with whom God bargained and sent into His vineyard—world. Their labor consisted of representing the Creator or householder, and giving us the Bible. The Psalmist has made the following record of the agreement: "He hath remembered his covenant for ever, the word which he commanded to a thousand generations. Which covenant He made with Abraham, and His oath unto Isaac; And confirmed the same unto Jacob for a law, and to Israel for an everlasting covenant." (Psalms 105:8-10.)

The covenant was made with Abraham, which was only a promise **to him** and **his seed,** but Abraham obtained not the promise. "His oath unto Isaac"; that is to say, God solemnly declared that He will carry out His agreement. But Isaac, even as his father, "obtained not the promise." He "confirmed" the same to "Jacob"; that is, He administered, settled, or established it. The covenant made with Abraham was realized by Jacob as a law. But "to Israel, **for an everlasting** covenant." Hence, Israel received the promise. Therefore, it was Israel that went to labor in the vineyard after they departed from Egypt. "According to the word that I covenanted with you when ye came out of Egypt, so my spirit remaineth among you: fear ye not." (Haggai 2:5.) Isaiah speaks of the vineyard which in itself was a symbol of the world. (Isa. 5.) Therefore, the householder's early hour call for laborers in His vineyard, applies to the call of Israel out of Egypt. Why is it called "early in the morning?" At that time Moses was writing the Bible, which is the light of the world. Therefore, very "early," for the Scriptures had just begun to be written. Thus the period since the Bible came is called the day, according to the parable. Which signifies that the written word of God is the light of the world.

Second Call in the Third Hour

"And when he had agreed with the laborers for a penny a day, he sent them into his vineyard." (Verse 2.) The wage agreed upon between the parties, is the promise of God to Israel. "And he went out about the third hour, and saw others standing idle in the market place, And said unto them: Go ye also into the vineyard, and whatsoever is right I will give you. And they went their way." (Verse 3, 4.) Having established the first call it would not be difficult to determine the second. Note that these were not of the same company, but "others," who were **idle.** If not Israel, then it can only be the Apostles and the Gentiles in the beginning of the Christian era, as recorded in Acts 13:46: "Then Paul and Barnabas waxed bold, and said, It was necessary that the word of God should first have been spoken to you: but seeing ye put it from you, and judge yourselves unworthy of everlasting life, lo, we turn to the Gentiles."

Note that there was no bargaining with the second company. They went, having confidence in the "Goodman" that they would receive whatever was right. The call of the Gentiles was not based upon any special agreement. They responded, trusting in God's generous promise to Israel, as it was recorded in the Scriptures. Therefore, the call of the Apostles, and the Gentiles, is represented by the "third hour call."

The Sixth and Ninth Hour Calls

"Again he went out about the sixth and ninth hour, and did likewise." (Matt. 20:5.) Each of the calls being at intervals, extending over the entire day, it is evident that they must come one after another at different periods. On each occasion there must be a call—message. If so, it cannot be merely a call of reformation—obedience to a former message. Therefore, the reformation by Luther could not be considered here, for it was only a revival to the message delivered before his time. Said Luther, "The just shall live by faith." Knox, Wesley, and Campbell could not enter in the parable, for they too had only a call for reformation (obedience) to the message (doctrines) delivered to the Gentiles—the early Christian church. The doctrine of the Holy Spirit by Knox, Grace by Wesley, and Baptism through immersion by Campbell were taught by the apostles. We shall present further proof from another angle to show the above stated reformers are not included in the parable.

As Israel and the Gentiles in the first and second calls comprised God's church in the vineyard, then the third, fourth, and fifth calls must represent the church in the vineyard as well. We turn the reader's attention to the "woman" with the crown of twelve stars of Revelation 12:1, 6, 14. She being a symbol of the church, was given the wings of an eagle to fly into the **wilderness** for 1260 days—years. Therefore, while she was in the wilderness there could have been no church **in the vineyard.** The long prophetic period has been fixed and accepted to be the period from 538 A.D. to 1798 A.D. Therefore, during the long wilderness journey of the "woman," there can be no call for laborers in the "vineyard." Thus, the three last calls in the parable must have met their fulfillment after 1798, at which time the "woman" was to return from the "wilderness." Consequently the following question is asked: If the church ("woman") was in the wilderness between the years 538 and 1798, in which period the above stated reformers did their wonderful work to bring about reformation by obedience to the Scriptures, were they not called out and sent by God? Answer.—Surely they were. There can be no doubt about it. Their work, character, and sacrifice answers the question. Think of Luther, the father of Protestantism, who risked his life like those of God's great servants in the past. God, by the hand of Luther, tore asunder the doors of darkness, brought an end to the terrible persecution and bloodshed of the saints of the most High, and caused the light in His written word to shine into the hearts of men. Had it not been for the earnest and zealous efforts of these godly reformers, the woman (church) would have been in the wilderness until this day, and there would have been no Protestantism. Thus, their unselfish service broke the power of despotism and by the imprisonment of the Pope terminated the long prophetic period. Therefore, God, through the service of these men was to bring the "woman" (church) from the wilderness and prepare the way for the third call, at the sixth hour.

The calls at the sixth, ninth, and eleventh hours, must be similar to that of the preceding ones—made by a special message, preached for the first time—which would have made it necessary on each occasion for another company—"laborers." The nature of these messages also must have been world wide, for they were sent into His "vineyard"—world. The third call therefore, represented by the sixth hour, must have come sometime after 1798 A.D., at which time the "woman" was due to return. Just such a message was presented to the world after A. D. 1798 and prior to A. D. 1844 in the preaching by William Miller of the 2300 days of Daniel 8:14. Therefore, the message by Miller was represented by the company hired at the "sixth hour."

"Again he went about the sixth and ninth hour, and did

likewise." (Verse 5.) Note that these words closely associate "the sixth and ninth hour" calls, while the other calls are separated. The significance is that these two messages represented by the "sixth and ninth hour," are to be closely joined to each other. Therefore, the ninth hour call must come after Miller's work came to an end. It was the Sanctuary truth, and the investigative judgment preached since 1844, bound in the first, second and third angel's messages of Revelation 14:6-11 Therefore, the Three Angel's Messages constituted that call in 1844.

The Eleventh Hour Call

The eleventh hour call is the last on record, and only an hour before sunset—millennium. The time for its deliverance to the world is shorter than any universal message ever given. Though the time is the shortest its area over the earth's surface is more extensive than any. Its speedy delivery is of the highest importance, for by it shall the world be judged.

God's servants shall have no time or desire for the cares of this world, for there is a city prepared for them whose builder and maker is God. As we have just enough time to get ready for translation, we must not let the enemy steal our precious moments. Because the work is so broad, its expansion so vast, and its importance so great, God has inspired modern science to invent, and build speedy equipment to quickly finish His work. "But thou, O Daniel, shut up the words, and seal the book, even to the time of the end: many shall **run to and fro,** and **knowledge shall be increased.** Many shall be purified, and made white, and tried, but the wicked shall do wickedly; and none of the wicked shall understand; but the wise shall understand." (Dan. 12:4, 10.)

The evidence in Christ's parable plainly reveals another call for laborers to the vineyard between the one in 1844, and the millennium; namely, at the eleventh hour. This being true, why is it, that the movement called out at the ninth hour (in 1844) has not forewarned the church that there is more truth to follow and another message, "call," to come? Has God neglected to give the warning and left His people in darkness? We answer the question by quoting the following testimonies: "In view of that great day, the Word of God in the most solemn and impressive language **calls** upon His people to arouse from their spiritual lethargy, and to seek His face with repentance and humiliation: 'Blow ye the trumpet in Zion, and sound an alarm in My holy mountain'!"—"The Great Controversy," p. 311.

"Then I saw another mighty angel commissioned to descend to the earth, to **unite** his voice **with** the **third angel,** and give power and force to his message. . . . This message seemed to be an **addition** to the third message, joining it as the midnight cry joined the second angel's message in 1844."—"Early Writings," p. 277. Again we read, "Be assured that there are **messages to come** from human lips, under the inspiration of the Holy Spirit. 'Cry aloud, spare not . . . **show** my people their **transgression,** and the house of Jacob their sins'."—"Testimonies to Ministers," p. 296. "Another message of **warning** and **instruction** was to be given the church."—"The Great Controversy," p. 425.

"Prophecy must be fulfilled. The Lord says: 'Behold, I will send you Elijah the prophet before the coming of the great and dreadful day of the Lord.' Somebody is to come in the spirit and power of Elijah, and when he appears, men may say: 'You are too earnest, you do not interpret the Scriptures in the proper way. Let me tell you how to teach your message'."—"Testimonies to Ministers," p. 475. "Behold, I will send you Elijah the prophet before the coming of the great and dreadful day of the Lord." (Mal. 4:5.) Has not God, through the "Spirit of Prophecy," as well as by the Scriptures, plainly forewarned His people that they must expect messages at any time? "As never before, we should pray not only that laborers may be sent forth into the great harvest-field, but that we may have a clear conception of truth, so that when the **messengers of truth shall come,** we may accept the message and respect the messenger."—"Testimonies for the Church," Vol. 6, p. 420.

If the warning has been given, why have men from the pulpit so persistently closed their eyes to the Word of the Most High, and opened their mouths in speaking fables to their congregation, by declaring that they have all the truth and need neither message nor prophet? Has not this lying and hypocrisy paved the way for a wholesale deception in the church by strengthening their confidence in that they have need of nothing and are on the way to heaven? Think of the prejudice and false security the message will have to break through. Think of the loss of life if the people should accept the decision of the leaders. Has not just such a terrible trap of deception ensnared the people of God in every movement called forth? Confidence in the leaders, and the acceptance of their decisions without investigation has deceived the people in every age. What will change the course now? How terrible the thought and how great the responsibility! May God help His people to search for light and truth for themselves, and may their zeal demand an explanation and an account of these things.

What is the message? The eleventh hour message is none

other than Revelation 18—the loud cry of the Third Angel. Quoting "Testimonies to Ministers," p. 59: "This same message [The Third Angel's] is to be proclaimed the **second time.** 'And after these things I saw another angel come down from heaven, having great power; and the earth was lightened with his glory." "This message is the last that will ever be given to the world; and it will accomplish its work."—"The Great Controversy," p. 390.

"Thus the message of the third angel will be proclaimed. **As the time comes for it to be given with greatest power, the Lord will work through humble instruments, leading the minds of those who consecrate themselves to His service. The laborers will be qualified rather by the unction of His Spirit than by the training of literary institutions. Men of faith and prayer will be constrained to go forth with holy zeal, declaring the words which God gives them.** The sins of Babylon will be laid open. The fearful results of enforcing the observances of the church by civil authority, the inroads of Spiritualism, the stealthy but rapid progress of the papal power,—all will be unmasked. By these solemn warnings the people will be stirred. Thousands upon thousands will listen who have never heard words like these. In amazement they hear the testimony that Babylon is the church, fallen because of her errors and sins, because of her rejection of the truths sent to her from heaven. As the people go to their former teachers with the eager inquiry, Are these things so? the ministers present fables, prophesy smooth things, to soothe their fears, and quiet the awakened conscience. But since many refuse to be satisfied with the mere authority of men, and demand a plain 'Thus saith the Lord,' the popular ministry, like the Pharisees of old, filled with anger as their authority is questioned, will denounce the message as of Satan, and stir up the sin loving multitudes to revile and persecute those who proclaim it."—Id., pp. 606, 607.

The eleventh hour call, in reality, is similar to that of the ninth. The ninth hour call is repeated with additional mention of the corruption in the churches; also light and force is added to it.

Why Stand Ye Idle?

The laborers were hired from the **"market place."** The market must refer to the church from which God calls His laborers for service. Note those hired in each instance were **idle.** The significance is that every message that has ever come to our world, came not by those in high position in the church. It was delivered by humble men, of whose services the church leadership thought they had little need. In every case the messages have been rejected by the foremost in the church. Mark the question asked by the householder, **"Why** stand ye all the day idle?" The significance is that they should have been at work. They say unto him "Because **no man** hath **hired us."** When the church leadership is corrupted, the work is controlled by **a** certain class, and a ban of restriction placed on all others. Thus, the very ones whom God wishes to use are thrust aside and remain idle.

The workers hired by such leadership are selected from the viewpoint of a technical education as a test of qualification, instead of Biblical knowledge, consecration, and absolute obedience to the whole truth. Such practices are contrary to Biblical instruction. We quote: "A bishop then must be blameless, the husband of one wife, vigilant, sober, of good behaviour, given to hospitality, apt to teach; Not given to wine, no striker, not greedy of filthy lucre; but patient, not a brawler, not covetous; One that ruleth well his own house, having his children in subjection with all gravity; (For if a man **know not how to rule his own house, how shall he take care of the church of God?)"** (1 Timothy 3:2-5.) The apostles in selecting men for sacred office, said: "Wherefore, brethren, look ye out among you seven men of **honest report, full** of the **Holy Ghost** and **wisdom,** whom we may appoint over this business." (The Acts 6:3.)

Moses spent forty years in the school of Christ. While keeping sheep he exchanged his Egyptian training for the knowledge and wisdom of the Great **I Am.** Thus he was fitted to lead His people out of Egypt. Paul was shown that his worldly wisdom derived in the school of men was harmful, and useless in the work of Christ, so the apostle declared: "And I, brethren, when I came to you, came not with **excellency** of **speech or of wisdom,** declaring unto you the testimony of God. For I determined not to know anything among you, save Jesus Christ, and Him crucified. And my speech and my preaching was **not with enticing words of man's wisdom,** but in demonstration of the **spirit and of power."** (1 Cor. 2:1, 2, 4.) Paul meant that he had determined to preach Bible and Bible only, which reveals Christ and Him crucified. Preached by the power of the Spirit of God, and not by wisdom of men. Thus, the learned apostle stooped to the level of the ignorant fishermen in human knowledge, at the same time climbing up with the eleven in divine wisdom, which in comparison earthly honor and human greatness sink into insignificance. Therefore, the sacred cannot be mingled with the common.

Said the householder, "Go ye also into the vineyard; and whatsoever is right, that shall ye receive." God asks men and women to arise and go to work in the vineyard, trusting in the value of His Word. "Provide neither gold, nor silver, nor brass in your purses, Nor scrip for your journey, neither two coats, neither shoes, nor yet staves: for the workman is worthy of his meat. And into whatsoever city or town ye shall enter, inquire who in it is worthy; and there abide till ye go thence." (Matt. 10:9-11.) "And He said unto them, When I sent you without purse, and scrip, and shoes, lacked ye anything? And they said, Nothing." (Luke 22:35.)

Mark the following point with care: From the ninth hour in 1844, to the twelfth, or close of probation, there are only three full hours. The number of hours symbolically denote that there is only enough probationary time from 1844 to the end, for one movement—three hours. The Scripture of Revelation 10:6 applies here: "That there should be time no longer." Every movement that God has called into existence since the world began, went just so far, and when He sent a message, or new light upon His Word, the leaders rejected it, and necessity gave birth to a new movement.

If the leaders in God's church at the present time should accept the eleventh hour call, it would be out of the ordinary. But should they reject it, God cannot start a new movement, for there is **"time no longer."** New movements generally start with a handful of people and require years to develop, and after a time corruption sets in. Consequently, He could never finish His work on earth with such a program. The words of the Master figuratively declare that the leadership in the movement called in 1844 will reject the eleventh hour message, for He says those who were about to be hired, were "standing **idle**"; that is, it was not those at work whom he hired.

If there is no time for a new movement, then there is but one solution to the perplexing problem, and that is to separate the "wheat" from the "tares" by smiting the class who are controlling the work and keeping God's people in bondage of sin. Therefore, the enemies of God are taken out of the way by the five men of Ezekiel 9. This subject is made clear in "The Shepherd's Rod," Vol. 1.

The Last First and the First Last

Coming back to our text: "A measure of wheat for a penny, and three measures of barley for a penny." (Rev. 6:6.) Why is the wheat mentioned first, and the barley last? Why not the reverse? Why three times as much barley for a penny to one of wheat? Or why not the reverse? The Scriptures are perfect and no flaw can be found in them. Therefore, there must be a reason for this order of arrangement, as well as for the quantity of each cereal. Barley ripens much earlier than wheat. Therefore, those hired first must be represented by the barley, otherwise the symbol could not be perfect. The barley, then, represents the Jewish nation, as they were hired first. Naturally the wheat must represent the ones called at the eleventh hour. It is marvelous how perfect the Scriptures are.

Why only two kinds of cereals brought to view? Why not five? The two cereals are sufficient to illustrate the thought and to clear the lesson. But the chief reason for only two is to draw attention to the first and last calls, because reference is made of but two Israels; namely, Israel after the flesh (the descendants of Abraham), and Israel after the spirit (the 144,000). But the object of the lesson is for the latter, who are hired at the eleventh hour, for the truth of the parable has never been understood by any other company.

Mark that the ones hired first worked all the day, but those hired last labored only one hour. For that reason the voice said, "three measures of barley" as against "one measure of wheat" for a penny—day's wage. The interval between each call was three hours. The "measures" denote the allegorical hours consumed in labor. The intervals of three hours between each call is a symbol of a full length of time allowed to each movement, or message, without specific meaning as to the number of years. Those called last, labored only one hour, but they too received equally as much. The generosity of the Goodman signifies that all God's servants are equally rewarded, not in proportion to their deeds, but according to the benevolence of the householder.

Now the question why the voice from the throne said, "One measure of wheat for a penny," first, and "three measures of barley for a penny," last, will be answered. Humanly speaking it should have been the reverse, for by the wheat is represented the last message (eleventh hour) and by the barley the first (early in the morning—Israel going out of Egypt). Had the voice reversed the enumeration of the cereals, it would have been wrong, for said Jesus: "So when even was come, the Lord of the vineyard saith unto his steward, Call the labourers, and give them their hire, beginning from the last unto the first. And when they came that were hired about the eleventh hour, they received every man a penny. But when the first came, they supposed that they should receive more; and they likewise received every man a penny. And when they had received it, they murmured against the goodman of the house, Saying, These last have wrought but one hour, and thou hast made them equal unto us, which have borne the burden and heat of the day. But he answered **one** of them and said, Friend, I do thee no wrong: didst not thou agree with me for a penny? Take that thine is, and go thy way: I will give unto this last, even as unto thee. Is it not lawful for me to do what I will with mine own? Is thine eye evil, because I am good? So the **last** shall be **first,** and the **first last:** for many be called, but few chosen." (Matt. 20:8-16.) Thus a measure of wheat for a penny, first, and three measures of barley for a penny, last. They that murmured represent that part of the Jewish nation who were unworthy, and the phrase, **"Friend,** I do thee no wrong . . . . Take that thine is, and go thy way," denotes the rejection of the nation.

Give Them Their Hire

Note that those who were hired last were paid first, and the first, last. As all were equally regarded, the ones hired first murmured, though they were paid in full. Their disdainful act denotes that the Jewish nation was unworthy of their hire, and the Goodman said to them, "Take that thine is, and go thy way." As ancient Israel is represented by the first call, as previously explained, to them the words apply, and as they were the ones who murmured, it proves the parable correct.

Why were the first paid last, and the last first? Answer.—The pay God's servants receive is eternal life, and is characterized by the penny. Therefore, those who are granted the assurance of a never ending life first, are those who were hired last, and according to the parable, it was the company called at the eleventh hour. They are those who are marked or sealed by the man with the writer's inkhorn of Ezekiel 9, or as John calls him, the angel with the seal of God; and he sealed, or marked, 144,000. (See Rev. 7.) This glorious company is the first who are granted the assurance of never tasting death. (See "The Shepherd's Rod," Vol. 1, pp. 22-24.) Thus they are paid first, but those who were called early in the morning (Israel after the flesh) are to be resurrected (the righteous) when Christ comes in the clouds, at which time they shall be given immortality. "So that the last shall be first, and the first, last." For this reason, those who were sealed and saved by the Third Angel's Message since 1844, are resurrected in the special resurrection before Christ comes. (See Dan. 12:2; "Early Writings," p. 285.)

Why Early in the Morning?

The evidence brought forth shows that the calls (messages) before Israel went out of Egypt were not included in the parable, and that the call of Israel was "early in the morning." Jesus has divided the history of the church in this instance into two equal parts of twelve hours each. In the parable He refers only to the part called **day,**—the period of the Bible. "Jesus answered, Are there not twelve hours in a day? If any man walk in the day, he stumbleth not, because he seeth the light of this world." (John 11:9.) Therefore, the period before the Bible came is called **night.** Not that God's people were left in darkness concerning **His word,** but that it was orally passed from father to son, while the written word is a direct revelation—light. Thus He has portrayed the history of His church on a twenty-four clock dial. We may better comprehend the study by a brief summary as we follow the chart on page 224.

There are only five calls in the parable; First, those who were called early—Israel out of Egypt; Second, those who went to labor in the vineyard at the third hour—the early Christian church; Third, the sixth hour call—William Miller and his coworkers; Fourth, the ninth hour call—the Third angel in his first cry after 1844; Fifth, the 11th hour call—the Loud Cry of the Third Angel's Message. As number "seven" is used in every one of God's finished acts to denote completeness, there must have been two such calls before Israel's time, otherwise it would show incompleteness in the proclamation of the gospel. "And Enoch also, the seventh from Adam, prophesied of these, saying, Behold, the Lord cometh with ten thousands of His saints." (Jude 14.) As Enoch had a world wide message of the coming of the Lord, his message is the first call. Noah's call is the second from creation. Therefore, "seven" in all, meaning perfect, finished, the end of the gospel.

Seven Universal Movements

Thus far we have referred to the calls only, but now we turn our attention to the movements. The start of the First movement is from the time Adam sinned to Enoch's message; Second, from Enoch to Noah; Third, from Noah to Moses; Fourth, from Moses to the apostles; Fifth, from the apostles to Miller; Sixth, from Miller to E. G. White; Seventh, from E. G. White to the end. From the last call to the end, being only one hour, it proves that there is no time for a new movement. And a new movement would throw the number seven out of its significance. Therefore, the old movement must be purified and march on.

The time allowed for each movement is marked on God's clock dial as three hours. The first three hours on the dial indicate from creation to the fall of Adam; consequently it leaves only twenty-one allegorical hours for human probation. **Seven** times three equal twenty-one; therefore, we have another reason why the angel said, "There should be time no longer."

Reason Why Three Hours to a Movement

The following fact further proves that the church history in this instance is represented by a twenty-four hour clock dial. If the call came to Israel early in the morning, at the twelfth hour, and the day closed at the following twelfth hour, called day, because the written word of God was in existence for light to the church, then the period that preceded the Bible is symbolically called night.

Some may question the evidence for allowing three hours to each incident— from creation to the fall of Adam, and again to Enoch and Noah. If God worked on the three hour schedule with the crucifixion of Jesus (see chart on page 22), and the same rule was followed in the period called "day," then He certainly would not follow another rule in the period called "night." The reason He has followed that particular rule is to present to His church the exact time of her history by periods.

Let us examine the evidence from another angle. The first man that sinned is called the first Adam. Now look at the clock dial; from the third hour in the dark part (fall of Adam) opposite to the third hour in the light part, and we see the second Adam (Christ crucified). Again, look at the sixth hour in the dark part of the clock dial (Enoch prophesying of the coming of Christ) **opposite to the sixth** hour of the light part, and there we see Miller also prophesying of the same event (coming of Christ). This is one of the reasons why God allowed Miller to proclaim the coming of Christ in 1844. Now look at the ninth hour, Noah predicting the end of the world in his generation, and opposite to the ninth hour in the light part, we see E.G. White prophesying of the end of the world in **this** generation. (And that is where this generation began.) And at the twelfth hour (Israel after the flesh going out of Egypt) and opposite the twelfth hour (sunset), we see Israel after the Spirit (finished product) going out of the world (Egypt). Therefore, there is no question but what the fall of Adam, the prophecy of Enoch, and Noah, came at the hours as shown on the chart.

Here we see another type. God's truth to the world **before the Bible came,** coincides with His truth **in the time of the Bible,** showing that God has but one truth, one Christ, and one gospel in all ages. Therefore, the idea taught by self-styled ministers of the gospel that God had one method of saving people before the Bible came into existence, another in the Old Testament time with the descendants of Abraham, and still another for the New and the Gentiles, etc., is a deception of the Devil and there is no truth in it. Not only the things written prove the truth and exposes the error, but even common reasoning tells us there can be no justice in such an ever-changing method of salvation—"For I am the Lord, I change not."

The twelfth hour on the dial, to the left, represents sunrise and on the right, sunset; the sixth hour in the light part, noon, and six in the dark part, midnight. The message at the sixth hour by Miller is called the Midnight cry (see "Early Writings," p. 277.) because it corresponds with that of Enoch. Said Jesus: "And at midnight there was a cry made, Behold, the bridegroom cometh: go ye out to meet him." (Matt. 25:6.) The sixth hour in the light part stands also as noon when the sun is in its full strength. The Bible began to rise at the twelfth hour and when the message by Miller was preached, represented by the sixth hour call, both Old and New Testaments had been compiled and published; thus it also denotes mid-day.

The message proclaimed by Enoch was a prophecy looking forward to 1844 when Jesus came into the most holy place with His saints for the investigative judgment. Therefore, the preaching by Miller was a fulfillment of the prophecy by Enoch. Thus it is called the Midnight Cry. As the subject of the judgment was not to be understood until after its session had commenced, it was impossible for Miller to make the proper application for the then-expected event. Note the grammatical expression Christ used: "There **was** a cry **made."** He uses past tense, proving the fact that the true meaning of Miller's message was to be understood after the call was made. There **"was,"** said He, instead of there **shall** be a "cry."

The evidence in this study proves the divinity of Christ, and His power in vision even to the smallest of details, in past, present and future. If such a truth as this, so plain and simple, so strong and certain in revealing the wonders of the Scriptures would not change the heart of the reader, then we conclude that nothing greater would be of any value. If the dead should arise from the grave, or even if an angel should descend from heaven, that class would attribute the power to the Devil. The Psalmist describes the Majesty of God's Word in the following language:

"I will worship toward Thy holy temple, and praise Thy name for Thy loving kindness and for Thy truth: for Thou hast **magnified Thy word above all Thy name.**" (Psa. 138:2.) Said Jesus: "If they hear not Moses and the prophets, neither will they be persuaded, though one rose from the dead." (Luke 16:31.)

The one hour of Revelation 17:12, in which time the horns of the scarlet-colored beast received power as kings, is the period from the eleventh hour call to the end of this world's history—from the eleventh to the twelfth allegorical hour.

WHY MILLER'S MISTAKE; WHAT IS THE FLOOD TO US?

Said Enoch: "Behold the Lord cometh **with ten thousands** of His **Saints."** (Jude 14.) This prophecy by Enoch is not the second coming of Christ in the clouds, for when He shall appear in glory He comes not "**with** His saints," but rather **for** His saints. Neither could it be of His coming **with his saints** on the other side of the millennium, for in such a case it could not have been a message to the antediluvian world. It would have been improper and without object, or lesson to that people, if Enoch should have preached to the world Christ's third coming before preaching His second coming for His saints. What then?

Enoch prophesied of the coming of the Lord to His temple in the most holy place in the heavenly sanctuary **with** His saints in figure (not bodily) for the investigative judgment to blot out their sins, of which event Malachi the prophet refers: "Behold, I will send my messenger, and he shall prepare the way before me: **And the Lord, Whom ye seek, shall suddenly come to His temple,** even the messenger of the covenant, **Whom ye delight in: behold He shall come,** saith the Lord of hosts. **But who may abide the day of His coming? And who shall stand when He appeareth? For He is like a refiner's fire, and like fullers' soap: And he shall sit as a refiner and purifier of silver: and He shall purify the sons of Levi, and purge them as gold and silver, that they may offer unto the Lord an offering in righteousness.'** (Mal. 3:1-3.) "Behold, I will send **My messenger,** and he shall **prepare** the way **before Me:** even the messenger of **the covenant."** The messenger is not the Lord Himself, but note that he is the one who shall prepare the way **for** the Lord. He is called the "messenger of the **covenant**" (agreement or promise). Since the Scripture is for the last days, this messenger of promise can be no other than the one whom the Lord has promised: "Behold, I will send you Elijah the prophet before the coming of the great and dreadful day of the Lord." (Mal. 4:5.)

The Lord came to His temple in the most holy place in 1844 for the judgment of the **dead,** which was a fulfillment of Daniel 7:9, 10. Malachi refers to the judgment for the living, which is of the same event (judgment). For the prophet says: "But who may abide the day of His coming? and who shall stand when he appeareth? for . . . he shall sit as a refiner and purifier of silver: And shall purify the sons of Levi, and purge them as gold and silver, that they may offer unto the Lord an offering in righteousness." (Verses 2, 3.) As the dead cannot be purified, or offer gifts, it is evident that it is the purification of the church, for "He shall purify the sons of Levi"—the priests—the 144,000. Furthermore the Lord says: "I will send my messenger," and as no messenger can be sent to the dead, it must be a message to the living.

Coming back to the prophecy by Enoch: "Behold the Lord cometh with **ten thousands** of His saints." The word "thousands" being in plural, does not reveal the number of saints that come with Him. But if the word **"ten thousands,"** have no numerical definition of any kind, then the word **"ten,"** would be vain repetition and foreign to the Scriptures. Therefore, we must look for a symbolical definition of the word. The number **"ten,"** has the same meaning as the **"ten virgins"** of Matthew 25, denoting **universal** (the church as a body). Thus it symbolically apprehends the saints collectively—all the saved from Adam to the end. Therefore, the prophecy by Enoch commenced its fulfillment in 1844, at which time the Lord came with the names and records of those who are sleeping in the grave, and when the investigation of the dead is finished, then He comes with the names of the living saints. First with the 144,000, and afterward with the "great multitude of all nations, and kindreds, and people, and tongues." (Rev. 7:9.) Therefore, the complete fulfillment of the prophetic words, "Behold the Lord cometh with ten thousands of His saints," shall be realized at the close of probation. Of this coming of the Lord (for the dead) William Miller was the messenger, and the message of Elijah the prophet—the messenger of the covenant—is the forerunner for His coming with the living saints, both of the same event—the judgment.

In "The Great Controversy," p. 426, referring to Christ's second advent, part of verse 14 is quoted with verse 15, to complete the sentence with the word "cometh"; that part of the verse "with ten thousands of His saints," apply to His coming to the temple before the "Ancient of days." The word "cometh" from verse 14, with verse 15, is applied to His second advent, the same as Zechariah 13:6. Verse (6) is applied to Christ's second coming and verse (7) to His crucifixion. Also note that the comment is on the fifteenth verse, about the judgments upon the wicked and not to the saints.

True, Enoch prophesied of the anti-typical day of atonement (our time), but if his message was without significance to the world before the flood, then his preaching would have been merely ostentatious. Therefore, what is true of his message now, was also true to the antediluvians; and if this statement is correct, there must be a perfect comparison of the world then, with the one now. The preaching of Enoch was followed by the preaching of Noah. While the ancient world did not have a perfect understanding of the coming of the Saviour, they too, like the present generation, were looking and waiting for Him who was to redeem them from sin and death, and to reinstate them in the garden of Eden. With their lips they professed a great longing for Him Whom they expected to see in His glory, but their attitude toward the glad news in the message by Enoch: "Behold the Lord cometh," brought to the surface that which was in their hearts. As it was generally expected that the Lord would come at that particular time, and as Enoch had not been given the light as to the manner of His coming, he proclaimed his message in perfect harmony with the popular view of that generation. Now the question is, what made them reject the message so long as its proclamation was in harmony with their expectations and they could not refute its truth? This question can be answered by the experience of John the Baptist.

"John did not fully understand the nature of the Messiah's kingdom. He looked for Israel to be delivered from her national foes; but the coming of the King in righteousness, and the establishment of Israel as a holy nation, was the great object of his hope."—"The Desire of Ages," p. 103.

It would have been unreasonable and an injustice to the chosen people of God if He should have left them in darkness concerning the time of the most important event of all church history—the coming of Christ. That part of the long prophetic period of the 2300 days (years) of Daniel 8:14, which pertained to the Jewish nation; namely, the **seventy weeks,** or 490 years, they perfectly understood, for: "It was **well known** that the **seventy weeks** of Daniel's prophecy, covering the **Messiah's advent,** were nearly ended; and all were eager to share in that era of national glory which was then expected."—Id., p. 133.

Light had been shining to the Jewish nation, and they were well informed of Him (to whom they had expended millions of dollars in sacrifices, and hundreds of years in ceremonial services), the time He should come, and the nature of His kingdom. As the rulers of the nation had fallen under sin they despised the corrections by the prophets. Thus the character of the then expected kingdom was misinterpreted, but the time they rightly understood and nationally accepted. As John had not been given light on what was to transpire **after** the Anointed One should come, he proclaimed the message in perfect harmony with the popular idea of the prophetic time, and of the coming kingdom. Now, since there was no controversy between the teachings of John the Baptist and the rulers of Israel, what made them reject his message?

"In the natural order of things, the son of Zecharias should have been educated for the priesthood. But the training of the rabbinical schools would have unfitted him for his work. God did not send him to the teachers of theology to learn how to interpret the Scriptures. He called him to the desert, that he might learn of nature, and nature's God.

"It was a lonely region where he found his home, in the midst of barren hills, wild ravines, and rocky caves. But it was his choice to forego the enjoyments and luxuries of life for the stern discipline of the wilderness."—Id., p. 101.

As the Scribes and Pharisees said of Christ and the apostles: We will not have these ignorant men reign over us, they poured the same accusations against John, and this was the undermining of their eternal welfare. Their second stumbling block came as "John's singular appearance carried the minds of his hearers back to the ancient seers. In his manner and dress he resembled the prophet Elijah. With the spirit and power of Elijah he denounced the national corruption, and rebuked the prevailing sins. . . . As a symbol of cleansing from sin, he baptized them in the waters of Jordan. Thus by a significant object-lesson he declared that those who claimed to be the chosen people of God were defiled by sin, and that without purification of heart and life they could have no part in the Messiah's kingdom. . . . John declared to the teachers of Israel that their pride, selfishness, and cruelty showed them to be a generation of vipers, a deadly curse to the people, rather than the children of just and obedient Abraham."—Id., pp. 104-106.

Thus the forerunner of Christ did, for he saw his people deceived, self-satisfied, and asleep in their sins. He longed to rouse them to a holier life. God does not send messengers to flatter the sinner. He delivers no message of peace to lull the unsanctified into fatal security. Because John warned his people of the danger and the doom of his nation, they hated him the more.

Now, what made the antediluvian world reject the message by Enoch? Enoch's message to the Old world was in like manner in perfect harmony with the popular acceptance of the "coming of the Lord", but as his work carried the same rebuke as that of John the Baptist, he also incurred the displeasure of his people. By turning from the message of salvation that was to blot out their sins (Enoch's prophecy of the judgment), they placed themselves under greater condemnation. By rejecting the only means for their salvation, they cut themselves loose from the Power that upholds all things, and thereby invited the terrible flood.

God, not willing that any should perish, commanded Noah to declare the danger before-hand, and provide means and facilities for those who wished to escape the ruin. But as they turned down the message by Enoch they did likewise with the message by Noah. As these messages were inspired by the Holy Spirit, they sinned against Him; therefore, it shall never be forgiven them.

Thus the message by William Miller was a fulfillment of Enoch's prophecy—also a duplicate. If this is correct, there must be a perfect comparison of one with the other. As Enoch did not fully understand the manner of the "coming of the Lord", and John the Baptist the character of the Kingdom that was to be set up, just so Miller misinterpreted the "cleansing of the sanctuary", and proclaimed the coming of the Lord to earth instead of to the Most Holy place. If some should charge Miller with being a false prophet, they may likewise accuse Enoch and John. Such blind and hasty conclusions is an attempt to overthrow the whole Bible.

Now the question arises, Why did God allow His servants to remain in darkness as to what was to transpire at the end of their message? There are several reasons. Enoch's and Miller's messages were similar to the forerunner of the first advent of Christ. John's message was to prepare the way of the Lord's coming, and not to explain the nature of His kingdom. So it was with Miller and Enoch. The second reason.—Had John been given light that Christ's kingdom was not of this world, it would have brought about extreme internal friction with his nation. Therefore, such a debatable question would have overthrown his work and rendered useless the message for His people. But as there was no argument as to what he taught his hearers, it left the sin-blinded leaders of Israel without an excuse. Had they accepted his message, and repented of their sins, it would have opened their spiritual eyesight, and the arrival of the **Anointed One** would have enlightened the rest of the way.

In Miller's time Christendom was no less ignorant of the sanctuary question than the Jewish nation was of Christ's kingdom. Therefore, had Miller been given light concerning the place to which Christ was to come at the end of the 2300 days; namely, to the Most Holy place for the judgment of the saints, his message would have brought forth many arguments and idle discussions. Thus the time and proclamation of the prophetic period would have been neglected, and his efforts frustrated. But in the manner he proclaimed his message he gave them no occasion for dispute, and as the enemies of God could not contradict his interpretation of the Scriptures, and refused to be interested in what he taught, it left them without excuse.

Thus the second angel's message of Revelation 14:8, was proclaimed immediately after the disappointment, Saying, "Babylon is fallen, is fallen." That is, the world in 1844 fell in the same manner as the one before the flood. The present world is called Babylon, because the kingdom of Babylon is the immediate one after the flood. Thus Babylon became the mother of the nations.

Our world stands at this present time in the same place as the one before the flood. The Old World was condemned by rejecting the message in its type, and the New in the anti-type. Note how remarkable the co-incidences: After the proclamation of the glad news (the coming of the Lord, by Enoch) was flatly ignored by the Old world and the preparation neglected, Noah declared the end of the world in his generation. The message by Miller was followed by identically the same declaration as that of Noah, as it was announced after 1844, "The end of the world in this generation."

As it was understood that Christ was to come to earth on the expected date, and the teaching remained uncontradicted that the return of the long expected Son of God was at hand, it should have been profoundly interesting to those who claimed the name of Christ as their only Saviour and Redeemer. If the praises which they proclaimed with their lips were also in their hearts, they would have gladly accepted the good news and made all possible preparation for the most glorious event in all history. But as they refused to be interested, they ridiculed, and flatly rejected it all—showing their true character and thus marking themselves as goats. Since the most exalted and promising news of celestial glory was rejected, and the messenger unappreciated in both cases (Old and Modern worlds), it is positive that whatever truth is presented, regardless of its magnitude or glory, these scoffers of today will not believe, and will thus bring condemnation upon themselves.

As God declared the danger to the Old world by the preaching of Noah in one generation, just so has He forewarned the world of its end in **this** generation. As provision was made before the flood for those who wished to escape the ruin, just so He has provided means and facilities for all who wish to evade the doom that confronts our world. Not to enter into an ark built by the hands of man, No, no, that was only a figure; but into "many man-sions" prepared by the Lord himself; not into an ark floating over mad waters; but into mansions resting on foundations of precious stones. The dreaded flood is a type of the dark millennium. As God's faithful people were saved then, so shall they be saved now; but the sinner now, shall perish as the sinner then.

The Flood a Type of the Destruction of the Wicked

If the flood is a type of the millennium, and the generation that perished then a type of the generation now living, then the number of days employed in the destruction of the Old world must be considered with the destruction of this present world.

"And the Lord said unto Noah, Come thou and all thy house into the ark; for thee have I seen righteous before me in **this** generation. For yet seven days, and I will cause it to rain upon the earth forty days and forty nights; and every living substance that I have made will I destroy from off the face of the earth. And Noah did according unto all that the Lord commanded him. And Noah went in, and his sons, and his wife, and his sons' wives with him, into the ark, because of the waters of the flood. And it came to pass **after seven** days, that the waters of the flood were upon the earth. In the six hundredth year of Noah's life, in the second month, the seventeenth day of the month, the same day were all the fountains of the great deep broken up, and the windows of heaven were opened. And the rain was upon the earth **forty** days and **forty** nights. And the flood was forty days upon the earth; And the waters increased, and bear up the ark, and it was lift up above the earth. And the waters prevailed upon the earth an hundred and fifty days." (Gen. 7:1, 4, 5, 7, 10-12, 17, 24.)

"And the waters returned from off the earth continually: and **after** the end of the hundred and fifty days the waters were abated. And the waters **decreased** continually until the tenth month: in the tenth month, on the first day of the month, were the tops of the mountains seen. And it came to pass at the end of the forty days, that Noah opened the window of the ark which he had made: And he sent forth a raven, which went forth to and fro, until the waters were dried up from off the earth. Also he sent forth a dove from him, to see if the waters were abated from off the face of the ground; but the dove found no rest for the sole of her foot, and she returned unto him into the ark, for the waters were on the face of the whole earth: then he put forth his hand, and took her, and pulled her in unto him into the ark. And he **stayed** yet other **seven** days; and again he sent forth the dove out of the ark; And the dove came in to him in the evening; and, lo, in her mouth was an olive leaf pluckt off: so Noah knew that the waters were abated from off the earth. And he **stayed** yet other **seven** days; and sent forth the dove; which returned not again unto him any more. And it came to pass in the six hundredth and first year, in the first month, the first day of the month, the waters were dried up from off the earth: and Noah removed the covering of the ark, and looked, and behold, the face of the ground was dry. And God spake unto Noah, saying, Go forth of the ark, thou, and thy wife, and thy sons, and thy sons' wives with thee." (Gen. 8:3, 5-13, 15, 16.)

After faithful Noah had sounded the warning to his generation and had completed the building of the ark, God commanded His servant to enter into it seven days before the rain had begun. As he, and all that were to go into the ark entered the wonderful boat that rested upon dry land with no seeming evidence that it would ever have a chance to float, the Lord closed the door.

Six days passed without any apparent sign of a flood, but in the end of the seventh day, the pouring rain from above and the gushing fountains from beneath dashed against each other, and Noah's prediction commenced its dreadful fulfillment in the devastation of the land. As the waters from above and the fountains from beneath covered the surface of the earth fifteen cubits upward, and destroyed every living thing by the end of the forty days and forty nights, they suddenly ceased; from terror to calmness, from fury to peace, as though satisfied with the accomplishment of victory over rebellion against truth and righteousness. For one hundred and ten days they neither increased nor decreased, but held their level by a miracle. When the total of one hundred and fifty seven days were fulfilled from the day Noah entered the ark, they began to abate; that is, the fountains of the deep opened their mouths to swallow them down in the bowels of the earth.

Now we go back to clear the apparent Scriptural complication in recording the duration of the flood and the confinement in the ark. "In the **six** hundredth year of Noah's life, in the **second** month, the **seventeenth** day of the month, the **same** day were **all** the fountains of the great deep broken up, and the windows of heaven were opened." (Gen. 7:11.) The second month and the seventeenth day of the month was the date of the solar year according to the antediluvian calendar when the raging flood began its violent rush against every living thing upon the earth. The same indignation of nature vehemently continued forty days, and when it had reached its climax and wiped out the inhabitants it suddenly quieted down. Adding forty days to the foregoing date would show that the rain ceased on the twenty-seventh day of the third month. "And the ark rested [quieted] in the seventh month, on the **seventeenth** day of the month, upon the mountains of Ararat." (Genesis 8:4.)

Therefore, from the day the rain started to the day the ark rested, (not on the ground but from drifting) was exactly five months. The same is recorded in verse three, "And the waters returned from off the earth continually: and after the end of the hundred and fifty days the waters were abated." This fact proves that the antediluvian monthly calendar consisted of thirty days to a month (5 x 30 =150).

"And the waters decreased continually until the tenth month: in the **tenth** month, on the **first** day of the month, were the tops of the mountains seen." (Verse 5.) That is, from the day the waters were abated to the day the mountains appeared, there were seventy-four days. (13) to complete the seventh month, (30) in the eighth, (30) in the ninth, and (1) day from the tenth month = 74 in all.

"And it came to pass in the six hundredth and first year, in the first month, the first day of the month, the waters were dried up from off the earth." (Verse 13.) That is, from the day the mountain tops had appeared to the day the waters returned to their proper place, there were ninety days—(29) to complete the tenth month, (30) in the eleventh, (30) in the twelfth, and (1) day from the first month of the commencement of the new year, making a total of ninety days.

The following record will give us the number of days to dry the earth's surface and solidify from the effects of the waters: "And in the second month, on the seven and **twentieth** day of the month, was the **earth** dried." (Verse 14.) Therefore, the earth had dried in the space of fifty-six days from the day the waters were taken away—(29) days to complete the first month, and (27) from the second month, making a total of (56) days.

The following is a summary and a grand total of days: (40) while raining, 110 to the time they began to subside, 164 days for the waters to recede in the bowels of the earth, and (56) for the earth to dry; making a total of 370 days; and seven before the flood had started, reaching a grand total of 377 days—twelve months and seventeen days in all (30 days to the month).

Certainly no one would suppose that this arrangement of the flood with fixed number of days to each act was thoughtlessly devised by a just and all wise God. Why should Noah and his family with all the living creatures that went into the ark be

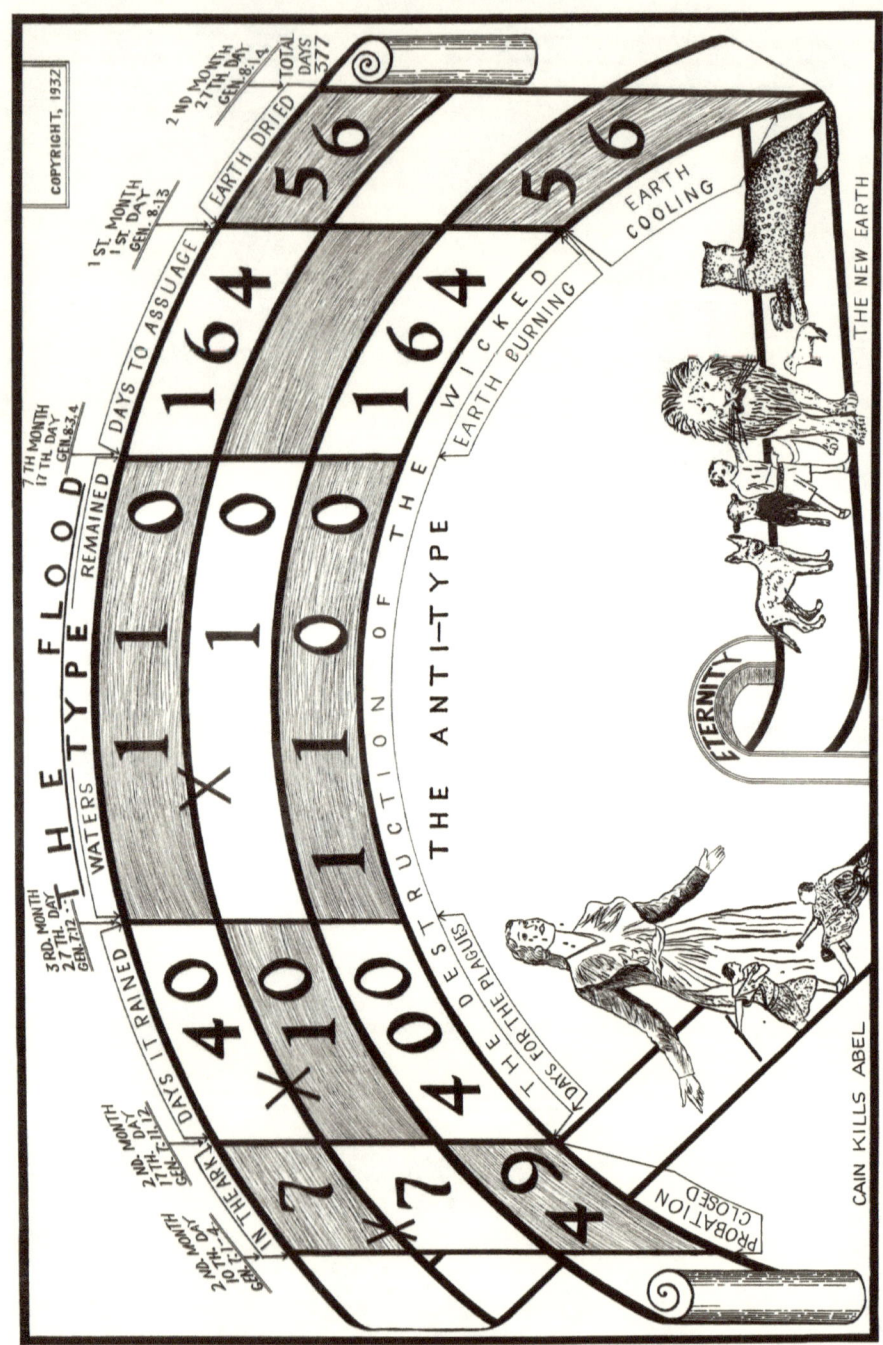

shut in seven days before the rain began? It would have been unwise and cruel on the part of God, also costly to Noah, and burdensome to all the inmates of the ark in prolonging their captivity if it had no object lesson for future generations. Why consume forty days to flood the earth while He could have done it in much less time? Why lengthen the captivity of His creatures in the ark, by restraining the liberty of the waters in their downward course, and compel them to keep their elevation fifteen cubits upward for 110 days? Or why not more or less? Why should He cause the waters to rise upward in forty days, and consume 164 (over four times as long) in going down? Is it not contrary to nature?

The earth had been under water for over ten months, and as the rushing torrents from underneath had violently inverted the form of the earth on their upward course, it had become one slimy mass of mud. But after the waters had descended into the lower lands, and in the bowels of the earth, He caused the earth to dry in but fifty-six days. Everything God did in connection with the flood was contrary to nature and to human judgment or reason. Unquestionably, it was thus devised for an object lesson for those upon whom the end of the world is come.

The following will not only prove that what has been said is correct, but it will also show that the closing of the door of the ark seven days before the destruction by the flood had begun, is a type representing the time from the close of probation to the commencement of the plagues. It will further prove that the rain of forty days and forty nights is a type of the destruction of the wicked in the plagues. The 110 days (after the rain had stopped and before the waters were abated) is a time-type of the wicked, both during the millennium and for one hundred years after. Also that the clearing of the earth from the waters is a type of the destruction of the wicked by fire (the second death) after the millennium, and the fifty-six days in which the earth was dried is a type of the cooling of the earth after its purification from sin and sinners.

As the above stated types are symbols of six different periodic events dealing with days, months and years, depending on the incident, their true meaning cannot be deciphered by comparison, neither would such method prove anything in this case, nor yet show Omnipotence in devising the type. Therefore, their true meaning is to be found by multiplication with Biblical numbers of special meaning to fit the incident and broaden the view. Also the lesson derived by such methods must prove correct and in perfect harmony from every angle one may figure; thus one thing proves another.

Therefore, we shall first consider the seven days (from the time Noah entered the ark to the commencement of the flood) of which we stated to be the type of the time between the close of probation and the commencement of the plagues. The method to be used in disclosing the length of time in the said period is also to indicate that human probation, and the completeness of the gospel proclamation has closed. The only fitting Biblical number that can be used to describe such incidents as well as to reveal the number of days from one event to the other, would be number seven. Therefore, we must multiply the type with the Biblical number of completeness. Thus, 7 x 7 = 49 days from the close of probation to the commencement of the plagues. Therefore, the falling of the plagues should be a signal to the wicked that they are lost! O, how great the disappointment to them, who, like the antediluvians hope to be saved, but find themselves lost.

A computation of like manner was employed to define the year of **jubilee.** Said the Lord: "And thou shalt number seven sabbaths of years unto thee, **seven** times **seven** years; and the space of the seven sabbaths of years shall be unto thee **forty and nine** years." (Lev. 25:8.) The fiftieth year while the land rested being also a type of the millennium (showing that the land shall keep a Sabbath-rest), a like computation is used. Therefore, at the beginning of the thousand years is the commencement of the jubilee in its anti-type. And as the land was returned to the lawful owners in the typical year of jubilee, just so it will be in the anti-typical—returned to the saints. "Thy people also shall be all righteous; they shall inherit the land forever, the branch of my planting, the work of my hands, that I may be glorified." (Isa. 60:21.)

The next number and event to deal with is the typical forty days and forty nights while it rained, in comparison with the anti-typical (the destruction of the wicked in the time of the plagues and to the second coming of Christ). The ruin of the wicked being world-wide we must multiply the type with a number signifying universal, so as to prove that the destruction shall include the four points of the compass. It has been previously proven that **ten** is the only fitting number; therefore, 40 x 10 = 400, thus bringing the total of 449 days, or one and one fourth years (15 months) from the close of probation to the coming of Christ to take His saints. This fact will be proven from another angle in connection with another study.

Since the two sections of the flood (7 x 7 = 49 and 10 x 40 = 400 days) bring us to the end of the world, then the third section (the 110 days while the waters kept their elevation fifteen cubits upward or from the time the rain ceased to when the waters abated) must be applied to the millennium. It also being universal, we are again obliged to multiply number **ten** with the type, 110 x 10 = 1100. The millennium being 1000 years long, and 100 years on the other side of it (after the resurrection of the wicked to their final destruction, see "The Shepherd's Rod," Vol. 1, page 164), making a total of 1100 years. This proves that the 1100 days derived by our multiplication are prophetic (a day for a year). Thus the remaining typical days of the deluge while the waters were on the decrease and the earth was clearing herself from the flood, must apply to the final destruction of the wicked and of the purification of the earth by fire.

Therefore, the typical number of days are literally applicable as the flood was, and as follows: From the day the waters were abated to when the tops of the mountains appeared, there were **seventy four days,** and **ninety** more until they all cleared away, making a total of 164; in which time the wicked and their works are burned to ashes. (Mal. 4:1.)

The remaining **fifty six** days (while the earth was drying) apply to the time the earth is cooling off; and as Noah went out from the ark, just so the saints shall walk out from the Holy City and possess the earth for ever and ever. "And the kingdom and dominion, and the greatness of the kingdom under the whole heaven, shall be given to the people of the saints of the most High, whose kingdom is an everlasting kingdom, and all dominions shall serve and obey Him. Hitherto is the end of the matter." (Dan. 7:27, 28.)

It is certain that nothing could fit so perfectly by accident. But think of such marvelous foresight in devising a wonder of this kind which could reveal by a living picture the future for thousands of years! Are not such evidences as these a token of love divine toward fallen beings! Gratitude swells from our hearts, words fail us, we can only exclaim with the Psalmist: "Thy word is a lamp unto **my** feet, and a light unto **my** path. I have sworn, and I will perform it, that I will keep thy righteous judgments." (Psa. 119:105, 106.)

It is not only wonderful to invent a lamp throwing out a light of such amazing candlepower, but it is also astonishing how our God can conceal His marvels from the eyes of wise and prudent men. Then in His own time He sets them upon high hills by which He is able to light the pathway of the searcher for truth, and by its glaring power blindfold the sight of the wicked. "Therefore the people that doth not understand shall fall." (Hosea 4:14.) "Light is sown for the righteous, and gladness for the upright in heart." (Psa. 97:11.)

Our God could have spoken to us direct by prophets as in times past, but it would have been impossible to transmit as much light to one generation. Neither could we comprehend its meaning as we can by these examples or symbols. Also knowing the great deception, unbelief and doubts of high minded men that were to arise, He has placed these marvels in the Bible to expose error and reveal truth, thus overthrowing the enemy of mankind; also leaving the hypocrites and the unbelievers without an excuse.

As every living thing perished in the time of the flood that was outside of the ark, just so in the dark millennium every living thing shall return to dust, except the devil and his angels. Though men are teaching a millennium of peace, their doctrine shall come to naught, and they shall lie down in sorrow except they repent.

Flood Coincides With the Passover and Crucifixion

Our God commanded Noah with his family, beasts, fowls, and creeping things to enter in the ark on preparation day—Friday. "In the selfsame day entered Noah . . . as God had commanded him: and the Lord shut him in" as the Sabbath drew on, being the tenth day of the second month. (Gen. 7:13, 16.) Seven days later, or at the beginning of the following Sabbath, being the seventeenth day of the month, "all the fountains of the great deep were broken up, and the windows of heaven were opened" and it rained upon the earth forty days and forty nights. The rain ceased on the twenty seventh day of the third month, in the end of the fourth day of the week—Wednesday after sunset. There is a remarkable coincidence between the flood and the passover week; also in connection with the crucifixion, resurrection, and ascension of Christ. Therefore, this divine providence is worthy of our earnest consideration. The Israelites were commanded to take the passover lamb apart from the flock on the tenth day of the first month, and were to kill it on the fourteenth day of the same month at even. (Ex. 12:3, 6.)

As Christ was crucified, buried, and resurrected within the passover week, the weekly cycle and the monthly calendar coincide as follows: The tenth day in which the lamb was to be taken from the flock, fell on the seventh-day Sabbath that year; which coincided with the day of the week and the month of Noah's first day of confinement in the ark. In the end of the fourteenth day of the month after Christ had observed the feast of the passover lamb, He was taken before the priests; died on Friday the sixteenth day of the month, was buried at the commencement of the seventeenth (Sabbath), which coincides with the commencement of the flood, and was resurrected on the eighteenth—Sunday. As He ascended on high forty days afterwards, it fell on Thursday the **twenty seventh day** of the second month; being the same day of the week, as that which followed the forty days of rain. Our previous explanation showed that the day, following the **forty days** of **rain,** depicted in type, the end of the world, being followed with the departure of the saints from the earth.

We may not presume that God had brought about these coincidences without an object in view. As the ceasing of the rain is a time type of the end of this world, so the ascension of Christ with those who were resurrected with Him, is a type of the ascension of the saints at the coming of the Lord. It also reveals that His coming would be on Wednesday, and the train of glory shall depart for the Heaven of heavens on Thursday. Again we are told that it would take the saints seven days to ascend to the throne of God, and that we shall rest a Sabbath on one of the planets while on the way. From this it is evident that Christ shall come in the middle of the week. So again we find that one thing proves another. Such close calculations of the schedule of events that are soon to transpire, make it evident that the end of all things is at hand; otherwise the information would not as yet have been submitted.

This light being transmitted by marvels of typical events, is a clear manifestation that there is a type for every incident of vital interest to the church of God; which are the only positive proofs and clear explanations of divine providences. As there is no type for that which is false, teachers of theories without a typical representation for their claims of so-called Bible truths, and those who believe in them, are as the blind leading the blind. The types are worked out to expose the error and reveal the truth. The honest ones will shun the devil by embracing the facts, and by walking in the light.

The passover lamb being separated from the flock on the tenth day, coincides with the separation of the righteous from the wicked in the antediluvian world. The day of Christ's burial coincides with the day of the commencement of the flood, also with the commencement of the plagues; and His ascension with the day after the rain ceased, also with the end of the world and the translation of the saints. These coincidences are perfect with the day of the week and of the month; but the one is a month earlier in the season than the other; the passover being in the **first** month, and the flood in the **second.** It has been explained that the passover is a type of the close of probation for the church, (see page 216-218) and the closing of the ark a type of the closing of probation for the world. Therefore, there are thirty typical days between one close of probation and the other. If we were given light on how to decipher these typical (30) days it seems it would reveal the exact number of years from the fulfillment of Ezekiel nine (Passover), to the final close of probation. This fact perhaps will not be made known until after the work of the gospel has closed. For a brief summary of the flood in type and anti-type, we draw the reader's attention to the chart on page 250.

The Significance of the First and the Second Month

The closing work for the church is signified by the **"first"** month, and the harvest for the world by the **"second"** month. As one truth reveals another, our attention is turned to Joel 2:23, 28, 29: "Be glad then, ye children of Zion, and rejoice in the Lord your God: for He hath **given** you the **former** rain moderately, and He will cause to come down for you the rain, the former rain, and the latter rain in the **first month.** And it shall come to pass **afterwards,** that I will pour out my spirit upon all flesh; and your sons and your daughters shall prophecy, your old men shall dream dreams, your young men shall see visions: and also upon the servants and upon the handmaids in those days will I pour out my spirit." Note that the "rain" comes first and the pouring out of His spirit **afterwards.** Therefore, the rain is one thing, and the pouring out of the spirit is another.

By the "rain" is represented great light on the Word of God that is to ripen the harvest and lighten the world with its glory—the angel of Revelation 18:1. The pouring out of the Spirit is the power that is to descend upon God's servants to carry on the work represented by the former and latter rain. "And upon all flesh" is the Spirit that is to convince the honest in heart of the truth and bring them into the church, of which Pentecost was a type. "And the floors shall be full of wheat, and the fats shall overflow with wine and oil"—represents a great harvest of souls that shall be garnered in by the result of the "rain" and the "Spirit." (Joel 2:24.)

The "rain" falls in the "first month"; that is, the month by which the closing work for the church is represented—the sealing time of the 144,000. Therefore, in that period of time (before Ezekiel Nine) a great light is to be revealed. It is remarkable to note the perfect grammatical order of the words at the time of their application, clearly dividing the Word of truth as though it were written just at the time the prophetic words are revealed.

"For He **hath given** you the former rain moderately" is the light of truth that is characterized by the **former rain** which must have fallen previous to the time of the latter rain. Therefore, the former rain is none other than the writings of the "Spirit of Prophecy." Further proof of this will be given in another chapter.

But note that the **falling** of the **former** rain is repeated with the **latter** rain: "And He **will** cause to come down for you the rain, the **former rain,** and the **latter rain** in the first month." Therefore, the **former rain** (Spirit of Prophecy) falls the second time—revealed more fully in the time of the "latter rain"—the first time independent of the latter rain, and the second time associated with the latter in the "first month" (preceding Ezekiel Nine). The meaning is, the truth recorded in the writings of the "Spirit of Prophecy" was not fully understood until the time of the latter rain. Thus the former rain comes again with the latter rain, and this is what brings about the "Loud Cry."

Cain and Abel

Another remarkable fact as it appears on the chart is the crime committed by Cain in slaying his brother Abel. These being the first two brothers and the first quarrel over religion, also the first murder in the human family, it certainly must hold out a lesson of great importance.

According to the law of the Bible the priesthood was to be made up from the first born of every family. Thus, by the rights of the law, Cain was the priest. The Lord himself stated this fact as He spoke to Cain saying: "And unto thee shall be his desire [margin, subject], and thou shall **rule** over him." (Gen. 4:7.) Therefore, these two men represent two classes of people. Since this fact cannot be denied, Cain must represent a class of leadership (priests), and Abel the true church-membership. It was Cain who rebelled against God by presenting a false sacrifice, and because Abel obeyed and worshiped in the manner prescribed by the Creator, he incurred the displeasure of his elder brother.

If the statement that Cain and Abel represent two classes of people is correct, then the same must be proven by historical facts. We stated that Cain who typified the leadership, persecuted him who typifies the true membership. Thus every section of God's church has apostatized through unconsecrated leadership, and every message that called for reformation was likewise, by them, thrown out of the church. In their blindness they were determined to keep the people ignorant of the truth and thus they persecuted the messengers and those who embraced the message and obeyed the truth. Therefore, necessity called forth one movement after another. How fearful the thought for those who bear this great responsibility! And how dangerous to the class who permit others to think and act for them! The class that accepts the decisions of others, whether for or against the truth, are deceived and robbed of eternal life, for they can have no experience of their own, no true conversion, no change of heart. My brethren: these words are not against you, for it is God speaking through His word of truth to save you from the bottomless pit. Will you not let Him work for you and for His people? Will you not be His sheep?

THE FIRST AND SECOND TEMPLE—TYPE
AND ANTI-TYPE

The apostle Paul speaking comparatively of Solomon's temple with the church, points to Christ as "the chief corner stone; in whom all the building fitly framed together" he says is "for an habitation of God through the Spirit." (Eph. 2:20-22.) David, looking prophetically forward to the construction of the first temple by his son, and also of its application to the church of Christ, says: "The Stone which the builders refused is become the head stone of the corner. This is the Lord's doing; it is marvellous in our eyes." (Psa. 118:22, 23.)

Speaking of the ancient temple the Scripture says: "And the house, when it was in building, was built of stones made ready **before** it was brought thither: so that there was neither hammer nor axe nor any tool of iron heard in the house, while it was in building." (1 Kings 6:7.) A peculiar stone which was prepared to fit the main corner of the temple, was disallowed; and though the **builders** refused the "head-stone" of the house, the Psalmist says: "This is the Lord's doing; it is marvellous in our eyes." By the refusal of the "stone," the Lord typified, and thus prophesied, the rejection of Christ by the Jewish nation. (See The Acts 4:10, 11.) For Jesus says: "The stone which the builders rejected, the same is become the head [stone] of the corner." (Matt. 21:42.) Therefore, if it is become the head of the corner, then it is evident that the first temple was a representation of a Spiritual house, and a type of the Christian church; Christ himself was represented by the chief corner stone "which the builders refused," as being both the head and the founder of the Christian church.

The Second Temple

In erecting the second temple, Haggai and Zechariah prophesied and strength-ened the hands of the people by the Word of God. The writings of both prophets bear evidence in every line, that the perfect fulfillment of their prophecy is to be realized in the last days of this world's history. As they have interwoven these predictions with the construction of the second temple, it is obvious that the literal model of the stately edifice has a spiritual meaning for the church in the closing work of the gospel. Zechariah, looking forward to the time of the spiritual temple (the last section of the church) and its construction, says: "Behold the man whose name is **the branch**; and he shall grow up out of his place, and he shall build the temple of the Lord: Even he shall build the temple of the Lord; and he shall bear the glory, and shall sit and rule upon his throne; and he shall be a priest upon his throne: and the counsel of peace shall be between them both. And they that are far off shall come and build in the temple of the Lord, and ye shall know that the Lord of hosts hath sent me unto you." (Zech. 6:12, 13, 15.)

"He shall bear the glory." To Christ belongs the glory of redemption for the fallen race. "Unto Him that loved us, and washed us from our sins in His own blood . . . . to Him be glory and dominion for ever and ever." (Rev. 1:5, 6.) He "shall sit and rule upon His throne; and He shall be a priest upon His throne." (Zech. 6:13.) "Christ, who is the faithful witness, and the first begotten of the dead, and the Prince of the kings of the earth." (Rev. 1:5.) "He shall be a **Priest** upon **His throne.**" It is obvious that the time predicted is some time after the crucifixion and before probation has closed; for He is **"a priest."** Christ, **"the branch," "shall** grow up out of His place"; that is, He was to spring up from the Jewish nation, "and He **shall** build the temple of the Lord." Therefore, the temple that "He shall build" could not have been the literal temple in ancient Jerusalem, for it was a temple that He is to build after His birth. "And they that are far off shall come and build **in** the temple of the Lord." As this was untrue with the literal temple, the words must apply to the anti-typical one. At that time the prophet says: "And many nations **shall** be joined **to** the Lord **in that day,** and shall be **My** people." (Zech. 2:11.) "In that day"; that is, in the time of the "Loud Cry," a great multitude shall be converted to the church. In chapter 13:8, it is stated that one-third of the inhabitants will **"come,"** and they are the ones who shall "build **in** the temple of the Lord," of which the literal one was a type.

Zechariah then saw the powers that had "scattered Judah, Israel, and Jerusalem" (the type, also the anti-type), symbolized by "four horns." Immediately afterward he saw the same horns as four carpenters (read Zech. 1:18-21), representing the agencies used by the Lord in restoring His people and the house of His worship, both in type and anti-type; that is, the Gentiles who scattered the church shall also come and build the same.

The Literal and Spiritual Distinction Between the Two Temples

The religious services in both temples were executed in the same manner, but in structural magnificence, both internal and external, Solomon's temple comparatively speaking, was by far the greatest. But the Lord by the mouth of Haggai the prophet, asked those who were then engaged in the construction of the house of God: "Who is left among you that saw this house [Solomon's temple] in her first glory? and how do ye see it now? Is it not in your eyes in comparison of it as nothing? The glory of this latter house shall be greater than of the former, saith the Lord of hosts: and in this place will I give peace, saith the Lord of hosts." (Haggai 2:3, 9.)

The literal grandeur of the second temple in comparison with the first was "as nothing," but the Word says: "The glory of this latter house shall be greater than the former." Literally this was untrue. Therefore, the glory of these two temples in comparison with each other, is not in their literal, visible form, but rather in their typical spiritual standing. Consequently, both temples cannot typify the same period of the Christian era, for one distinctly differs from the other. Since this is true, then the type shows that the Christian church in this instance is divided in two sections. So then, in type the second temple denotes that the latter section of the church is to be by far the greater, which in comparison the former stands as nothing.

These two sections of church history were also pointed out in the vision on Patmos. To John was shown the true Spiritual Church of God in all ages, in a symbol of a woman. To her were given two wings of a great eagle that she should fly into the wilderness for 1260 days (years). The wilderness represents the dark ages, in which time she was out of civilization (from 538 A.D. to 1798 A.D.) Therefore, this prophetic period of 1260 years, split the true church in two sections; namely, from the crucifixion to 538 A.D. and from 1798 A.D. to the end of time. Thus the first section, or as it is called, the apostolic church, was typified by the first temple; and the last section by the second temple. This is not saying that God had no true people between the years of 538 A.D. and 1798 A.D. for the Word says, "She is **nourished** for a time, and times, and a half a time." (Rev. 12:14.) The lesson taught here is that, the first section of the church in the first few centuries was endowed with the true Sabbath—"daily"—and sanctuary truth; but prior to 538 A.D. the truth was "trodden under foot." (Dan. 8:12, 13.) The second section after the fulfillment of the 1260 year period denotes that she was again to be endowed with the truth that was "cast to the ground," and the reformation between these two sections (from 538 A.D. to 1798 A.D.) of the church, or "woman," was to prepare the way for her return, or for the restoration of the truth. For both temples, by which these two sections were typified, represent a worship with the Sabbath and the sanctuary truths.

First Temple Literally Greater, But the Second Spiritually

There was something glorious with both temples; and the greatness of the one was as "nothing" in comparison with the other. The first visibly exceeded the second, and the second spiritually exceeded the first; but the glorious gift to both was unsurpassable. As the one represents the early Christian church, and the other the last section of the same church, it is evident that both sections were endowed with great glory; but the glory of the early church was literal, and of the latter spiritual, according to types.

The early Christian church was literally greater, because Christ, the "Head stone of the corner," appeared at that time in His visible human form. Thus the literal magnificence of Solomon's temple was a perfect symbol! But the type reveals that the glory of the early church was as nothing in comparison with the latter section of the same church. Therefore, the visible presence of Christ (in His human form) in the early church, was as nothing in comparison with His invisible presence in the closing work of the gospel church!

We think of the wonderful miracles—the casting out of devils, the healing of the sick, and the raising of the dead! We marvel as we think of His resurrection, ascension, and of the glorious demonstration on the day of Pentecost! But all these wonders will be as nothing in comparison with the divine manifestations of greater splendor in the harvest time!

Let us not suppose that when Christ appears in the clouds the infirmities of the saints are to be removed. This work must be done previous to that time, after which immortality shall be granted. "He that believeth in me, the works that I do," said Jesus, "shall he do also; and greater works than these shall he do." (John 14:12.) The perfect fulfillment of these words are yet future and must be fulfilled before His second advent. "For this corruptible must put on incorruption, and this mortal must put on immortality. So when this corruptible shall have put on incorruption, and this mortal shall have put on immortality, then shall be brought to pass the saying that is written, Death is swallowed up in victory." (1 Cor. 15:53, 54.)

Therefore, in the time of the "Loud Cry," miracles are wrought—the sick will be healed, the eyes of the blind shall be opened, the deaf shall hear, the tongue of the dumb loosed, and the lame shall leap for joy! What a glorious sight! Those who have never seen light, to behold the glory of the Lord! They who have never heard a sound, now listening to the glorious melodies of the angels' harps, and the singing of the saints! What a thrill! What bliss! "And God shall wipe away all tears from their eyes; and there shall be no more death, neither sorrow, nor crying, neither shall there be any more pain: for the former things are passed away." (Rev. 21:4.)

"Behold, I shew you a mystery; We shall not **all** sleep, but we shall all be changed, in a moment, in the twinkling of an eye, at the **last** trump; for the trumpet shall sound, and **the dead shall be raised incorruptible,** and we shall be changed. For this corruptible must put on incorruption, and this mortal must put on immortality. . . . Then shall be brought to pass the saying that is written, Death is swallowed up in Victory." (1 Cor. 15:51-54.)

As the living saints witness the dead of all ages rising from their dusty beds, it will bring joy indescribable. Then to behold friends and loved ones as they meet each other, clothed in glorious incorruptible bodies, marching through space via sinless planets, and finally into the Heaven of heavens! What a glorious train of immortal beings—saints and angels, and the King of kings, the Lord of lords, "the everlasting Father, and the Prince of Peace," in the midst of them! Swiftly flying from the sin-cursed earth to the Center of centers in but "seven" days, while it would take "light" millions of years to make a trip of such incomprehensible distance! Can you perceive of an object moving with such tremendous velocity! God forbid that we should rob ourselves of glory like this. An hour's time lived in heaven, without sin, pain or tears, fear or death, is worth more than a thousand years in tents of wickedness.

My brethren, to obey the Word of God, and be true to principle for your own good, is not asking too much of you. Will you let self and sin rob you of a crown of life? Your human wisdom and worldly knowledge will prove to be as black as darkness itself, if you should allow the wily foe to rob you of the celestial bliss that should be yours throughout the ceaseless ages of eternity.

Though the early Christian church suffered terrible persecution, she prospered wonderfully. The three thousand converted on the day of Pentecost "of such as should be saved," was marvelous to behold. But the speedy growth of the first section of the church, in comparison with the second and last is to be as

nothing, according to the type. Therefore, the same is proven by the prophetic Word of God through the prophet Zechariah, and as the prediction was interwoven with the construction of the second temple, or with the type of the second section of the church, of which we speak at this particular time, the application of the following Scriptures must be correct:

"Sing and rejoice, O daughter of Zion: for, lo, I come, and **I will dwell in the midst of thee,** saith the Lord. And many nations shall be joined **to** the Lord in **that day,** and **shall be my people:** and **I will dwell in the midst of thee."** (Zech. 2:10, 11.) "Yea, many people and **strong nations shall come to seek the Lord** of hosts in **Jerusalem** [the church without reference to location], and **to pray before the Lord."** (Chapter 8:22.) "Therefore thy gates shall be open continually: they shall not be shut day nor night; that men may bring unto thee the forces [margin, wealth] of the Gentiles, and that **their kings** may be brought." (Isa. 60:11.) "And it shall come to pass, that in all the land, saith the Lord, **two parts** therein shall be cut **off** and **die;** but the **third** shall be left therein. And I will bring **the third part through the fire,** and will **refine** them as silver is refined, and will try them as gold is tried: they **shall** call on **my name,** and **I will hear them: I will** say, **it is My people:** and **they shall say, the Lord is my God."** (Zech. 13:8, 9.)

What is three thousand converts in one day in comparison to **one third** of the people saved of this present generation! Gathered in during the last hours of probationary time! Truly then, it can be said, the glory of the first temple, or first section of the church, was **as nothing** in comparison with the second. The last section of the church in the time of the **"loud cry"** is indeed the **harvest** time and the end of the world.

The early Christian church was a converted righteous church; nevertheless, the tares and the wheat were to grow together **"until the harvest."** (Matt. 13:30.) These words, **"until the harvest,"** cannot be mistaken; therefore, at the commencement of the harvest the separation takes place. Thus the church in the time of the **"loud cry"** is to be a pure and holy church, without spot, or wrinkle, or any such thing: a church without guile. If the foregoing statement is correct then the same must be found in the prophetic Word of God.

My brethren I beg of you hear the voice of the Good Shepherd: "Awake, awake; put on thy strength, O Zion; put on thy beautiful garments, O Jerusalem, the holy city: for **henceforth** [from now on] there shall **no more** come unto thee the **uncircumcised** and the **unclean.** Shake thyself from the dust; arise, and sit on thy throne, O Jerusalem: loose thyself from the bands of thy neck, O captive daughter of Zion." (Isa. 52:1, 2; A.R.V.) As these words are so plain, how can we doubt, or misconstrue their meaning?—It must be that the church of God is asleep in the dust! Thy God is calling thee, O Zion. God's church, "the only object on earth upon which He bestows His supreme regard" is in captivity; she is bound by her "neck" to "men of good words and fair speeches." Hear the Words of thy God, O Zion; arise and sit on thy throne for thou shall judge nations. Why make flesh thy arm? Is not thy God able to save thee? Is not the "Word of thy God quick, and powerful, sharper than a two-edged sword, piercing even to the dividing asunder of soul and spirit, and a discerner of the thoughts and intents of the heart?" "For Zion's sake will I not hold my peace, and for Jerusalem's sake I will not rest, **until** the **righteousness** thereof go forth as **brightness,** and the **salvation** thereof **as a lamp** that **burneth.**" My brethren, **"go** through, **go** through the gates; **prepare ye the way of the people;** cast up, cast up the **highway;** gather **out** the stones; **lift up a standard for the people."** (Isa. 62:1, 10.)

"The remnant of Israel [the 144,000] shall not do iniquity, nor speak lies; neither shall a deceitful tongue be found in their mouth: for they shall feed and lie down, and none shall make them afraid." (Zeph. 3:13.) "In **that day** shall there be upon the bells of the horses [those that carry the gospel] **holiness unto the Lord;** and the **pots** [in whose possession is the truth] in the Lord's house shall be like the bowls before the altar [pure and undefiled]. Yea, **every pot** in Jerusalem [the church] and in Judah [the leading part of the church] shall be **holiness unto the Lord of hosts;** and all they that sacrifice [offering] shall come and take of them, and seeth therein [they who administer in sacred things], and in **that day** there shall be **no more** the Canaanite [unconverted] in the house of the Lord of hosts." (Zech. 14:20, 21.) This is the church that is represented in Revelation 12:17, "Which keep the commandments of God, and have the testimony of Jesus Christ." The "woman" represents the church as a body. "The remnant of her seed" are the 144,000 against whom the dragon makes war. The war is waged against them, because they are the earthly leaders and founders of the movement. "Of her seed" signifies that they are part of "the woman," or in other words, the 144,000, and the great multitude, is but one movement—one family.

To the saints of this holy church the benediction is pronounced: "Blessed are they that do His commandments, that they may have a right to the tree of life, and may enter in through the gates into the city." (Rev. 22:14.)

Jacob, the father in type of Israel the true, dreamed on the way to Padan-Aram, "And behold a ladder set up on the earth, and the top of it reached to heaven: and behold the angels of God ascending and descending on it. And he was afraid, and said, How dreadful is this place! this is none other but the house of God, and this is the gate of heaven." (Gen. 28:12, 17.) Jacob's dream was prophetic of a time when there will be a complete connection and constant communication with heaven and earth—the **"loud cry"** of the third angel's message—the harvest time. To that glorious church these words apply: **"This** is the house of God and the gate of heaven." Only by the gospel proclamation through that Spiritual house can God save His people. There is to be One fold, One Shepherd, One Lord, One Truth to embrace, One salvation to accept, One road to travel, One gate to pass through, One train to take, and One time to depart, One Heaven to enter, One people, and One holy family. There can be no other way!

"It is impossible to give any idea of the experience of the people of God who shall be alive upon the earth when celestial glory and a repetition of persecutions of the past are blended. They will walk in the light proceeding from the throne of God. By means of angels there will be constant communication between heaven and earth."—"Testimonies for the Church," Vol. 9, p. 16.

The Time for Building the Anti-Typical Temple (Church)

We partially explained that the two literal temples, successively built in ancient Jerusalem, were types of two sections of the Christian church. The wide literal and spiritual contrast of these two typical structures was explained comparatively with type and anti-type. Though we could have greatly enlarged on the subject, we have eliminated excessive reading by briefly stating the facts, endeavoring to paint a more comprehensive pen-picture of this most vital lesson to Christendom.

The question before us is, when will the anti-type meet its perfect fulfillment? In the preceding paragraphs it was explained that the first section of the Christian church ended in 538 A.D.; and the second must commence after 1798 A.D., at which time the "woman" was supposed to return from the wilderness.

A close study of the type is the only possible way to clear the truth, not only of the foregoing question, but also of the following ones: If the "woman" was to return from the wilderness to the vineyard (civilization) after the end of the prophetic period of 1260 years, what transpired in 1798 to prove that "she" came back in that year? As the imprisonment and death of the pope answers one side of the question and clears the end of the prophetic period, where is the sign to show that the "woman" returned from the wilderness? If the accepted interpretation of the "woman" is a symbol of the church, and if she was in the "wilderness" from 538 A.D. to 1798 A.D., what about the four great denominations that were raised up prior to that time; namely, Lutherans, Presbyterians, Methodist, and Christian? Were they not the "woman" (church)? Bible students have failed to clear this mystery because of their lack of light on the Word of God. A great searchlight by the power of the Spirit shining through the types, is the only medium that can remove the obstruction and clear the way to an understanding of these and many other mysteries that are considered incomprehensive and that baffle the human mind. Therefore, the temple type of the church (woman) is the only channel by which these questions can be answered.

The "temples" and the "woman" represent the church as a body; or in other words, the symbol of the woman is a revelation of the types (temples), and the temples are symbolical prophecies of the "woman"—church. It will be noticed that the separate members of that church are represented by the composite substance of the temples: "As **lively stones** are built up a spiritual house, an holy priesthood, to offer up spiritual sacrifices acceptable to God by Jesus Christ." (1 Peter 2:5.) "So we being many, are **one** body in Christ, and every one members one of another." (Rom. 12:5.) "In whom all the building fitly framed together groweth unto an holy temple in the Lord." (Eph. 2:21.) Therefore, these two temples represent both—the church, and Christ. Christ, our High Priest, is prefigured by the "chief-corner-stone," and His priestly administration by the ceremonial or sanctuary service of these two literal temples.

The earthly sanctuary service for the salvation of the human race, in types and symbols, reveals Christ's administration in the heavenly. Which was made up of two laws; namely, the "ten commandment" and the "ceremonial" laws. The tables of the ten commandments were put **in** the ark, and the ceremonial or the law of Moses was placed **on the side** of the ark. (See Deut. 10:2; 31:26.) Why two laws? The moral law points out the sin, "for by the law is the knowledge of sin." (Rom. 3:20.) "For where no law is, there is no transgression." (Rom. 4:15.) But the ceremonial law "was added because of transgressions till the seed should come to whom the promise was made." (Gal. 3:19.) Which was the remedy to heal the sinner and set him free from the condemnation of the moral law. When Christ (the **seed**) came, He took this law of ordinance (the law of Moses) "out of the way, nailing it to the cross." (Col. 2:14.) The earthly administration of the law of ordinance could not give life of itself, because it was only a shadow of the true. Therefore, at the crucifixion of Christ it ceased and the heavenly one, which was foreshadowed by the earthly, began. The literal sanctuary service of both temples were identical.

Therefore, these two temples are types of two sections of the Christian church with the anti-typical sanctuary service made up of these two laws—moral and ceremonial. The first section of the Christian church, from the crucifixion to about 538 A.D., was endowed with just such a sanctuary; that is, they had a perfect knowledge of the work in the heavenly to that time, and their faith corresponded with its service. But in 538 A.D. the faith of this divine administration was thrown out from the church, or as Daniel puts it, "trodden under foot" (Dan. 8:13), and substituted by a **pagan priesthood,** with **pagan ceremonial,** and moral **laws,** or papal service, and Sunday worship. Therefore, as the first temple typified the first section of the early Christian church with faith in a true sanctuary service, just so, the second temple has prefigured the last section of the same church with faith in a sanctuary service that would be identical with the first.

The foregoing explanation answers one of our questions. The Protestant churches which were raised up before the "woman" returned from the wilderness were in total darkness concerning the sanctuary service. Therefore, they are not represented by the "woman," or by the "temple," for, as we stated before, the typical temples represent both sections of the church with **two divine laws;** namely, moral and ceremonial. Thus the "woman" represents a church that keep the "commandments of God—moral law, and have the testimony of Jesus Christ"—ceremonial law or the plan of salvation revealed in the light of "The Spirit of Prophecy." (Rev. 12:17.) The reformers, before the "woman" returned from the wilderness, were divinely called out as a preparatory step to bring her back to the "vineyard"; that is, to establish a true anti-typical temple service—true church worship.

As Solomon's temple was robbed of the sacred vessels and destroyed by Nebuchadnezzar, king of Babylon, ancient Babylon became a type; and had it not been so, there would have been no modern Babylon—the anti-type. (Rev. 18:2.) As there is no controversy as to who these two Babylons are, it is not difficult to unmask the mystery; and the proof of one will also clear the other. If the claim in this study is correct that Solomon's tem-

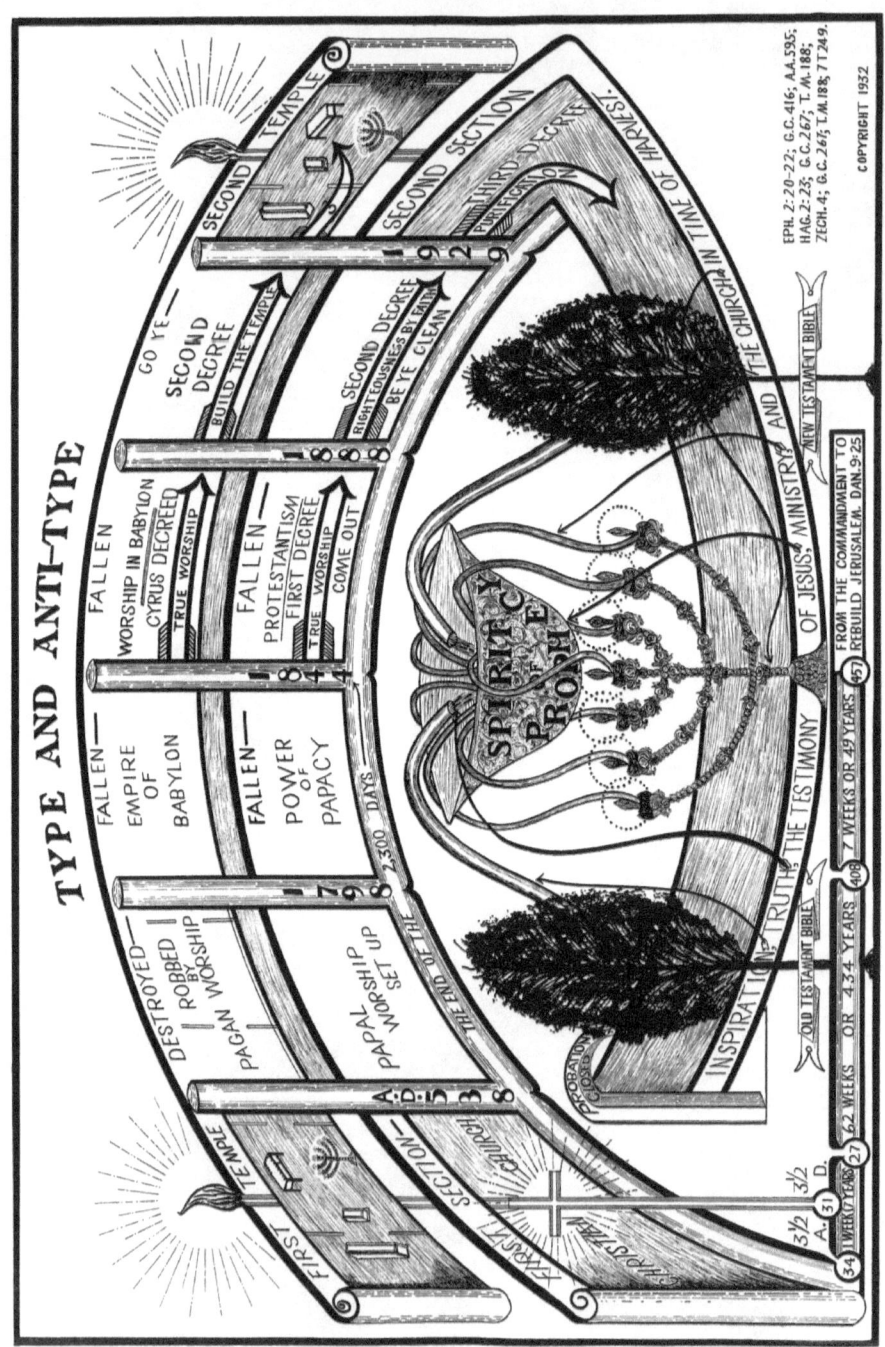

TYPE AND ANTI-TYPE

SECOND TEMPLE

SECOND SECTION

GO YE—
SECOND
DECREE
BUILD THE TEMPLE

RIGHTEOUSNESS BY FAITH
SECOND DECREE
BE YE CLEAN

THIRD DECREE

FALLEN—
WORSHIP IN BABYLON
CYRUS DECREED
TRUE WORSHIP

FALLEN—
PROTESTANTISM
FIRST DECREE
TRUE WORSHIP
COME OUT

FALLEN—
EMPIRE
OF
BABYLON

FALLEN
POWER
OF
PAPACY

2300 DAYS

DESTROYED—
ROBBED
BY
PAGAN WORSHIP

PAPAL
PAPALSHIP
WORSHIP SET UP

THE END OF THE

FIRST TEMPLE

A.D. 5 3

INSPIRATION TRUTH, THE TESTIMONY OF JESUS, MINISTRY AND THE CHURCH IN TIME OF HARVEST.

SPIRIT OF PROPHECY

OLD TESTAMENT BIBLE
NEW TESTAMENT BIBLE

FROM THE COMMANDMENT TO
REBUILD JERUSALEM. DAN. 9:25

7 WEEKS OR 49 YEARS
62 WEEKS OR 434 YEARS
457
408
27
3½ 3½ A. 31
1 WEEK 7 YEARS
34

EPH. 2:20–22; G.C.416; AA.595;
HAG. 2:23; G.C.267; T.M.188;
ZECH. 4; G.C.265; T.M.188; 7 T.249.

COPYRIGHT 1932

270

ple was a type of the first section of the Christian church, then there must be a perfect comparison with type and anti-type.

As type destroyed type, so anti-type must have destroyed antitype; that is, ancient Babylon (the type of the papacy) robbed and destroyed Solomon's temple (the type of the early Christian church) and led Israel into captivity. This symbolical prophecy met its perfect fulfillment in 538 A.D. when the papacy went forth and destroyed the church (Christian), robbed them of the truth, and led the followers of Christ into captivity (subject to papal rule). As the true sanctuary worship was abolished by ancient Babylon at the captivity of Israel, with the destruction of the temple, just so the papacy did away with the truth and strategically supplanted here on earth, the meaning of the mediatorial work of Christ in the heavenly sanctuary, of which the ceremonial system of the first temple was a type in the period before the judgment began. Thus the second temple represents the time while the judgment was in session. And as the sacred vessels were carried from the sanctuary and set up in a pagan temple in a heathen land, just so the papacy trod down the "truth" and set up a pagan priesthood in a so-called Christian church during the dark ages, while the "woman" was in the wilderness, which was typified by the **heathen land**—Babylon.

Our second co-incident is the fall of the Babylonian monarchy by the conquest of the Medo-Persian kings. Let it be remembered that in the night of Belshazzar's drunken feast, Cyrus and Darius took the kingdom and slew the king. The fulfillment of the type in the anti-type, which co-incides with the imprisonment of the pope in 1798 A.D., and followed by his death. Therefore, the death of Belshazzar who defied the God of heaven and earth, is a type of the pope who blasphemed for a "time, times and a half a time," fulfilling Daniel 7:25 and Revelation 13:10. At which time the prophetic 1260 years of the "woman's" wilderness journey ended.

Again we refer back to the type. With the death of Belshazzar the captivity of God's people ended, and they were made free; this co-incides with the termination of the 1260 years of the persecution against God's people by the papacy—church and state. The fall of the Babylonian monarchy was not the thing that built the temple in Jerusalem, but it was a preparatory step to it. As the death of Belshazzar was a preparatory step toward the establishment of a true temple worship, just so the death of the pope was a preparatory step toward the establishment of a true church-worship. If so, then the type clearly shows that nothing could have happened to the church in 1798 A.D. to signify that the "woman" had returned from the wilderness. This brings us to a third co-incidence.

Cyrus was a heathen worshiper at the time he conquered Babylon; but his attention was turned to the fulfillment of the Scriptures, and was shown that his name was written in the sacred volume years before he was born, and that he had fulfilled the words of the prophet Isaiah: "Thus saith the Lord to His anointed, to Cyrus, whose right hand I have holden, to subdue nations before him; and I will loose the loins of kings, to open before him the two leaved gates; and the gates shall not be shut; I will go before thee, and make the crooked places straight: I will break in pieces the gates of brass, and cut in sunder the bars of iron: And I will give thee the treasures of darkness, and hidden riches of secret places, that thou mayest know that I, the Lord, which **call** thee **by thy name,** am the God of Israel. . . . I have surnamed thee, **though thou hast not** known me." (Isa. 45:1-4.) "That saith of Cyrus, He is my shepherd, and shall perform all my pleasure: even saying to Jerusalem, thou shall be built; and to the temple, Thy foundation shall be laid." (Isa. 44:28.)

Thus his heathen heart was changed, and with gratitude he inscribed the words: "Thus saith Cyrus, the king of Persia, the Lord God of heaven hath given me all the kingdoms of the earth; and He hath charged me to build Him an house at Jerusalem, which is in Judah." (Ezra 1:2.) After his conversion he recognized that the pagan worship in Babylon was false. Therefore, he proclaimed throughout the realm of Babylon: "The Lord God of Israel, He is the God, which is in Jerusalem. . . . Also Cyrus the king brought forth the vessels of the house of the Lord, which Nebuchadnezzar had brought forth out of Jerusalem, and had put them in the house of his gods; Even those did Cyrus, king of Persia, bring forth by the hand of Mithredath the treasurer, and numbered them unto Sheshbazzar, the prince of Judah." (Verses 3, 7, 8.) Thus the pagan worship of Babylon was declared false some time after the death of Belshazzar and the fall of his empire. Therefore, Cyrus made a decree to build the house of God in Jerusalem. So much for the type, now our attention is turned to its fulfillment in the anti-type.

According to the type, we must look for a proclamation some time after 1798 A.D. that would brand the so-called Christian churches as being Babylon and their worship false. This is just what happened. Immediately after 1844 A.D. the second angel's message of Revelation 14:8 was proclaimed, saying: "Babylon is fallen, is fallen, that great city, because she made all nations drink of the wine of the wrath of her fornication." Therefore, it is evident that light shining through the types is the only medium that can explain these prophetic mysteries in the Word of God. With the proclamation of the fall of Babylon, it was announced that the so-called Christian festivals, such as Sunday keeping, Christmas, and Easter, also baptism by sprinkling, and other false doctrines were unbiblical and of pagan origin. But as ancient Babylon failed to renounce the pagan system of worship, and adopt the worship of the only true God, just so, present day Christendom has refused to reform or turn from these practices. The true mediatorial work of the heavenly sanctuary, jointly with the Seventh-day Sabbath as it was then taught, is also unheeded!

Three Decrees Issued Before Temple Was Built

Though Cyrus freely offered his resources to finance the construction of the house of God and its sacred service, and authoritatively commanded that it must be built, the Samaritans, or factitious Jews, frustrated the progress of the foundation and retarded its completeness. Therefore, though the message (decree) in 1844 was proclaimed to build the house of God and restore true worship according to the law and the prophets, the type reveals that the progress has been frustrated, and its completeness retarded by factitious Jews—untrue Seventh-day Adventists. This fact is plainly stated in the "Testimonies for the Church," Vol. 5, p. 217:

"I am filled with sadness when I think of our condition as a people. The Lord has not closed Heaven to us, **but our own course of continual backsliding has separated us from God.** Pride, covetousness, and love of the world have lived in the heart **without** fear of banishment or condemnation. . . . The church has turned back from **following Christ her leader,** and is steadily **retreating toward Egypt.** Yet few are alarmed or astonished at their want of spiritual power."

False Accusations and Excuses

These unconverted Seventh-day Adventists when told of these facts, not to criticize or to find fault with them, but to arouse them from the terrible stupor of deception and false security, begin to make excuses in the following manner: "We are God's people." "This is God's church." "There is no other movement to follow. "It is wicked to accuse the church militant." "You are setting time." "You must not tear down but build up." "Shun them which make divisions." "There shall be no more prophets." "We have all the truth and there is no need of more."

My brethren, as you have trimmed your lamps, will you not also avail yourselves of the "extra oil" (truth), and act like men who are looking for their Lord to come? No one denies the fact of your being God's people, but remember that the Jews also were once His people. No one wishes to affirm that it is not God's church, but is this the only time He has ever had a church? We do not claim that there is another movement to follow. But is not the Word of the "True Witness" saying, "I **will** spue thee out of my mouth?" If calling the church militant to a reformation by anointing their eyes with eyesalve that they may see, that the shame of their nakedness do not appear, is wicked as you say, then against whom are you speaking? And what other means can He use to call to repentance this Laodicean, "rich, and increased with goods, and have need of nothing" condition? "And knowest not that thou art wretched, and miserable, and poor, and blind, and naked?"

Is the one who calls for obedience to the truth according to the Word of God tearing down, or the ones who have broken every true principle of the message we bear? Who has caused divisions? Is it he who calls for obedience to the Word, or the one who refuses to hear a call from Heaven? Do you recall that the Christian church was split in seven reformatory sections because the messages were rejected? Who is the one that should be "shunned?" Is it he who accepts truth regardless of where it comes, or the one who allows prejudice to bar his mind from receiving the truth? Your claim of having all the truth, and that there is need of none, is denying every word written to the church. It is rejecting in advance every message of truth or light God may choose to send. It is shutting God out, and cutting the church loose from His stretched out arm. It is a preparatory step toward sinning against the Holy Ghost. Your assertion that there shall be no more prophets, is casting off before hand the latter rain and the **"loud cry!"** It is denying the Word in its prophetic form, for we read: "And it shall come to pass afterward, that I will pour out my spirit upon all flesh; and your sons and your daughters **shall prophesy,** your old men shall dream dreams, your young men shall see visions." (Joel 2:28.)

My brethren is there anything so fearful as this ungodly practice committed by men who are supposed to be watchmen on the walls of Zion? If you count yourselves unworthy of the everlasting kingdom, will you not take your hands off the church of God? Will you not grant religious freedom to the sheep and let them make their own decision? Why not do as you would have others do unto you? It is hard for you to kick against the pricks. Will you not say, Lord what wilt thou have me to do? Do you know that the blood of the lost sheep shall be required at your hands?

Your accusations against setting time is like a man talking when out of his mind. What definite time has been set? Do you mean Ezekiel, chapter four? If so will you not study the subject a little closer than you have and see what it says? Do you not see that the prophetic period had already ended when the statement was made? Or do you mean to say that God knows not the length of time from one event to another, and that He **must not** put it in the Bible? Do you not see that the coincidences recorded in "The Shepherd's Rod," Vol. 1, pp. 212, 213, proves the interpretation of Ezekiel four to be correct, or truth would not have come?

You will also note on page 222, that the 430 prophetic years originally applied to Abraham and his seed, overlap the 430 of Ezekiel 4. The 430 years of Ezekiel should terminate in 1929, or 1930, but the perfect fulfillment of the prophetic period of Abraham in its anti-type is yet in the future (going out of Egypt). The chart on page 212, 213, shows its termination in 1930, for as we stated before, it is outlined by the coincidences which perfectly fit the prophecy of Ezekiel. As it is impossible to make a time chart without any date to go by, we have used these coincidences, and it is stated that the date is indefinite. (See chart on page 133.) Ezekiel's prophecy is intended to point forward to the announcement of the predicted reformation, and the one through Abraham, to its completion (Ezekiel nine).

"Then shall the seers be ashamed, and the diviners confounded: yea they shall all cover their lips; for there is **no answer of God.** But truly I am full of power by the Spirit of the Lord, and of judgment, and of might, to declare unto Jacob his transgression, and to Israel his sin. Hear this, I pray you, ye **heads** of the house of Jacob, and princes of the house of Israel, that abhor judgment, and per-vert all equity. They build up Zion with blood, and Jerusalem with iniquity. The heads thereof judge for reward, and the priests thereof teach for hire, and the prophets thereof divine for money. **Yet** will they **lean** upon the Lord, and say, Is not the Lord **among us? None** evil can come upon us. Therefore shall Zion for your sake be plowed as a field, and Jerusalem shall become heaps, and the mountain of the house as the high places of the forest." (Micah 3:7-12.)

Objections Against the Channel God May Use

History proves that many have risen against the channel God has used to re-veal His Holy Word. So it is now. Some say:

"If God will speak to His people, He may do so through one of our leading men." That may be so, but where is the evidence that He cannot call a more humble instrument from the flock of his sheep? Historical facts prove that He seldom reveals himself through great men. Why should He change His method now? Others throw reflections against God's servants because of their external appearance, nativity, or rudiments of speech, etc. My brethren, will you limit the Father and Creator of the human race by your restrictions to a nation, man or country, by your narrow minded and self-conceited wisdom? The heart that conceives such unreasonable theologies through self-esteem, is like the proud pharisee in comparison with the penitent publican. These wise and self-digni-fied ideologists are the most ignorant ones, for by so doing, they allow the father of self-exaltation to rob them of life, and eternity. While such men are blinded to their own destruction, they are very wise and useful agents for the enemy of souls. For by their usurpation they carry a never ending influence like a "pebble thrown in the lake; a wave is formed, and another and still another, and as they increase, the circle widens, until it reaches the very shore."

What influence would your "words of life" have upon others if you think your dignity so great, and that of theirs so insignificant? Your actions are speaking louder than your words, saying to the poor of the flock: Look on us, and see yourselves as nothing. If a wrong act is committed against one sheep for pour-ing forth the straight truth, the others would be treated likewise. To such shep-herds the following words are spoken:

"Ye eat the fat, and ye clothe you with the wool, ye kill them that are fed: but ye feed not the flock. The diseased have ye not strengthened, neither have ye healed that which was sick, neither have ye bound up that which was broken, neither have ye brought again that which was driven away, neither have ye sought that which was lost; but with force and with cruelty have ye ruled them." (Ezek. 34:3, 4.)

The Second Decree To Build "The Temple"

By suppression the adversaries of God brought the work of the first decree to a stop. But in due time Cyrus' decree was renewed by Darius the king, and "Zerubbabel the son of Shealtiel, and Jeshua the son of Jozadak, and began to build the house of God which is at Jerusalem: and with them were the prophets of God helping them." (Ezra 5:2.)

But though this second decree carried additional power against the temple foes, they made the Jews cease by force of arms. The type by the second decree unmistakably reveals that there should have been another message after 1844, which with additional mention should have declared—go forward by faith, endeavor to establish a clean church and a true worship by obedience to the Word of God (righteousness by faith). The type also discloses that this second message would have been defeated and the work frustrated. Now note how perfectly the type coincides, reveals the truth, and exposes the schemes of the devil. In 1888 just such a message (decree) went forth, but the leaders at that time rejected it as the following testimonies prove: "The Lord in His great mercy sent a most precious message to His people. This message was to bring more prominently before the world the uplifted Saviour, the sacrifice for the sins of the whole world. It presented justification through faith in the Surety; it invited the people to receive the righteousness of Christ, which is made manifest in **obedience** to **all** the commandments of God. Many have lost sight of Jesus."—"Testimonies to Ministers," p. 91.

The message was delivered with the power of the Spirit, says the messenger: "I shall never again, I think, be called to stand under the direction of the Holy Spirit as I stood at Minneapolis. The presence of Jesus was with me. All assembled in that meeting had an opportunity to place themselves on the side of truth by receiving the Holy Spirit, which was sent by God in such a rich current of love and mercy. But in the rooms occupied by some of our people were heard ridicule, criticism, jeering, laughter. The manifestations of the Holy Spirit were attributed to fanaticism. . . . The scenes which took place at that meeting made the God of heaven ashamed to call those who took part in them His brethren. All this the heavenly Watcher noticed, and it was written in the book of God's remembrance."—"Special Testimony to Review and Herald Office", pp. 16, 17, written in 1896.

"They began this satanic work at Minneapolis. Afterward, when they saw and felt the demonstration of the Holy Spirit, testifying that the message was of God, they hated it the more, because it was a testimony against them. . . . Yet these men have been holding positions of trust, and have been molding the work after their own similitude, as far as they possibly could."—"Testimonies to Ministers," p. 80.

"But if . . . they nourish the same spirit that marked their course of action both before and after the Minneapolis meeting, they will fill up to the full the deeds of those whom Christ condemned when He was upon earth. The perils of the last days are upon us. Read Matt. 25:14."—"Testimonies to Ministers," p. 79. We also present a written testimony from an eye-witness: "The

1888 message backed up by Sr. White as the message of the hour . . . few of the leaders recognized it as such. Almost as a unit they rebelled, even claiming those men had unduly influenced Sr. White in their favor by some unseen power, thus they rejected the Spirit of Prophecy. . . . These two men (Elders Jones and Waggoner) with Sr. White . . . were rejected the use of the big tabernacle. . . . Thus you see not only (90%) but nearly (95%) of our leaders rebelled."

The Third Decree To Build "The Temple"

As the first and second decrees by the kings of Medo-Persia had failed to complete the construction of the temple and restore the sacred typical service, a third decree was set forth, then the king added: "Also I have made a decree, that whosoever shall alter this word, let timber be pulled down from his house, and being set up, let him **be hanged** thereon; and let **his house be made a dunghill** for this. And the God that hath caused his name to dwell there **destroy all kings and people,** that shall put to their hand to **alter** and **to destroy** this house of God which is at Jerusalem. I Darius have made a decree; let it be done with speed. . . . And the elders of the Jews builded, and they prospered through the prophesying of Haggai the prophet and Zechariah the son of Iddo. And they builded, and finished it, according to the commandment of the God of Israel, and according to the commandment of Cyrus, and Darius, and Artaxerxes king of Persia. And this house was finished on the third day of the month Adar, which was in the sixth year of the reign of Darius the king." (Ezra 6:11-15.)

It will be noticed that the third decree threatened the lives of disloyal men and nations: "Whosoever shall alter this word," said the king, "let his house be made a dunghill for this." So much for the type. Now we come to the anti-type. The type reveals that the messages of 1844 and 1888 are to be followed by a third one. But according to the type, the third message is to be a severe one. A message that will demand obedience and enforce executive judgment upon those who would oppose its decree. And according to the type, it is the third message that will accomplish its mission.

In 1929 just such a message came to the Seventh-day Adventist church, and it was put in writing and published in 1930, entitled "The Shepherd's Rod," Volume 1. And as the message went to all the sisterhood of churches (as far as possible) throughout the world, the man clothed with linen, which had the writer's inkhorn by his side, was told: "Go through the midst of the city, through the midst of Jerusalem [the church], and set a mark upon the foreheads of the men that sigh and that cry for all the abominations that be done in the midst thereof [in the church]. And to the others he said in mine hearing, Go ye after him through the city, and smite: let not your eye spare, neither have ye pity: Slay utterly old and young, both maids, and little children, and women: but come not near any man upon whom is the mark; and begin at my sanctuary [Conference]. Then they began at the ancient men [Elders] which were before the house." (Ezek. 9:4-6.)

On this Scripture was the message based, prophetically declaring, that 144,000 will be marked, and the balance now in the church must suffer the consequences except they repent and march on with the truth of God. But though not one of the entire denomination has been able to contradict the truth of the 144,000 as a whole, or even in part, nor have they dared refute the charge regarding the fostered abominations in the midst of them, they have risen against the message and prefer to hold to their abominations just as the enemies of God opposed the construction of the temple to the very last. As the decree by the king of Me-do-Persia declared to the foes of the house of God, saying: "Whosoever shall alter this word let his house be made a dunghill for this." Just so the Word of God has declared now, "slay utterly old and young, both maids, and little children, and women." If such a message as this would not convince the professed people of God to do better, then what can do it? Nevertheless, as God's purpose was carried out in the type, just so it will be in the anti-type. It is remarkable to note how perfectly the anti-type coincides with the type.

There was no change made in the decrees of Cyrus and as it was but a renewal from time to time, so it has been with the anti-type. Thus there can be no change with the Third Angel's Message, but great light and power shall be added to it. "Fearful is his work! Awful is his mission. He is the angel that is to select the wheat from the tares, and seal, or bind, the wheat for the heavenly garner."—"Early Writings," p. 118.

The Time For the Establishment of the True Church

In Haggai 2:23, speaking of the construction of the "type" (second temple) but looking prophetically forward to the fulfillment of the anti-type (the church in her purity), the Word of God by the prophet came to Zerubbabel who laid the foundation of the type (temple), and of whom the Word says is a signet or sign for the anti-type. We read of what God is to do at that time:

"For thus saith the Lord of hosts; Yet once, it is a little while, and I will shake the heavens, and the earth, and the sea, and the dry land; And I will shake all nations, and the desire of all nations shall come: and I will fill this house with glory, saith the Lord of hosts. The silver is mine, and the gold is mine, saith the Lord of hosts. The glory of this latter house shall be greater than of the former, saith the Lord of hosts: and in this place will I give peace, saith the Lord of hosts." (Haggai 2:6-9.)

"And I will overthrow the throne of kingdoms, and I will destroy the strength of the Kingdoms of the heathen; and I will overthrow the chariots, and those that ride in them; and the horses and their riders shall come down, every one by the sword of his brother." (Verse 22.)

It is evident by this Scripture that this glorious church is to be established at the close of this world's history when the earthly kingdoms shall come to their end. While interpreting Zechariah's vision, the angel spoke of Zerubbabel, saying: "The hands of Zerubbabel have laid the foundation of this house; his hands also shall finish it." (Zech. 4:9). That is, the founders of the anti-type which were typified by Zerubbabel, laid the foundation in 1844. Zerubbabel being "a signet" to the anti-type (by laying the foundation and finishing the house), denotes that the finishing of the spiritual house (the completeness of the church of God—numbering of the saints) is to be accomplished in one generation (in the life of a man, commencing in 1844.)

The Power of God's People To Build His House

"Thus saith the Lord of hosts; If thou wilt walk in my ways, and if thou wilt keep my charge, then thou shalt also judge my house, and shalt also keep my courts, and I will give thee places to walk among these that stand by. Hear now, O Joshua the high priest, thou, and thy fellows that sit before thee: for they are men wondered at: for, behold, I will bring forth my servant the **branch.**" (Zech. 3:7, 8.) "And they shall be as mighty men, which tread down their enemies in the mire of the streets in the battle: and they shall fight, because the Lord is with them, and the riders on horses shall be confounded." (Zech. 10:5.)

"Blow ye the trumpet in Zion, and sound an alarm in my holy mountain: let all the inhabitants of the land tremble: for the day of the Lord cometh, for it is nigh at hand; A day of darkness and of gloominess, a day of clouds and of thick darkness, as the morning spread upon the mountains: a great people and a strong;

there hath not been ever the like, neither shall be any more after it, even to the years of many generations. A fire devoureth before them; and behind them a flame burneth: the land is as the garden of Eden before them, and behind them a desolate wilderness; yea, and nothing shall escape them. The appearance of them is as the appearance of horses; and as horsemen, so shall they run. Like the noise of chariots on the tops of mountains shall they leap, like the noise of a flame of fire that devoureth the stubble, as a strong people set in battle array. Before their face the people shall be much pained: all faces shall gather blackness. They shall run like mighty men; they shall climb the wall like men of war; and they shall march every one on his ways, and they shall not break their ranks: Neither shall one thrust another; they shall walk every one in his path: and when they fall upon the sword, they shall not be wounded. They shall run to and fro in the city; they shall run upon the wall, they shall climb upon the houses; they shall enter in at the windows like a thief. The earth shall quake before them; the heavens shall tremble: the sun and moon shall be dark, and the stars shall withdraw their shining." (Joel 2:1-10.) "The earth", "sun", "moon", and the "stars" have no connection with Matt. 24:29. The prophetic signs of the stated planets shall find their complete fulfillment before the commencement of the millennium.

The Result of Obedience to God's Word

"Thus saith the Lord of hosts; It shall yet come to pass, that there shall come people, and the inhabitants of many cities: And the inhabitants of one city shall go to another, saying, Let us go speedily to pray before the Lord, and to seek the Lord of hosts: I will go also. Yea, many people and strong nations shall come to seek the Lord of hosts in Jerusalem, and to pray before the Lord. Thus saith the Lord of hosts; In those days it shall come to pass, that ten men shall take hold out of all languages of the nations, even shall take hold of the skirt of him that is a Jew, saying, We will go with you: for we have heard that God is with you." (Zech. 8:20-23.)

The meaning of the "**ten** men" is the same as the "**ten** virgins" of Matthew 25:1. The ten virgins signify the church as a body; and the "men" symbolically denote those who are to be converted to the church, and that they shall come from all languages, and nations. "Even shall take hold of the skirt of him that is a Jew"; that is, the one who is a Jew represents Christ in the person of His saints (the 144,000), "His skirt" represents truth or the church as a whole, by which the 144,000 are symbolically clothed.

"And it shall come to pass, that in all the land, saith the Lord, two parts therein shall be cut off and die; but the third shall be left therein. And I will bring the third part through the fire, and will refine them as silver is refined, and will try them as gold is tried: they shall call on my name, and I will hear them: I will say, It is my people: and they shall say, The **Lord** is my **God.**" (Zech. 13:8, 9.)

"Therefore thy gates shall be open continually; they shall not be shut day nor night; that men may bring unto thee the forces of the Gentiles, and that their kings may be brought." (Isa. 60:11.)

ZECHARIAH 4

The anti-typical symbols of the second temple (the type), were shown to Zechariah in vision, and recorded in the fourth chapter of his prophecy as follows:

"And the angel that talked with me came again, and waked me, as a man that is wakened out of his sleep. And said unto me, What seest thou? And I said, I have looked, and behold a candlestick all of gold, with a bowl upon the top of it, and his seven lamps thereon, and seven pipes to the seven lamps, which are upon the top thereof: And two olive trees by it, one upon the right side of the bowl, and the other upon the left side thereof. So I answered and spake to the angel that talked with me, saying, What are these, my lord? Then the angel that talked with me answered and said unto me, Knowest thou not what these be? And I said, No, my lord. Then he answered and spake unto me, saying, This is **the word of the Lord** unto Zerubbabel, saying, Not by might, nor by power, but by my spirit, saith the Lord of Hosts. . . . And I answered again, and said unto him, What be these two olive branches which through the two golden pipes empty the golden oil out of themselves? And he answered me and said, Knowest thou not what these be? And I said, No, my lord. Then said he, These are the two anointed ones, that stand by the Lord of the whole earth." (Verses 1-6, 12-14.)

Thus the **word of God** is represented by these symbols. Therefore, the interpretation of them is to reveal the manner of communicating the Word of God to Zerubbabel. Not to the Zerubbabel that was engaged in building the typical temple, for he was orally instructed by the prophets Zechariah and Haggai. Therefore, as the significance of these prophetic symbols were not understood by them, they must be applicable to those who are to be engaged in building the anti-typical, or spiritual temple (church), as it was previously explained.

Each one of these symbols must be separately deciphered by uncontradictory evidence, and their significance must constitute the method by which God is to communicate His Word to His servants. It has been previously stated that all the books of the Bible meet, and end in the book of Revelation. Therefore, the revelation of Zechariah's prophecy must be found there also.

We quote: "The seven stars are the angels of the seven

churches: and the seven candlesticks which thou sawest are the seven churches." (Rev. 1:20.) It will be noticed that the messages to the seven churches are not addressed to the **candlesticks** (the church as a body), but to the **angels,** saying, "And unto the angel of the church of the Laodiceans write." (Rev. 3:14.) This angel is not a heavenly angel, for he is at **fault**—under condemnation and about to be spued out, except he repent. It is this angel who has charge of the **candlestick** (church). Therefore, the **seven angels** denote the leadership of the seven churches, and the candlesticks are the symbols of the seven churches. Thus, the churches in this instance are symbolized by candlesticks. Therefore, the candlestick in Zechariah's vision denotes the **church** as a body.

The revelation of the **olive trees** is found in the eleventh chapter and the fourth verse: "These are the two **olive trees,** and the **two candlesticks** standing before the God of the earth." The olive trees and the two candlesticks are the **two witnesses.** (See verse 3.) Zechariah also states that "These are the two **anointed** ones, that stand by the Lord of the whole earth." (Zech. 4:14.) Therefore, these two olive trees, and two candlesticks are inseparable, for they both "stand by the Lord of the **whole** earth." The **two** candlesticks in this instance represent God's church in two sections, and each one has an **olive tree.** The angel interpreted them to Zechariah as the Word of God to Zerubbabel. Therefore, the **two candlesticks** represent the **Old** and **New Testament** churches (Jewish and Christian). And the **two olive trees** are symbols of the **Old** and **New** Testament Bible (the Word of God to Zerubbabel). These two witnesses "shall prophesy a thousand two hundred and three score days (from 538 A. D. to 1798 A. D.) clothed in sackcloth." (Rev. 11:3.) "The two Witnesses represent the Scriptures of the Old and New Testament."—"The Great Controversy," p. 267.

Thus we have a candlestick for each of the two sections of God's church while the Scriptures were being written. One candlestick and one olive tree to the Jewish, and one candlestick and one olive tree for the apostle's, and seven for the remaining history of the church to the time of the separation of the tares from the wheat, or to the commencement of the harvest. Thus the candlestick (church) in Zechariah's vision is the tenth, denoting a universal church; depicting the living church that shall unite with **all** the saints since the world began—which will join with the church of the entire universe of God! This candlestick in Zechariah's vision is a glorious one, which in comparison, all others stand as "nothing"—in perfect harmony with the second temple, which in comparison the first stood as "nothing."

The Two Golden Pipes

True then, the candlestick represents the church, and the two olive trees the Old and New Testament Scriptures. Now, "What be these two golden pipes," which "empty the golden oil out of themselves?" We quote from "Testimonies for the Church," Vol. 7, p. 249: "The inner lamp must be supplied with the oil that flows from the **messengers of heaven through the golden tubes into the golden bowl.** The Lord's **communication** never comes to man in vain." Therefore, the **two golden pipes** that empty the golden oil into the golden bowl are God's messengers of inspiration through whom present truth is revealed, and the only true interpreters of the Scriptures. The oil represents the revealed Word of God from the Bible as it is explained through His appointed servants, and the bowl describes the publications into which these revelations are compiled. This is the "Testimony of Jesus—"the Spirit of Prophecy." (Rev. 12:17; 19:10.) The revelation which John received is called "The Testimony of Jesus." (See Rev. 1:9.) Therefore, the testimony of Jesus is also the Spirit of Prophecy, because his testimony is revealed only by the Holy Spirit through a human channel. Thus the Scripture interpreted by Inspiration, is the only testimony that can be, "the testimony of Jesus"—**truth without error.**

The Seven Lamps

If the candlestick represents the church as a body, then the seven lamps thereon must denote the sisterhood of churches scattered throughout the denomination. The Biblical number of completeness takes in the entire movement as a whole. This fact is also proven by the following quotation: "When the anointed ones empty themselves through the golden pipes, the oil flows out of themselves into the golden bowl, to flow into the lamps, the **churches**."—"Testimonies to Ministers," p. 337.

The Seven Golden Tubes

If the "golden bowl" is that which contains the inspired interpretation of the Scriptures or the writings of the Spirit of Prophecy, and the lamps or churches are supplied with oil **from the bowl** through the seven golden tubes, then the ministry is represented by the tubes, whose duty is to feed the entire church with the inspired Word of God only. This fact also is proven by the "Spirit of Prophecy," as we read: "The golden oil represents the Holy Spirit. With this oil God's ministers are to be constantly supplied, that they, in turn, may impart it to the church."—Id.,

p. 188. Note, the seven tubes (Ministry) draw the oil from the golden bowl, not direct from the olive trees (Scriptures).

This divinely illustrated lesson is too plain to be misunderstood, or its meaning misconstrued. The only safe way by which God's servants and His church can be free from error, full of faith, without guile in their mouth (all speak the same thing), is the never erring guide— "The Spirit of Prophecy." The acceptance of so-called truth, without inspiration, is the devil's trap of deception, and they who advocate such fallacious teachings are the hardest and most impossible ones to rescue from Satan's bottomless pit; for he makes them believe that confession of their errors would disqualify them for teachers, and dishonor their high standing.

He who denies inspired **interpretation** of the Scriptures is denying the office of the Holy Spirit, and is sinning against Him—committing the unpardonable sin!

This golden candlestick is the most remarkable symbol in the Bible pertaining to the church of God. Its arrangement with complete number of lamps, bowl, tubes, and pipes, all of gold, with its two olive trees emptying themselves of the golden oil in the golden bowl, reveals that the last section of God's church, is to be the most glorious church in all ages. This "continued communication" by the Holy Spirit to the church, represented by the olive branches emptying the "Golden Oil out of themselves" into one Golden Bowl, and its complete set of **Supply Tubes** from the bowl to all its lamps, is to bring every part of the entire body in perfect harmony; a church without guile.

This prophetic symbol unmistakably points forward to a heavenly agency absorbing human weakness and imperfection into everlasting glory. "A glorious church, not having spot, or wrinkle, or any such thing; but that it should be holy and without blemish." (Eph. 5:27.) A church that keeps "the commandments of God, and have the testimony of Jesus Christ." "Clad in the armor of Christ's righteousness, the church is to enter upon her final conflict. 'Fair as the moon, clear as the sun, and terrible as an army with banners,' she is to go forth into all the world, conquering and to conquer."—"Prophets and Kings," p. 725. (Song of Sol. 6:10.) To this "candlestick" is the promise: "Behold, I will make thee a new **sharp** threshing instrument having teeth: thou shalt thresh the mountains, and beat them small, and shalt make the hills as chaff." (Isa. 41:15.)

The "one stone"—the church—shall have complete vision of heavenly glory: "For behold **the stone** that I have laid before

Joshua; upon **one stone shall be seven eyes:** behold, I will engrave the graving thereof, saith the Lord of hosts, and I will remove the iniquity of that land in one day. In that day, saith the Lord of hosts, shall ye call every man his neighbor under the vine and under the fig tree." (Zech. 3:9, 10.) To the servants of God (the church) is granted to possess the earth, and restore the land to the saints, to whom it originally belonged. Thus, "They shall sit every man under his vine and under his fig tree; and none shall make them afraid: for the mouth of the Lord of hosts hath spoken it." (Micah 4:4.)

"And they shall be as mighty men, which tread down their enemies in the mire of the streets in the battle: and they shall fight, because the Lord is with them, and the riders on horses shall be confounded." (Zech. 10:5.) "Not by might, nor by power, but by my Spirit saith the Lord of hosts." (Zech. 4:6.)

"And in that day will I make Jerusalem a burdensome **stone** for all people: all that burden themselves with it shall be cut in pieces, though all the people of the earth be gathered together against it. . . . In that day shall the Lord defend the inhabitants of Jerusalem; and he that is feeble among them at that day shall be as David; and the house of David shall be **as God,** as the angel of the Lord before them." (Zech. 12:3, 8.) "And it shall come to pass, that in all the land, saith the Lord **two** parts therein shall be cut off and die; but the **third** shall be **left** therein. And I will bring the **third** part through the fire, and will refine them as silver is refined, and will try them as gold is tried: they shall call on my name, and I will hear them: I will say, It is my people: and they shall say, The Lord is my God." (Zech. 13:8, 9.)

"Glorious things are spoken of thee, O city of God." (Psa. 87:3.) "Cry out and shout, thou inhabitants of Zion: for great is the Holy One of Israel in the midst of thee." (Isa. 12:6.) "Sing and rejoice, O daughter of Zion: for, lo, I come, and I will dwell in the midst of thee, saith the Lord." (Zech. 2:10.)

What Is Inspired and What Is Not?

Cunning men under the power of the great deceiver, with good words and fair speeches have sought to overthrow the faith of the saints in the word of God by almost innumerable interpretations of the Scriptures, and multiplicity of sects; making it nearly impossible for one to find his way out through the confusion, and thus keeping him in ignorance of the truth. God, knowing beforehand of these cunning devices, has prophetically illustrated the truth by this candlestick in its assemblage of parts, symbolically showing that the truth of the Bible is revealed by Inspiration only. Written words can be misconstrued, but symbols can not. Thus making it possible for both learned, and unlearned, to immediately distinguish the difference between truth and error.

The question may arise with some, How can I determine what is inspired, and what is not? The prophetic word of God is capable of answering the question and clearing the confusion, dividing the one from the other as wheat is separated from the chaff. First, "to the law and the testimony: if they speak not according to this word, it is because there is **no light in them**" (uninspired). (Isa. 8:20.) Second, the churches who were in existence prior to 1844, fell with the proclamation of the second angel's message (Rev. 14:8), showing that God would **no longer** reveal Himself through that channel. Therefore, every theory, and offshoot or sect that has sprung from the denomination's in existence at that time, **is false** with no light in them. This is also proven by the fact that nearly all the authors or founders of these theories and movements make no claim of inspiration.

The prophecy of Ezekiel, chapter four (explained in "The Shepherd's Rod," Vol. 1, pp. 115-133), proves that Luther, Knox, Wesley, Campbell, Miller, and E. G. White were divinely called. It is also proven by the parable of Matthew 20 that Luther, Knox, Wesley, and Campbell were not given light on prophetic truth, but were inspired to call for reformation on certain truths which were revealed before their time, and had been "trodden underfoot." It is further proven by the same parable that through Miller and White, prophetic truths were revealed which had never before been taught. (See pages 227, 228). It is also shown by Ezekiel's prophecy that light and truth on the Scriptures would continue for 390 years; that is, from 1500 A. D. to 1890 A. D.; and then it was to cease for forty years. (See "The Shepherd's Rod," Vol. 1, pp. 114-133.)

Thus, while the 1844 movement proclaimed that light had ceased to be revealed through all other sects, it is shown by Ezekiel's prophecy that light was to continue with the latter, up to the year 1890. This fact also is self-evident, for the Seventh-day Adventist denomination has had no additional light on the Scriptures in the stated forty years. Therefore, any theory, or so-called truth, that might have been advanced by some within this (S. D. A.) denomination that had not been revealed prior to 1890, is **also false;** though some things were written in the Spirit of Prophecy, they were not to be understood until 1929. The truths revealed prior to 1844, and up to

1929, are found in the writings of the "Spirit of Prophecy," and that which is not written there, is of no value. Not until our minds have been cleared from all these false theories can we comprehend the truth. In other words the Laodiceans must confess that the charge against them is true—"wretched, and miserable, and poor, and blind, and naked"; and by acceptance of the truth they would anoint their eyes "with eyesalve"; for it is the **"true witness** speaking, and his Word must be correct." Find your explanations "in the Bowl," and you will have no trouble in knowing the truth, or of avoiding the ever ready trap of deception. Thus the difficulty in knowing the difference between truth and error is eliminated.

THE RIVER OF EZEKIEL'S VISION

It was previously explained that Zechariah's prophecy is applicable to the church in the time of the **"Loud Cry."** Thus it becomes present truth. We quote from Zechariah 12:8: "In that day shall the Lord defend the inhabitants of Jerusalem; and he that is feeble among them at that day shall be as David; and the **house of David shall be as God,** as the angel of the Lord before **them"**—before the great multitude of Revelation 7:9.

The church in her purity is called by these Scriptures, "The house of David." Therefore, this term becomes one of the names of the church in the time of the "Loud Cry." Thus the church under this name shall be as God before the people. The meaning here is the same as in Exodus 7:1, "And the Lord said unto **Moses** See, I have made thee **a god** to Pharaoh: and Aaron thy brother shall be thy prophet" (servant). That is, "Thou shalt represent My person, and act like God by requiring obedience to thy commands, and by punishing disobedience with such punishment as none but God can inflict; to which end thou shalt have **My** omnipotent assistance." This is the commission to the church in the time of the harvest. The apostle Peter was vested with such divine power when he said: "Thou has not lied unto men, but unto God. And Ananias, hearing these words, fell down, and gave up the ghost. . . . And it was about the space of three hours after, when his wife, not knowing what was done, came in. Then Peter said unto her . . . . behold, the feet of them which have buried thy husband are at the door, and shall carry thee out. Then fell she down straightway at his feet, and yielded up the ghost: and the young men came in, and found her dead, and, carrying her forth, buried her by her husband." (The Acts 5:4, 5, 7, 9, 10.)

"In that day there shall be a **fountain** opened **to** the **house of David** and **to** the **inhabitants of Jerusalem for sin and for uncleanliness."** (Zech. 13:1.) Note that this **fountain** is able to wash away two things; first **sin,** and second **uncleanness.** What is the difference between the one and the other? "Sin is the **transgression** of the **law."** (1 John 3:4.) And the result of sin is the decay of the body. "Speak unto the children of Israel, and say unto them, When any man hath a running issue out of his flesh, because of his issue **he is unclean."** (Lev. 15:2.) The Biblical term for sickness is, **"Uncleanness."** Also, taking into the body in the form of food of that which is forbidden by the Word of God, is **transgression of the law,** and corruption of the **body** (uncleanness).

"Wherefore come out from among them, and be ye separate, saith the Lord, **and touch not the unclean** thing; and I will receive you." (2 Cor. 6:17.) "For this ye know, that no whoremonger, nor unclean person, nor covetous man, **who is an idolater,** hath any inheritance in the kingdom of Christ and of God. **Let no man** deceive you with vain words: for **because of these things** cometh the wrath of **God upon the children of disobedience.** Be not ye therefore partakers with them. For **ye were** sometimes darkness, but **now are ye light in the Lord:** walk as children of light. . . . And have **no fellowship** with the unfruitful workers of darkness, but rather reprove them." (Eph. 5:5-8, 11.) God is able to heal the soul and the body; but He will not heal the latter before He has healed the former—"sin" first, then "uncleanness." "I will also save you from **all** your **uncleanness:** and I will call for corn, and will increase it, and lay no famine upon you." (Ezek. 36:29.) The power that is able to wash away the filthiness of any man, is **"opened** to the **house** of **David** and to the inhabitants of Jerusalem" and is represented by the **"fountain"** of Zechariah's prophecy.

Says Ezekiel: "In the five and twentieth year of our captivity," and "in the fourteenth year after that the city was smitten, in the selfsame day the hand of the Lord was upon me, and brought me thither." (Ezek. 40:1.) As recorded in the forty-seventh chapter, Ezekiel was shown in vision certain particulars of the temple building some years before the Israelites were made free from Babylonian captivity. It has been previously explained that the Temple erected after their captivity was a type of this particular church in the time of the **"loud cry"**—"house of David." Therefore, the river coming out from the temple according to Ezekiel's vision is applicable at this time, and is but the expansion of this "fountain" that is to be in the "house of David" the church. "From this **fountain** flows the mighty river seen in Ezekiel's vision."—"Counsels on Health," p. 210. Thus far we have explained the application of this "fountain," the place and the time; also that the mighty river seen in Ezekiel's vision flows from it. Now we shall study the meaning of this mighty river.

Ezekiel 47

Verse 1: "Afterward he brought me again unto the door of the house; and, behold, waters issued out from under the threshold of the house eastward: for the forefront of the house stood toward the east, and the waters came down from under from the **right** side of the house, at the south side of the altar." As the waters came from the south side of the altar, and then went toward the east, it shows clearly that they proceeded from the **north,** which symbolically denotes that whatever the meaning of the "waters" may be, they come from the throne of God, for It is "in the sides of the **north.**" (Isa. 14:14; Psa. 48:2; 75:6.)

While Ezekiel's attention was turned to the interior where he first saw the waters, he says: "Then brought he me out of the way of the gate northward, and led me about the way unto the utter gate by the way that looketh eastward; and, behold, there ran out waters on the right side. And when the man that had the line in his hand went forth eastward, he measured a thousand cubits, and he brought me through the waters; the waters were to the ankles. Again he measured a thousand, and brought me through the waters; the waters were to the knees. Again he measured a thousand, and brought me through; the waters were to the loins. Afterward he measured a thousand; and it was a river that I could not pass over: for the waters were risen, waters to swim in, a river that could not be passed over. And he said unto me, Son of man, hast thou seen this? Then he brought me, and caused me to return to the brink of the river. Now when I had returned, behold, at the bank of the river were very many trees on the one side and on the other. Then said he unto me, These waters issue out toward the east country, and go down into the desert, and go into the sea: Which being brought forth into the sea, the waters shall be healed. And it shall come to pass, that everything that liveth, which moveth, whithersoever the rivers shall come, shall live: and there shall be a very great multitude of fish, because these waters shall come thither; for they shall be healed; and everything shall live whither the river cometh. And it shall come to pass, that the fishers shall stand upon it from En-gedi even unto En-eglaim; they shall be a place to spread forth nets; their fish shall be according to their kinds, as the fish of the great sea, exceeding many. But the miry places thereof and the marishes thereof shall not be healed; they shall be given to salt. And by the river upon the bank thereof, on this side and on that side, shall grow all trees for meat, whose leaf shall not fade, neither shall the fruit thereof be consumed: it shall bring forth new fruit according to his months, because their waters they issued out of the sanctuary: and the fruit thereof shall be for meat, and the leaf thereof for medicine." (Ezekiel 47:2-12.)

It will be noticed that as Ezekiel first saw the waters by the side of the altar, they were of little significance in comparison

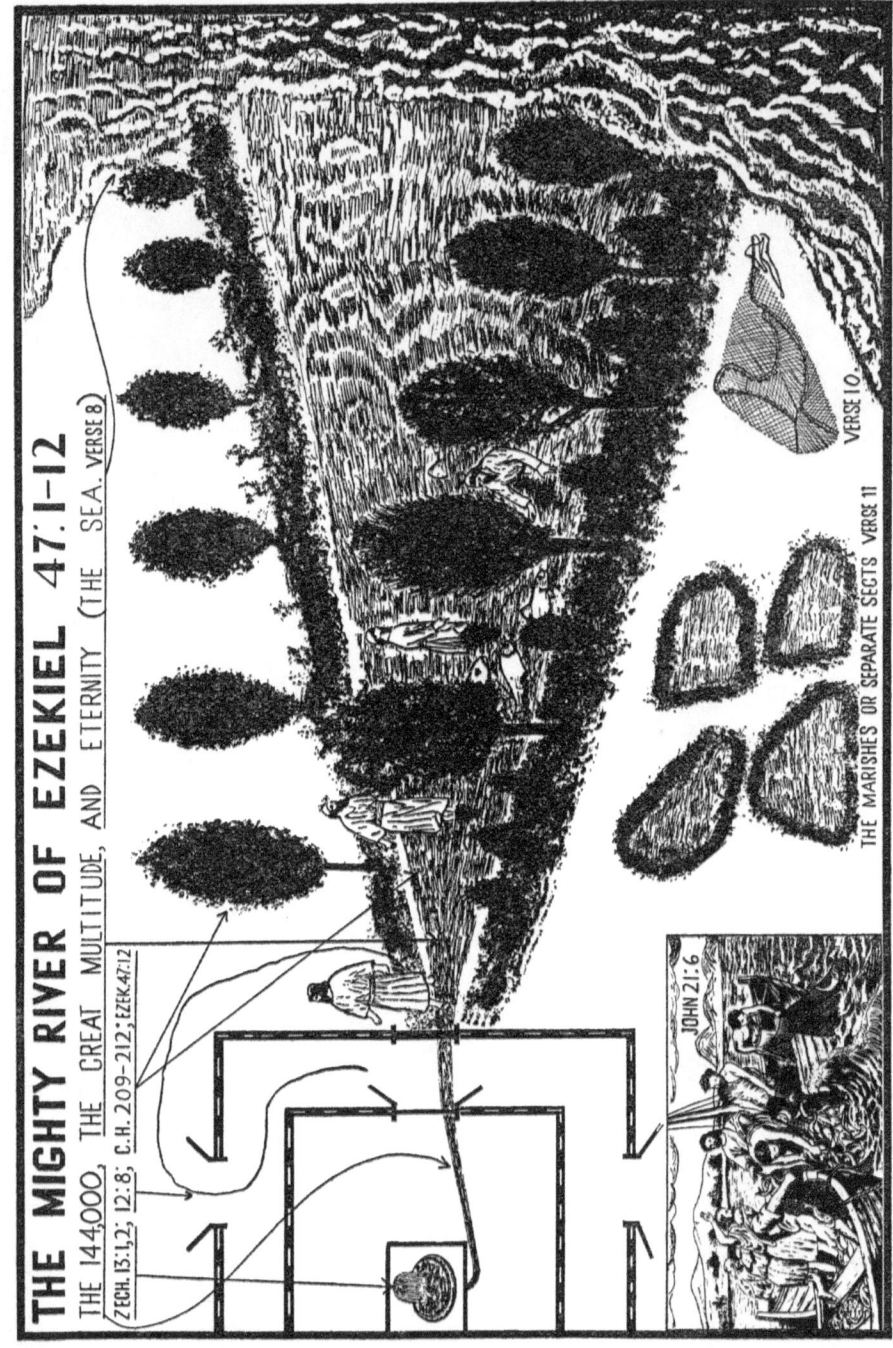

THE MIGHTY RIVER OF EZEKIEL 47:1-12
THE 144,000, THE GREAT MULTITUDE, AND ETERNITY (THE SEA. VERSE 8)
ZECH. 13:1,2; 12:8; C.H. 209-212; EZEK.47:12

VERSE 10.

THE MARISHES OR SEPARATE SECTS VERSE 11

JOHN 21:6

294

with that which he saw outside the gate. As the tiny rivulet immediately swells into a mighty river, it represents something of very rapid growth. These waters denote the same as the waters in Revelation 17:15, "Peoples, and multitudes, and nations, and tongues." For the angel said to Ezekiel: "Which being brought forth into the sea, the waters **shall be healed.**" (Verse 8.) Therefore, these waters represent a very great multitude "which no man could number" that shall be healed from sin and disease, saved in the time of the **"loud cry"** through the ministry of the "house of David" (the church). As Ezekiel could not swim this river, the symbol is in perfect harmony with Revelation 7:9, "A **great multitude,** which no man could number, of all nations, and kindreds, and people, and tongues . . . clothed with white robes, and palms in their hands."

Note that the reason the waters are healed, is because they are "brought forth into the **sea.**" If the mighty river represents the saints from the earth, then the **sea** must be a symbol of the sinless worlds (inhabitants) in the universe of God. As the **river** is brought into the **sea,** it denotes that the saints shall come in contact with the eternal nations who know not sin, and being "brought forth," we must be "healed" before we meet each other! The facts of this symbol prove that this is the last section of God's church—the church that shall be translated without tasting death! Get ready, get ready, get ready, we are now standing on the wings of eternity—life that shall never cease.

The waters that make up this mighty river represents a multitude of saints endowed with healing power from the throne of God; for the Word says, "And everything **shall live** whither the **river cometh.**" (Verse 9, last part.) This healing is not indefinite, but permanent; for we read: "And it shall come to pass, that everything that **liveth,** which **moveth,** whithersoever the river shall come, **shall live**" (eternally).

After the angel had measured three times a thousand cubits, says Ezekiel: "And he said unto me, Son of man, hast thou seen this? Then he brought me, and caused me to return to the brink of the river. Now when I had returned, behold, at the bank of the river were **very many trees** on the one side and on the other. And by the river upon the bank thereof," said the angel, "on this side and on that side, shall grow **all trees for meat,** whose leaf shall not fade, neither shall the fruit thereof be consumed: it shall bring forth new fruit according to his months, because their waters they issued out of the sanctuary: and the **fruit thereof** shall be **for meat,** and **the** leaf thereof **for medicine.**" (Verses 6, 7, 12.)

The value of the leaves and the fruit of these trees is identically the same as the **tree** of **life** according to Revelation 22:2, "And on either side of the **river,** was there **the tree of life,** which bear twelve manner of fruits, and **yielded her fruit every month:** and the **leaves of the tree** were for the **healing of the nations."** The significance is that the church of God (house of David) is endowed with power from the **throne** to offer **life eternal** with no taste of death to those who accept the truth, and are willing to become a part of this mighty river. As this is the only section of God's church that has been granted the authoritative gospel of permanent healing and life everlasting, the Word declares: **"He that is feeble** among them at that day **shall be as David; and the house of David shall be as God,** as the angel of the Lord before them." (Zech. 12:8.)

"And there shall be a very great multitude of fish, because these waters shall come thither. . . . And it shall come to pass, that the fishers shall stand upon it from En-gedi even unto En-eglaim. . . . Their fish shall be according to their kinds, as the fish of the great sea, exceeding many." (Ezek. 47:9, 10.) The fish represent those who are to be converted to the church — "river." "And everything shall live whither the river cometh." (Verse 9.) The ministry is symbolized as the **fishers,** "And Jesus said unto them, Come ye after me, and I will make you to become fishers of men." (Mark 1:17.) The apostles at one time left the gospel net and ceased to be fishers of men, as they went fishing for gain, "and that night they caught nothing. But when the morning was now come, Jesus stood on the shore. . . . then Jesus saith unto them, Children, have ye any meat? They answered Him, No. And He said unto them, Cast the net on the right side of the ship, and ye shall find. They cast therefore, and now they were not able to draw it for the multitude of fishes." (John 21:3-6.) Success never fails when the command of the Master is obeyed. If the ministry had been constantly inquiring of Jesus where and how to cast the **net,** there would have been a multitude of "fish"—converts —and never a lack of "meat"—means.

"For the forefront of the house stood **towards the east."** (Ezek. 47:1.) The position of the house proves that it represents a true worship, for thus God's chosen people were instructed to build their temples. Israel worshipped God with their backs toward the east to remind them that they should have no respect for sun worship and idolatry.

"Then said he unto me, These waters issue out towards the east country, and go down into the desert, and go into the sea." (Verse 8.) It is remarkable to note how perfect these symbols are in each instance. This direction of the compass denotes that the message of the **"loud cry"** is to start eastward when it is first revealed. The church membership being largely east of California, and across the Atlantic, naturally the message must start toward the east. This symbolical prophecy reveals that the message of the **"loud cry"** is to originate in California. Thus fulfilling the prophetic words of the "Spirit of Prophecy" in a letter to Elder E. E. Andross: "I feel confident Elder Andross, that the brethren in **Southern California** will find a blessing in reviewing the teachings of the Scripture concerning the 144,000 and bringing to bear upon these teachings whatever light there may be in the published writings of the Spirit of Prophecy, and as prayerful consideration is given the matter in all its bearings, I believe that God will make the truth sufficiently clear to make possible the avoidance of needless and unprofitable questions not vital to the salvation of precious souls."

East being the Biblical direction of idolatry, it also signifies that the message is headed toward the conversion of sinners and destruction of idolatry. "And it shall come to pass in **that day,** saith the Lord of hosts, that I will cut off the names of the idols out of the land, and they shall no more be remembered: and also I will cause the prophets and the unclean spirits to pass out of the land." (Zech. 13:2.)

The angel measured **four** times a **thousand** cubits eastward (a thousand—"ten" times one hundred). Why four times a thousand? Why not more or less? It has been previously explained that number "ten" is a symbol of universal, and the number **four** completeness of the earth or the four points of the compass. Thus it symbolically denotes that the message is world wide; and while it starts toward the east, it spreads from pole to pole, and completely encircles the earth (10 x 100 = 1,000—four times.) In perfect harmony with the words of Christ: "And this gospel of the kingdom shall be preached in **all** the **world** for a witness unto **all** nations; and **then** shall the **end** come." (Matt. 24:14.)

"But the miry places thereof and the marishes thereof shall not be healed; they shall be given to salt." (Ezek. 47:11.) The "marishes" and the "miry places" represent denominations and sects separate of the "**mighty** river," and that they shall not be saved, or healed. "Turned to salt," means eternally lost, as was Lot's wife. "And as it was in the days of Noe, so shall it be also in the days of the Son of man. . . . Likewise also as it was in the days of Lot. . . . **Remember Lot's wife."** (Luke 17:26, 28, 32.)

"And it shall come to pass, that the fishers shall stand upon it from En-gedi even unto En-eglaim; **they** [the two cities] shall be a place to spread forth nets." (Ezek. 47:10.) These two cities reveal that the fish are caught in two places, En-gedi (S. D. A. church) where the 144,000 are gathered—the **first** fruits. En-eglaim (Babylon or the world) where the great multitude of Revelation 7:9 are gathered. The diagram on the chart, page 294, represents the S. D. A. church (En-gedi) as it becomes the "House of David," and the place of the river (En-eglaim) denotes the world. The stream from the fountain where it first starts to the east gate, represents the 144,000, and the river stands for the great multitude. "There is a river, the streams whereof shall make glad the city of God, the holy place of the tabernacles of the most High. God is in the midst of her; she shall not be moved: God shall help her, and that right early." (Psa. 46:4, 5.)

JUSTIFICATION BY FAITH; WHAT IS IT?

All the blessings written in the preceding chapters are apprehended in the following

Though this most important subject is the simplest of all Biblical truths, it has been widely confused, and largely misunderstood. The example of one man's experience in the things of God and his justification by faith, should clear the widespread confusion, and remove the veil which has been drawn over the eyes of the faithful. "To that also which is of the faith of Abraham; who is **the father of us all.** (As it is written, I have made thee a **father of many nations**), before Him Whom he believed, even God, Who quickeneth the dead, and calleth those things which be not as though they were." (Rom. 4:16, 17.)

When the method pursued by Abraham is followed, then, and then only, can any one of us be justified; there is no other way. "And if ye be Christ's then are ye Abraham's seed, and heirs according to the promise." (Gal. 3:29.) **"If ye were Abraham's children, ye would do** the works of Abraham." (John 8:39.) Let us take notice of Abraham's faith, experience, and justification. **"Hearken to me, ye that follow after righteousness,** ye that seek the Lord: look unto the rock whence ye are hewn, and to the hole of the pit whence ye are digged. **Look unto Abraham your father."** (Isa. 51:1, 2.)

In the following it will be noticed that Abraham responded **without hesitation** to **all** God commanded him to do: "Now the Lord said unto Abram, Get thee out of thy country, and from thy kindred, and from thy father's house, unto a land that I will shew thee. . . . **So Abram departed,** as the Lord had spoken unto him. . . . And the Lord appeared unto Abram, and said, Unto thy seed will I give this land: and there **builded he** an **altar unto the Lord,** who appeared unto him." (Gen. 12:1, 4, 7.) "And the Lord said unto Abram, after that Lot was separated from him, Lift up now thine eyes, and look from the place where thou art northward, and southward, and eastward, and westward: for all the land which thou seest, to thee will I give it, and to thy seed for ever. And I will make thy seed as the dust of the earth: so that if a man can number the dust of the earth, then shall thy seed also be numbered. Arise, walk through the land in the length of it and in the breadth of it; for I will give it unto thee. Then Abram removed his tent, and came and dwelt in the plain of Mamre, which is in Hebron, and **built there an altar unto the Lord."** (Gen. 13:14-18.)

"And God said unto Abraham, Thou shalt keep my covenant, thou, and thy seed after thee in their generations. This is my covenant, which ye shall keep, between me and you and thy seed after thee; Every man child among you shall be circumcised. . . . And Abraham took Ishmael his son, and all that were born in his house, and all that were bought with his money, every male among the men of Abraham's house; and circumcised the flesh of their foreskin **in the selfsame day, as God had said unto him."** (Gen. 17:9, 10, 23.)

"And God said unto Abraham, Let it not be grievous in thy sight because of the lad, and because of thy bondwoman; in all that Sarah hath said unto thee, hearken unto her voice; for in Isaac shall thy seed be called. **And Abraham rose up early in the morning,** and took bread, and a bottle of water, and gave it unto Hagar, putting it on her shoulder, and the child, and sent her away." (Chapter 21:12, 14.) "And it came to pass after these things, that God did tempt Abraham, and said unto him, Abraham: and he said, Behold, here I am. And He said, Take now thy son, thine only son Isaac, whom thou lovest, and get thee into the land of Moriah; and offer him there for a burnt offering upon one of the mountains which I will tell thee of. **And Abraham rose up early in the morning,** and saddled his ass, and took two of his young men with him, and Isaac his son, and clave the wood for the burnt offering, and rose up, and went unto the place of which God had told him. . . . And Abraham built an altar there, and laid the wood in order, and bound Isaac his son, and laid him on the altar upon the wood. And Abraham stretched forth his hand, and took the knife to slay his son. And the angel of the Lord called unto him out of heaven, and said, Abraham, Abraham: and he said, Here am I. And he said, Lay not thine hand upon the lad, neither do thou anything unto him: for now I know that thou fearest God, seeing thou hast not withheld thy son, thine only son from me . . . . And the angel of the Lord called unto Abraham out of heaven the second time, And said, By myself have I sworn, saith the Lord, for because thou hast done this thing, and hast not withheld thy son, thine only son: That in blessing will I bless thee, and in multiplying I will multiply thy seed as the stars of heaven, and as the sand which is upon the sea shore; and thy seed shall possess the gate of his enemies; And in thy seed shall all the nations of the earth be blessed; **because thou hast obeyed my voice."** (Gen. 22:1-3, 9-12, 15-18.)

"Abraham believed God, and it was imputed unto him for righteousness: and he was called the **friend of God."** (James 2:23.) By simply doing the things that God asked of him he obtained this record: "Because that Abraham obeyed my voice, and kept my charge, my commandments, my statutes, and my laws." "In thy seed shall all the nations of the earth be blessed." (Gen. 26:5, 4.) Having childlike faith in the Word, and doing all God has said, is the only sanctification and righteousness that is Christ's. Such are the children of Abraham, and to them is the promise. They openly declare that the blood of Christ has the power to save them from the bondage of sin, and from the condemnation of the law. They shall inherit the land for ever and ever. These are the Israel of God. There are no others, and this only is righteousness and sanctification by faith.

SCRIPTURAL INDEX

The charts on pages 22, 64, 74, 84, 128, 150, 204, 224, 250, 270 and 294 can be obtained at a reasonable price. Size about 18x22 inches. Convenient for teaching. Address the publishers.